NEW YORK, NEW YORK
CUSTOM HOUSE RECONSTRUCTION

(9 Dec. 1719–31 Dec. 1723)

William Taylor Easter II

HERITAGE BOOKS
2017

HERITAGE BOOKS
AN IMPRINT OF HERITAGE BOOKS, INC.

Books, CDs, and more—Worldwide

For our listing of thousands of titles see our website
at
www.HeritageBooks.com

Published 2017 by
HERITAGE BOOKS, INC.
Publishing Division
5810 Ruatan Street
Berwyn Heights, Md. 20740

Copyright © 2017 William Taylor Easter II

Heritage Books by the author:
New York, New York - Custom House Reconstruction (9 Dec. 1719–31 Dec. 1723)
Philadelphia, Pennsylvania - Custom House Reconstruction (22 Dec. 1719–7 Jan. 1724)

All rights reserved. No part of this book may be reproduced or transmitted in any form or by any means, electronic or mechanical, including photocopying, recording or by any information storage and retrieval system without written permission from the author, except for the inclusion of brief quotations in a review.

International Standard Book Numbers
Paperbound: 978-0-7884-5797-5

Contents

	Page
Preface	I – VIII
Known Arrival & Departure Ports	IX
Average Passage Length & Ship Type / Sizes	X
Data Coverage For All Custom Houses	XI – XIV
Group - ?	1 – 7
Group – A	8 – 11
Group – B	12 – 14
Group – C	15 – 16
Group – D	17 – 18
Group – E	19 – 23
Group – F	24
Group – G	25 – 26
Group – H	27 – 29
Group – I	30
Group – J	31 – 33
Group – K	34
Group – L	35
Group – M	36 – 40
Group – N	41
Group – P	42 – 45
Group – R	46 – 47
Group – S	48 – 53
Group – T	54 – 55
Group – U-V	56
Group – W-Y	57 – 59
Group – Multi	60 – 68
Interact – 1	69 – 72
Interact – 2	70
Interact – 3	71
Interact – 4	72
Interact – 5	73
Interact – 6	74
Interact – 7	75
Interact – 8	76
Interact – 9	76
Interact – 10	77
Interact – 11	77
Interact – 12	78
Interact – 13	78
Interact – 14	79
Interact – 15	79
Interact – 16	80 – 87
Interact – 17	80 – 87
Interact – 18	81
Interact – 19	82
Interact – 20	83 – 84
Interact – 21	85 – 86
Interact – 22	87 – 88
Interact – 23	89 – 90
Interact – 24	91 – 92
Interact – 25	93 – 95
Interact – 26	96 – 97
Interact – 27	98 – 99
Interact – 28	100 – 102
Interact – 29	103 – 105
Interact – 30	106 – 108
Interact – 31	109 – 112
Shared Index – Captains & Ships	113
Index – Captains	114 – 118
Index – Ships	119 – 122
Index – Sources	123

- Group - (?-W) : Single Captain : Single Ship (1 To 1)
- Group - Multi : Single Captain : Multi Ships (1 To Many)
- Interact : Single Captain : Multi Ships & Multi Captains : Single Ship (Many To Many)

Preface

In genealogy we all know we are working on a puzzle that has no picture. When we look at the data, it is only a piece at a time, one date, one place, and one person. We can not get a whole grasp of what is going on. Think of a mosaic photo, if you look at it close up you see one small photo, but it is not what the overall photo looks like, if you take a few steps back it all comes into focus. That is what I have done with this book. I have tried to give you a picture for all the puzzle pieces that are between December 9,1719 – December 31,1723 for the Port of New York. You will see that getting a complete list of ships and their travels is the start of building a complete set of passenager records for this time period. More data is available for this time period than people think there is. Throughout the preface, I will explain how this data is laid out.

This is one of the first books for reconstructing a nearly complete list of ships and their voyages across the Atlantic and West Indies to and from New York. The data in this book was originally intended for the purpose of just reconstructing the records for the Custom House of just New York. But it had a different outcome when it was completed. It showed partial Arrival and Departure records for ships for years in a row to other ports besides New York. It shows interactions between ships and captains that previously were not known about.

Once you start looking over all the Arrival and Departure dates, you will start seeing how captains traded off with other captains. You will see how captains selected their own preferred Routes.

I have covered the dates of December 9,1719 – December 31,1723. In total there are 1489 days. Out of the sources I used, all days were covered, which gives a 100% coverage for the New York Custom House. On the coverage map, you will see 14 days for the American Weekly Mercury for New York is missing, I used the *Boston Gazette* to fill in those dates. If you look at Preface X-XIII in this book you will see the coverage for the Custom Houses. You will see the missing data is in 7 day sections. So Arrival, Entered Out, Cleared Out, did not happen all in the same 7 days span, so in turn, you end up getting at least 2 out of the 3 events that happened for a ship. So in the given time span you end up getting all captains and ships that interacted with the New York Custom House. Lets go a step farther and look at the partial data from captains and ships. In total there were 347 captains and 376 ships that interacted with the Custom House in the given date range. There were 32 partial captains, which means some data was missing from giving a 100% identification on those people, and there were 37 ½ partial ships. So you have 90.78% coverage on captains, and 90.03% coverage on ships. So lets add all this into account when giving a more detailed coverage %... When you take all three sections into account you have a 93.60% coverage for the given date range.

This list started out with around 2348 captains with 2348 ships. After cross-referencing names, ships, ship types, dates, and ports, the list was combined down to 347 Captains and 376 Ships, two rules were followed:

Rule 1 – Assume all captains / masters with the same name are the same captain / unless ship name and ship type and / or arrival & departure dates comfirm otherwise.

Rule 2 – Assume all ships with same name and ship type are the same ship / unless captain name and / or arrival & departure dates confirm otherwise.

The following is a list of the totals of the years and how many captains and ships interacted with New York & Philadelphia. I thought I would include the totals for both so you will see the total completion. Because both books cover the same time period and share captains and ships. A shared index has been given in front of the main index in the back of the book. The shared Captains & Ships are also in the main index.

New York – Total #		1720	1721	1722	1723
Captains: 347	Dates: 2348	Captains: 164	Captains: 139	Captains: 148	Captains: 143
Ships: 376	Ports: 2219	Ships: 157	Ships: 132	Ships: 140	Ships: 137

Philadelphia - Total #		1720	1721	1722	1723
Captains: 294	Dates: 1453	Captains: 142	Captains: 116	Captains: 115	Captains: 99
Ships: 288	Ports: 1518	Ships: 130	Ships: 113	Ships: 102	Ships: 87

Combined - Total #

New York – Captains: 326   New York – Ships: 351
Shared – Captains: 21   Shared – Ships: 25
Philadelphia – Captains: 273   Philadelphia – Ships: 263
Total – Captains: 620   Total – Ships: 639

Combined Completion % - December 9,1719 – December 31,1723 / New York & Philadelphia

			Total Coverage:
Captains: 620	Partial: 39	Missing Data: 6.29%	**94.46%**
Ships: 639	Partial: 55 ½	Missing Data: 8.68%	
Coverage Days: 2972	Missing: 49	Missing Data: 1.64%	

Known Arrivals – 1721, 1722 & 1723								
King George	29 Apr 1721	Passengers	1+	?	Dec 1722	Passengers	100+
Crown Galley	3 Jun 1721	Slaves	117+	Jolly	9 Dec 1722	Passengers	3+
Sunderland	20 Apr 1722	Passengers	25+	Greyhound	24 Dec 1722	Palatines	1+
Hannah	16 Jun 1722	Passengers	1+	Phenix Galley	17 Jun 1723	Passengers	1+
Hopewell	13 Jul 1722	Passengers	1+				
Blessing	29 Oct 1722	Palatines	200+				
TOTAL: 450							

To give you a idea of what data is available when the next book comes out for, Boston, Massachusetts for the same time span. For the coverage day completion for the next book. See chart below.

Combined Coverage Day Completion % - December 9,1719 – December 31,1723 / New York, Philadelphia, & Boston.

			Total Coverage:
Coverage Days: 4458	Missing: 70	Missing Data: 1.57%	**98.43%**

You may be asking now, what can I do with this data, we now have data for 2923 days with the first two books and 4388 Days of Custom House records for Colonial America with Boston when it's completed, between the given dates. You can now begin the reconstruction of the passenger list for these ships because now you have a nearly complete list of Captains and Ships to compare against, with the records you do find for people between the date given. For example: You have someone from Ireland, now pull out every ship that came from Ireland from 1720 – 1723 from all three major ports, you go from 1000 Ships down to 8 ships lets says. All because we have a nearly complete record now. As you can see, much of the preface in this book is the same as in my previous book. I have changed a few parts throughout the preface with additional information, and also to reflect examples of New York.

1. Known Arrival & Departure Ports: The West Indies section has been updated with more detailed locations for each port. Island Sub Groups have been added there and they have also been added throughout the rest of the book, to show finer detail on where to search for records if they are needed for a ship.

2. Average Passage Length & Ship Type / Sizes: This section has doubled in size, giving a more detailed look on the length it took ships to travel from port to port.

3. Data Coverage For All Custom Houses: This section has turned from a single page to four pages, giving the reader a wealth of information on where to find information on ships for a given date range. I thought including by all the data I used to reconstruct not just this book but the Philadelphia one as well and future books, the complexity of what has been done will now become clear. Also 7 ports are shown not just one like the first book.

4. On this page of the preface you can see I have given detailed stats on the total completion with Philadelphia & New York together, having both books will give you a nearly complete picture of two of the major ports from December 9,1719 – December 31,1723 for ships in Colonial America

Now you will see what each items means in the charts so you know how all the captains and ships interact.

Group	Ship				Captain / Master		Passage	Arrival / Departure 1		Passage	Arrival / Departure 2		Page
?	Year	Name	Type	Burden	First Name	Last Name	Length	Port	Arrival / Entered Inwards	Length	Port	Arrival / Entered Inwards	1
	MSTR ID#								Custom In / Entered Out			Custom In / Entered Out	
	SHIP ID#	Registry Location						State / Country	Custom Out / Cleared Out		State / Country	Custom Out / Cleared Out	
									Departure			Departure	
	Source						Notes						

Section: 1 / Group / Multi / Interact

- Group
- Multi — These 3 can show up in the first box to let you know what group they are in.
- Interact

Section: 4 & 6 / Passage

Passage — This will have the length of passage or a symbol to show connection to the next port.

Section: 2 / Ship

- Year — The years covered by the current ship being looked at.
- MSTR ID# — Captain / Master ID Number
- SHIP ID# — Ship ID Number
- Name — Name of Ship
- Type — Type of Ship / Sloop, Scallop, Brigantine, etc...
- Burden — Weight of Ship / 100 Ton, 120 Tons, etc...
- Registry Location — If location is known where ship is registred.

Section: 5 & 7 / Arrival & Departure

- Port — This is to show what port was for arrival or departure.
- State / Country — This is to show what state in Colonial America, or other country.
- Arrival / Entered Inwards — Date or Week ship entered port.
- Custom In / Entered Out — Date or Week ship entered customs to load or unload cargo.
- Custom Out / Cleared Out — Date or Week ship cleared customs for departure.
- Departure — Date or Week ship left port.

Section: 2.5 / Source

Source — Source number and page or issue number to locate data in source.

Section: 5.5 / Notes

Notes — Any notes available for passengers or other important data.

Section: 3 / Captain / Master

- First Name — First name of captain
- Last Name — Last name of captain

Section: 8 / Page

Page — Page number of current page.

Dates

[? ? 1700] --------------- If you see a date in [ ] with a ? for the day or month then only partial data was available for event.
[? Jan 1700]

[7 Jan 1700] --------------- When you see a date in [ ] it is a Post Date, event happen in the last 7 days. Example / 1 Jan – 7 Jan 1700

(14 Jan 1700) --------------- When you see a date in ( ) it is a Double Post Date, event happen in the last 14 days. Example / 1 Jan – 14 Jan 1700

> *Philadelphia, Decemb. 26.*
> The New York Post defigns to perform his Stage for this Winter-Quarter only once a Fortnight; fo that now every other Paper, during that Time, will contain the material Advices he brings.

Note: Winter Months – Stage from New York to Philadelphia carrying the custom house shipping news only traveled every 2 weeks in the winter quarter. Post has 14 days of shipping news.

(Fortnight = 2 Weeks / 14 Days)

When you see the coverage data in the preface for New York that is why you see it covering 14 days.

XX [7 Jan 1700] XX --------------- If you see dates in gray, that means it shows where the next captain continues or came from with the ship. To show how the two captains interacted when one enters the port and the other takes over.

7 Jan 1700 --------------- Exact date of event known when only a date is shown.

Port Names

Port Names --------------- If you see a port that is wrttien as New York, [New York], only the data not in [ ] was given in the source data. The [ ] data is based off of what was in the source.

Passage

Days / Weeks --------------- In the passage section you may see days or weeks for the voyage length.
> --------------- Data was complete to show next arrival & departure port for ship.
[>] --------------- Enough data was complete to calculate next arrival & departure port for ship.

Preface

III

The example to the right shows what [>] is used for. There is data that we know that is from the week of [26 Jun 1721] this ship cleared customs in New York, and was headed to Curacao. Then on 16 Oct 1721 the same ship entered New York from Jamaica.

So by looking at this small example, it also shows that we do not have the information between Curacao and Jamaica. On average it takes about a month in port to enter customs, clear customs and depart.

>	New York	[7 May 1721]	>	Curacao	
		[12 Jun 1721]			
	[New York]	[26 Jun 1721]		[Leeward Antilles]	
[>]	Jamaica		>	New York	16 Oct 1721
					(19 Dec 1721)
	[Greater Antilles]			[New York]	(1 Jan 1722)

We know thst documented passages from Curacao and New York are (17 – 26 Days) & Jamaica and New York are (22 - 35 Days), you can look at preface page IX to see the average passage times. By looking at the example chart below you see it would calculate out to this ship having 25 days to complete its trip back to New York. So this will validate that this example is correct.

New York	Departure	20 – 26 Jun 1721
Passage		21 – 28 Days**
Curacao	Arrival	16 Jul 1721**
Port Layover Delay – 1 Month		
Curacao	Departure	16 Aug 1721**
Passage		7 Days**
Jamaica	Arrival	21 Aug 1721**
Port Layover Delay – 1 Month		
Jamaica	Departure	22 Sept 1721**
Passage		25 Days**
New York	Arrival	16 Oct 1721

	** Calculated Dates	

>	New York	[7 May 1721]	>	Curacao	16 Jul 1721
		[12 Jun 1721]			
	[New York]	[26 Jun 1721]		[Leeward Antilles]	16 Aug 1721
[>]	Jamaica	22 Aug 1721	25 Days	New York	16 Oct 1721
					(19 Dec 1721)
	[Greater Antilles]	22 Sept 1721		[New York]	(1 Jan 1722)

American Weekly Mercury: Issue 10 / 16 Feb 1720

Newspaper issues used Quaker dates – this issue was 1719 / 1720

Note 1: When a ship winters at a port, the port layover can increase to 3 to 5 months from December to April if they dock at New York. The reason is the ice that blocked the river during the 1700's was a lot greater than it is today.

Note 2: If a ship does not winter in New York, they will leave by December and go to the West Indies and return by April.

New York February the 16th. 1719.

On Thursday last, Capt. Willson in Sloop Mary Sayled out of this Road for Jamaica, but there being little Wind Could gett no further then the Narrows, about nine at Night the Wind Sprung up at North West and blew prety frelh, but by realon of the Ice which was in the River Could not gett out, it Continued the next day blowing hard and it was Extream Cold. the Sloop was in great Danger : by Realon of the great quantity of Ice which was in the River, But on Sunday (with abundance of Difficulty) they gott back into the Road, the Malter and three of his Men having their hands and feet Froze.

The next two examples will explain how captains and ships interact and switching out captains to new ships.

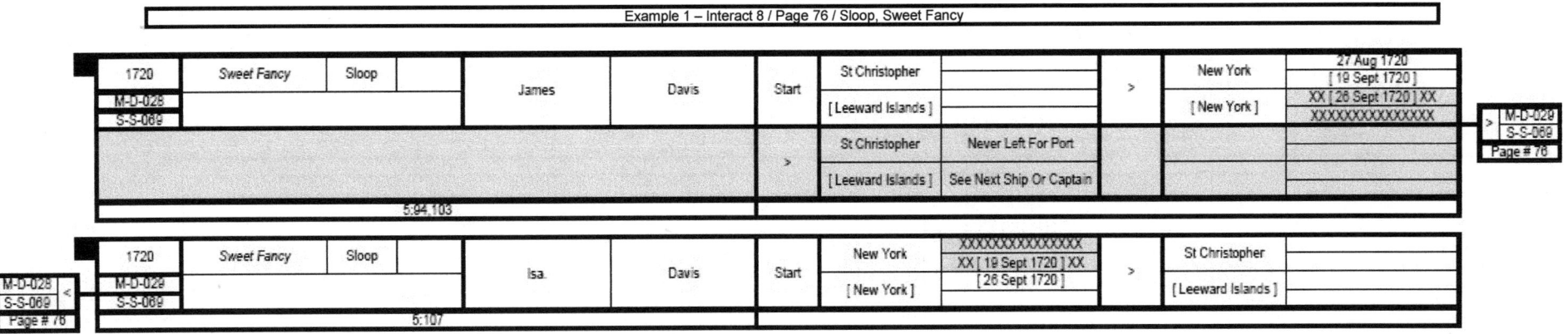

Example 1 – Interact 8 / Page 76 / Sloop, Sweet Fancy

You can see from the example, that the sloop, *Sweet Fancy* was in

New York the week of 19 Sept 1720, Issue 40 of *The American Weekly Mercury*.

New York the week of 26 Sept 1720, Issue 41 of *The American Weekly Mercury*.

This is just a small example – Interact 8 / Page 76 only has 2 captains and 1 ship.

But the captains were different. The reason for this is, James Davis never left with the Sweet Fancy. He stayed in New York and Isa. Davis took over the role as Captain, then took the ship to St Christopher. If you only look at the first entry in Issue 40 you only would think that James Davis was captain. That he did take the ship to St Christopher and you would be looking for the wrong captain if you needed to trace records. A issue later if you even would see it in the massive amount of data that the captain ended up changing. You may just think that there was just another ship going to the same place but in fact they were the same ship.

Black Circles – When you see a box on the end of a ship with a Master ID & Ship ID – matches the next Captain that took over the role as captain on that ship.

Gray Circles – When you see a box on the front of a ship with a Master ID & Ship ID – matches the pervious Captain of that ship.

Corrections

V

After more research and before this book was published, as I am writing the Boston Custom House Reconstruction book, there is a correction that needs to be listed.
Master: M-S-007 / Ship: S-F-006 : Was listed in the Philadelphia Book and is shown below in the chart and is shared with Boston so it is listed in the next book as well.. But with a correction.. To give a
little background for this correction, it needs to be explained.. And I want to make sure it was in the New York book so this data is not confused with the New Jersey & New York area.

This ship like others in the New York book and the next book for Boston did a transfer with a closely located Custom House. This happened in two locations on the east coast of Colonial America.
Salem & Boston Massachusetts / Perth Amboy, New Jersey & New York, New York. These ports were so close or even across the harbor from one another that they acted as one harbor, and shared ship
traffic.

So I have given a example where it was published in the Philadelphia , Pennsylvania – Custom House Reconstruction (22 Dec 1719 – Jan 1724) , where it was listed as Salem, New Jersey where in
fact it was Salem Massachusetts.

This error happen for the following reason, "Archives of the State of New Jersey Vol 11 Copyright 1894", when this book was published the author made a mistake in his newspaper extracts in relation
to New Jersey. The extracts that have "Custom House, Salem" are in fact Salem, Massachusetts. I only checked the years 1719 – 1723 so there could be many more errors. In my opinion the "Archives of
the State of New Jersey Vol 11 Copyright 1894" should not be trusted unless you do your research from the original source records. I did not use it but for this one ship, so I did not have to make any more
corrections.

"Archives of the State of New Jersey Vol 11 Copyright 1894"

American Weekly Mercury	Page 49	Custom House Salem Apr 9 1720 – This is Salem, Massachusetts **NOT** Salem, New Jersey
American Weekly Mercury	Page 49	Custom House Salem Apr 23 1720 – This is Salem, Massachusetts **NOT** Salem, New Jersey
American Weekly Mercury	Page 51	Custom House Salem Jun 25 1720 – This is Salem, Massachusetts **NOT** Salem, New Jersey
American Weekly Mercury	Page 53	Custom House Salem Sept 17 1720 – This is Salem, Massachusetts **NOT** Salem, New Jersey
American Weekly Mercury	Page 57	Custom House Salem Jul 22 1721 – This is Salem, Massachusetts **NOT** Salem, New Jersey

"American Weekly Mercury Copyright 1720"

American Weekly Mercury	Issue 38	Custom House Salem Aug 27 1720 – This is Salem, Massachusetts **NOT** Salem, New Jersey

"Boston Gazette Copyright 1720"

Boston Gazette	Issue 17	Custom House Salem Apr 9 1720 – This is Salem, Massachusetts **NOT** Salem, New Jersey

Matches

If you just look at one newspaper you will not see the pattern that shows up in the ships dates. When you look at 800 issues together you will see from American Weekly Mercury, The New England Courant,
Boston News Letter & The Boston Gazette. That they had to have time to set the type for the print. So they had to have the post from the custom house 2 days before the paper was printed. That is why
when you look at the coverage map I have given in the preface, I show the post dates not the issue dates.

Boston Gazette	Issue 17	Publication Date: Apr 11, 1720	Salem, MA – Ships News: Apr 9, 1720	Data Matches
American Weekly Mercury	Issue 19	Publication Date: Apr 28, 1720	Salem, MA – Ships News: Apr 9, 1720	

As you can see it took 19 days to get the shipping news from Salem, Massachusetts to publish it in the American Weekly Mercury. So this is the validation to show the Salem Custom House Data in
"Archives of the State of New Jersey Vol 11" is for Massachusetts and not New Jersey.

Orginialy Published

1720	Fortune	Ship				Start	Topsham		9 Weeks	Philadelphia	19 May 1720 [9 Jun 1720] [21 Jul 1720]
M-S-007 S-F-006				Richard	Stevens		[England]			[Pennsylvania]	
						>	Boston		>	Salem	[27 Aug 1720]
							[Massachusetts]			[New Jersey]	
						>					
							Spain				
	5:53,56,60,79,96							(Known Passengers / Settlers) Philadelphia / Inward – 19 May 1720 – Count Many+			

Corrcted Version

1720	Fortune	Ship				Start	Topsham		9 Weeks	Philadelphia	19 May 1720 [9 Jun 1720] [21 Jul 1720]
M-S-007 S-F-006				Richard	Stevens		[England]			[Pennsylvania]	
						>	Boston	[13 Aug 1720] vv Transfer vv	>	Salem	vv Transfer vv [27 Aug 1720]
							[Massachusetts]	vv Transfer vv vv Transfer vv		[Massachusetts]	
						>					
							Spain				
	5:53,56,60,79,96 / 21:857							(Known Passengers / Settlers) Philadelphia / Inward – 19 May 1720 – Count Many+			

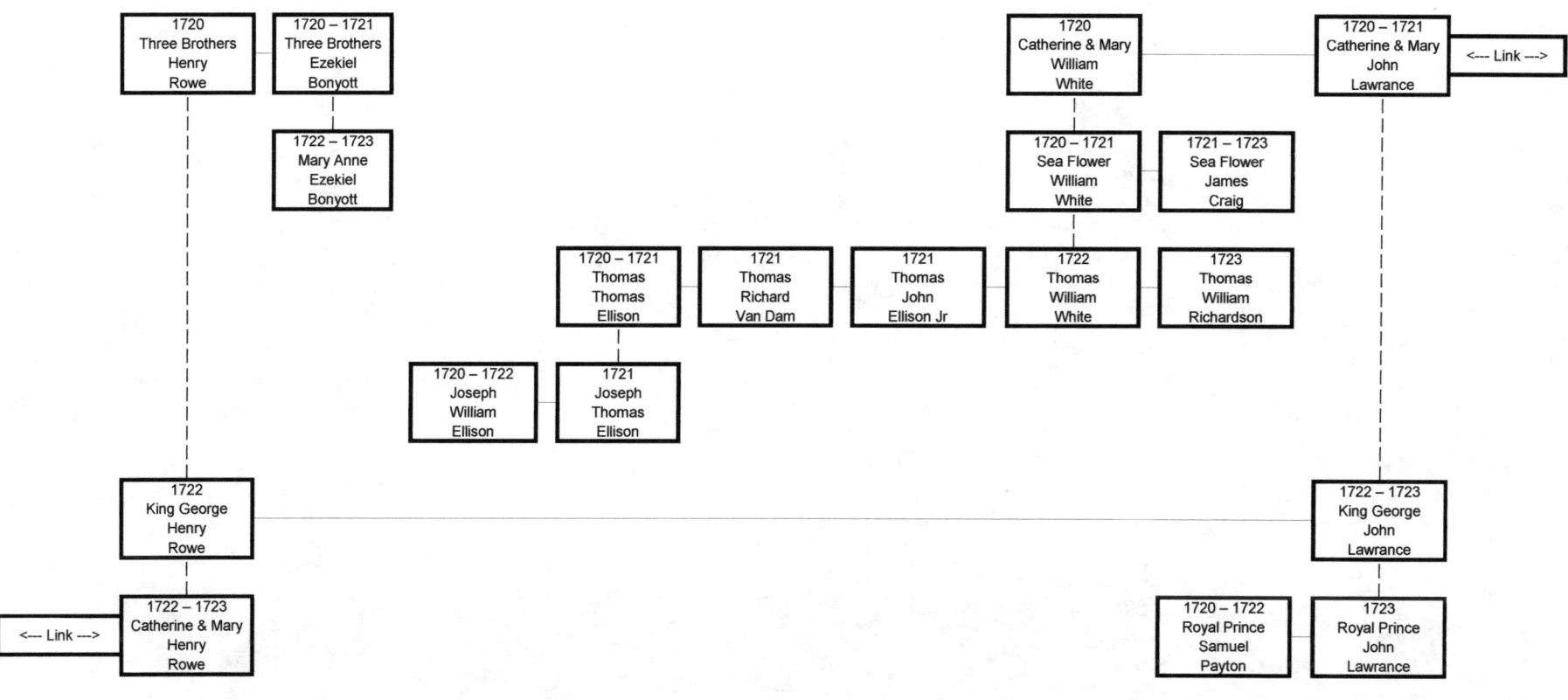

Preface

This is a scan of a 1720c map from Johann Baptist Homann of Germany, centered on the Rhine River Valley. This map is 19" x 22" in whole. I have scanned the top left 10" x 7" section to show from Rotterdam, and down a section of the Rhine River Valley. I am putting this in the book to show where most of the passengers of the 1720's would have traveled through. This map is out of my personal collection of books, documents, & maps.

Copyright © 2017 William Taylor Easter II

This is a photo of a book of prayers in German from 1721. With the owner signing and dating.
This book is out of my personal collection of books, documents, & maps.

This is a example of one of the few personal items that a Palatine would have brought with them on their ship passage to Colonial America.

Johann Christian Naumann – 1722

Book measures – 3 1/4" x 5 3/8"

IX

North America

St Johns	Newfoundland
Placentia	Newfoundland
Cape Sable	Nova Scotia
Annapolis Royal	Nova Scotia
Canso	Nova Scotia
New England	
Winter Harbor	Maine
Cape Porpoise	Maine
Piscataqua River	New Hampshire
Portsmouth	New Hampshire
Salem	Massachusetts
Boston	Massachusetts
Nantucket	Massachusetts
Nantasket	Massachusetts
Cape Ann	Massachusetts
Newport	Rhode Island
Rock Island	Rhode Island
Saybrook	Connecticut
Hartford	Connecticut
New London	Connecticut
New Haven	Connecticut
Albany	New York
New York	New York
Long Island	New York
Perth Amboy	New Jersey
Sandy Hook	New Jersey
Salem	New Jersey
Burlington	New Jersey
Cape May	New Jersey
Philadelphia	Pennsylvania
Upland / Chester	Pennsylvania
Delaware River	
Capes of Delaware	
New Castle	Delaware
Prime Hook	Delaware
Lewes	Delaware
Cape Henlopen	Delaware
Annapolis	Maryland
Wye River	Maryland
South River	Maryland
Patuxent	Maryland
Potomac	Maryland
Choptank	Maryland
Sinepuxent	Maryland
Capes of Virginia	
Cape Charles	Virginia
James River	Virginia
Accomack	Virginia
York River	Virginia
Lynnhaven Bay	Virginia
	North Carolina
Roanoke Island	North Carolina
Bath Town	North Carolina
	South Carolina
Charles Town	South Carolina
St Augustine	Florida

Unknown

Leogand	Location Unkn
New Castle	Location Unkn
Cales	Location Unkn

American Coasters

Known Arrival & Departure Ports of the 1720's

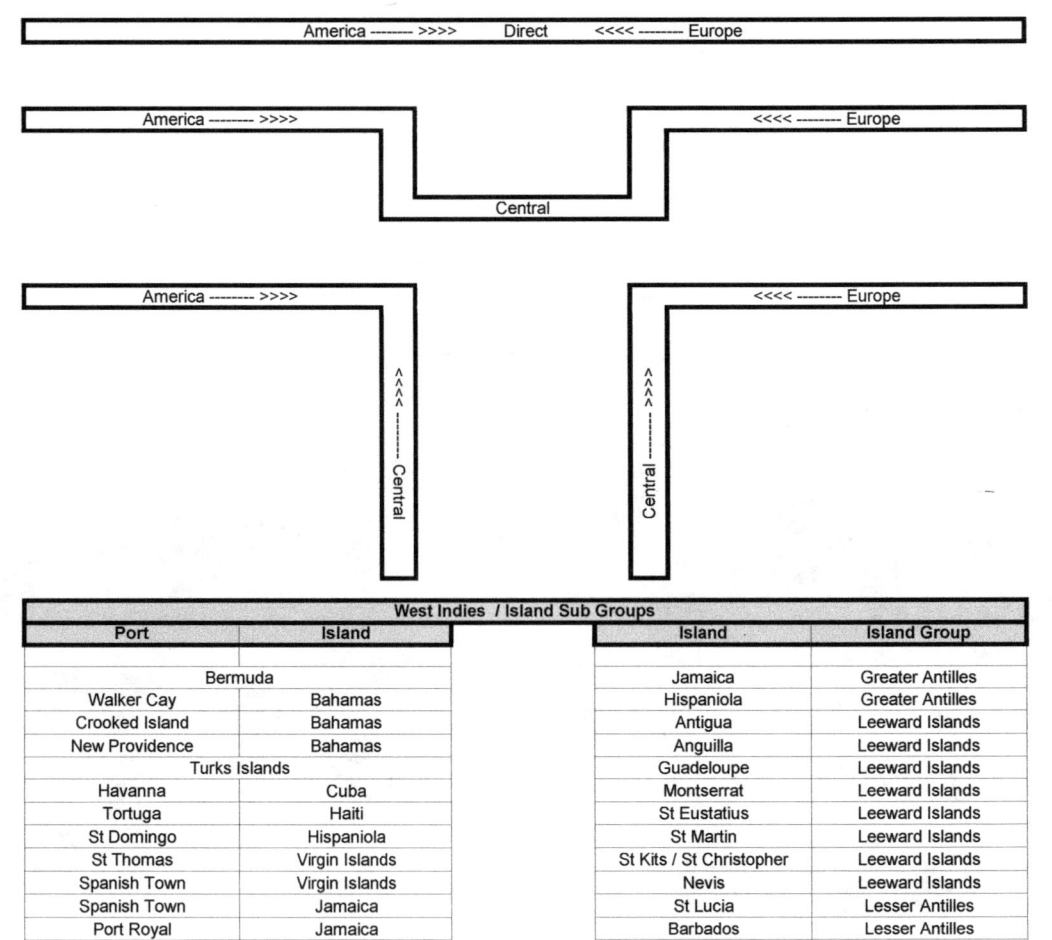

America -------- >>>>   Direct   <<<< -------- Europe

America -------- >>>>   <<<< -------- Europe

Central

America -------- >>>>   <<<< -------- Europe

^^^^ -------- Central

Central -------- ^^^^

West Indies / Island Sub Groups

Port	Island	Island	Island Group
Bermuda		Jamaica	Greater Antilles
Walker Cay	Bahamas	Hispaniola	Greater Antilles
Crooked Island	Bahamas	Antigua	Leeward Islands
New Providence	Bahamas	Anguilla	Leeward Islands
Turks Islands		Guadeloupe	Leeward Islands
Havanna	Cuba	Montserrat	Leeward Islands
Tortuga	Haiti	St Eustatius	Leeward Islands
St Domingo	Hispaniola	St Martin	Leeward Islands
St Thomas	Virgin Islands	St Kits / St Christopher	Leeward Islands
Spanish Town	Virgin Islands	Nevis	Leeward Islands
Spanish Town	Jamaica	St Lucia	Lesser Antilles
Port Royal	Jamaica	Barbados	Lesser Antilles
Saltertuda	[Location Unkn]	Martinique	Lesser Antilles
Pettiguavis	[Location Unkn]	Curacao	Leeward Antilles
St John	Antigua	Bonaire	Leeward Antilles
St George	Grenada		

There are 6 types of ships – they are sorted by their preferred travel ports.

1. American Coasters : Ships that only stayed on the coast of North America.
2. America – Direct – Europe : Ships traveled from America to Europe.
3. America – Central – Europe : Ships traveled from America to West Indies then Europe.
4. America – Central : Ships that traveled to and from America and West Indies, without going to Europe.
5. Europe – Central : Ships that traveled from Europe to West Indies, without going to America.
6: Europe Coasters : Ships that travel from England to Portugal or other coastal ports.

Note: In the Philadelphia Book – I had Salt Island, Jamaica which was for Saltertuda, I have now switched it to Location Unkn. Based off new information from research I am thinking its in the Leeward Islands. If more information is found it will be published in the next book.

Europe

Great Britain	
Isle of May	Scotland
Glasgow	Scotland
Montrose	Scotland
Dublin	Ireland
Lisburn	Ireland
Belfast	Ireland
Cork	Ireland
Londonderry	Ireland
Swansea	Wales
Milford Haven	Wales
Hull	England
Whitehaven	England
Torbay / Torquay	England
Plymouth	England
Exon / Exeter / Topsham	England
Cowes	England
Dartmouth	England
Dover	England
Deal	England
Bristol	England
Barnstable	England
London	England
Harwich	England
Gravesend	England
Falmouth	England
Liverpool	England
Dolyserne	England
Sussex	England
Southampton	England
Isle of Wight	England
Land's End	England
English Channel	
Amsterdam	Holland
Rotterdam	Holland
La Rochelle	France
Bilbao	Spain
Cadiz	Spain
Alicante	Spain
Oporto / Porto	Portugal
Lisbon	Portugal

Azores / Western Islands

Faial Island	Portugal
Madeira Island	Portugal
Terciera Island	Portugal

Africa

Africa
Canary Islands

South America

Bay of Campeche
Campeche
Bay of Honduras
Gulf of Honduras
Honduras
Suriname
Cayenne, French Guiana
Cape Catoche, Mexico

Europe Coasters

Average Passage Length & Ship Type / Sizes

Departure – North America

Departure		Passage	Arrival	
	Rhode Island	4 Days	New York	New York
	Rhode Island	13 Hours	New York	New York
Philadelphia	Pennsylvania	18 Days	Barbados	
Philadelphia	Pennsylvania	7 Days	Bermuda	
Philadelphia	Pennsylvania	35 Days	London	England
	Virginia	2 Days	Philadelphia	Pennsylvania
Charles Town	South Carolina	10 Days	Philadelphia	Pennsylvania
	South Carolina	9 Days	New York	New York
	South Carolina	8 Days	New York	New York
	South Carolina	7 Days	New York	New York
	North Carolina	18 Days	Perth Amboy	New Jersey

Departure – Europe

Departure		Passage	Arrival	
Cork	Ireland	10 Weeks	New York	New York
	Great Britain	10 Weeks	New York	New York
	Holland	11 Weeks	New York	New York
Downs	England	7 Weeks & 3 Days	New York	New York
Plymouth	England	6 Weeks	Piscataqua River	
Plymouth	England	7 Weeks	Philadelphia	Pennsylvania
Plymouth	England	9 Weeks	Philadelphia	Pennsylvania
Bristol	England	10 Weeks	New York	New York
Bristol	England	11 Weeks & 3 day	Philadelphia	Pennsylvania
Bristol	England	13 Weeks	Philadelphia	Pennsylvania
Land's End	England	5 Weeks	New York	New York
Madeira Island	Portugal	29 Days	New York	New York
Madeira Island	Portugal	5 Weeks	New York	New York
Madeira Island	Portugal	6 Weeks	New York	New York
Madeira Island	Portugal	6 Weeks & 5 Days	New York	New York
Madeira Island	Portugal	9 Weeks	New York	New York
Milford Haven	Wales	6 Weeks	New York	New York
Swansea	Wales	15 Weeks	New York	New York
Exeter / Topsham	England	9 Weeks	Philadelphia	Pennsylvania
London	England	11 Weeks	Philadelphia	Pennsylvania
London	England	10 Weeks	New York	New York

Ship Types

Sloop	Tons: 3, 8,10,15, 22, 30, 32, 55	
Ship	Tons: 100,130,150, 160, 200, 240	
Boat	N / A	
Galley	N / A	
Pink	N / A	
Schooner	N / A	
Scallop	N / A	
Snow	N / A	
Brigantine	N / A	

Departure – West Indies & South America

Departure		Passage	Arrival	
Bermuda		28 Days	New York	New York
Bermuda		16 Days	Philadelphia	Pennsylvania
Bermuda		10 Days	New York	New York
Bermuda		8 Days	New York	New York
New Providence	Bahamas	12 Days	New York	New York
New Providence	Bahamas	14 Days	New York	New York
New Providence	Bahamas	25 Days	New York	New York
Jamaica	Greater Antilles	22 Days	New York	New York
Jamaica	Greater Antilles	25 Days	New York	New York
Jamaica	Greater Antilles	26 Days	New York	New York
Jamaica	Greater Antilles	27 Days	New York	New York
Jamaica	Greater Antilles	28 Days	New York	New York
Jamaica	Greater Antilles	35 Days	New York	New York
Jamaica	Greater Antilles	35 Days	Philadelphia	Pennsylvania
Jamaica	Greater Antilles	5 Weeks	Boston	Massachusetts
Jamaica	Greater Antilles	7 Weeks	New York	New York
St Thomas	Virgin Islands	6 Weeks	New York	New York
St Thomas	Virgin Islands	12 Days	New York	New York
St Thomas	Virgin Islands	17 Days	New York	New York
St Thomas	Virgin Islands	19 Days	New York	New York
St Thomas	Virgin Islands	20 Days	New York	New York
St Thomas	Virgin Islands	29 Days	New York	New York
St Thomas	Virgin Islands	21 Days	New York	New York
St Christopher's	Leeward Islands	20 Days	New York	New York
St Christopher's	Leeward Islands	22 Days	New York	New York
St Martin	Leeward Islands	40 Days	New York	New York
Nevis	Leeward Islands	14 Days	New York	New York
Nevis	Leeward Islands	16 Days	New York	New York
Antigua	Leeward Islands	20 Days	New York	New York
Anguilla	Leeward Islands	14 Days	New York	New York
Barbados	Lesser Antilles	6 Weeks	New York	New York
Barbados	Lesser Antilles	30 Days	Hartford	Connecticut
Barbados	Lesser Antilles	17 Days	New York	New York
Barbados	Lesser Antilles	18 Days	New York	New York
Barbados	Lesser Antilles	20 Days	New York	New York
Barbados	Lesser Antilles	21 Days	New York	New York
Barbados	Lesser Antilles	22 Days	New York	New York
Barbados	Lesser Antilles	24 Days	New York	New York
Barbados	Lesser Antilles	31 Days	New York	New York
Barbados	Lesser Antilles	22 Days	Perth Amboy	New Jersey
Barbados	Lesser Antilles	18 Days		Rhode Island
Barbados	Lesser Antilles	16 Days	Philadelphia	Pennsylvania
Curacao	Leeward Antilles	7 Weeks	New York	New York
Curacao	Leeward Antilles	17 Days	New York	New York
Curacao	Leeward Antilles	19 Days	New York	New York
Curacao	Leeward Antilles	20 Days	New York	New York
Curacao	Leeward Antilles	21 Days	New York	New York
Curacao	Leeward Antilles	25 Days	New York	New York
Curacao	Leeward Antilles	26 Days	New York	New York
Suriname	South America	25 Days	New York	New York

Data Coverage / 9 Dec 1719 – 31 Dec 1723

The data in this chart is the information used for the reconstruction of both the Philadelphia & New York Custom Houses, and supplementary data for Salem, Boston, Rhode Island, Connecticut & New Jersey Ports to fill in data from the Philadelphia & New York ships that interacted with them. This is not all the available data, this is only the data I was able to acqurie to date. These dates are the coverage for the shipping news not the issue dates.

***** - No Data Available / When you see this, it is only for the current newspaper, it has already been searched and no data was found for that week for that port.

Legend

///	Data May Be Available	/	Partial Data Available	>	Captains Only	L	Local Only
X	Complete Data Available	*	No Data Available	S#	Check Sources	I	Inbound Only

Complete Data	Captain Names & Ship Names & Arrival, Departure Ports
Partial Data	Captain Names & Arrival, Departure Ports and with or without Ship Names
Captains Only	Captain Names Only & Arrival, Departure Ports no Ship Names
Local Only	Captain Names Only & Arrival, Departure Ports no Ship Names / No Outbound Besides Local

Boston Gazette			Boston News Letter			Boston Gazette			New England Courant			American Weekly Mercury			Boston News Letter			Boston Gazette			American Weekly Mercury			American Weekly Mercury & Source 45			American Weekly Mercury			American Weekly Mercury			American Weekly Mercury		
1719																																			
Salem – MA			Boston – MA												Newport – RI									New London – CT			New York – NY			Perth Amboy – NJ			Philadelphia – PA		
*****	*****	*****	11-22	11-28	815>/	*****	*****	*****	*****	*****	*****	No Date		1>	11-21	11-27	/////	*****	*****	*****	11-21	11-27	*****	11-18	11-24	*****	*****	*****	*****	*****	*****	*****	*****	*****	*****
*****	*****	*****	11-29	12-5	816>/	*****	*****	*****	*****	*****	*****	11-29	12-5	2>	11-28	12-4	/////	*****	*****	*****	11-28	12-4	*****	11-25	12-1	*****	12-3	12-9	1X	*****	*****	*****	*****	*****	*****
*****	*****	*****	12-6	12-12	817>/	*****	*****	*****	*****	*****	*****	12-6	12-12	*****	12-5	12-11	/////	*****	*****	*****	12-5	12-11	*****	12-2	12-8	*****	12-10	12-22	2X	*****	*****	*****	*****	*****	*****
12-13	12-19	/////	12-13	12-19	818>/	12-13	12-19	/////	*****	*****	*****	12-13	12-19	5X	12-12	12-18	/////	12-12	12-18	/////	12-12	12-18	5X	12-9	12-15	S45/				*****	*****	*****	12-16	12-22	1X
12-20	12-26	/////	12-20	12-26	819>/	12-20	12-26	/////	*****	*****	*****	12-20	12-26	*****	12-19	12-25	/////	12-19	12-25	/////	12-19	12-25	*****	12-16	12-22	*****	12-23	1-5	4X	*****	*****	*****	12-23	12-29	2X
12-27	1-2	*****	12-27	1-2	820>/	12-27	1-2	3X	*****	*****	*****	12-27	1-2	7X	12-26	1-1	820>	12-26	1-1	3X	12-26	1-1	7X	12-23	12-29	*****				*****	*****	*****	No	Data	3
1720																																			
1-3	1-9	*****	1-3	1-9	821>/	1-3	1-9	4X	*****	*****	*****	1-3	1-9	8X	1-2	1-9	/////	1-2	1-9	5X	1-2	1-9	9X	12-30	1-5	*****	1-6	1-18	6X	*****	*****	*****	12-30	1-8	4X
1-10	1-16	*****	1-10	1-16	822>/	1-10	1-16	5X	*****	*****	*****	1-10	1-16	9X	1-10	1-16	/////	1-10	1-16	/////	1-10	1-16	*****	1-6	1-12	*****				1-8	1-14	*****	/////	/////	5
1-17	1-23	*****	1-17	1-23	823>/	1-17	1-23	6X	*****	*****	*****	1-17	1-23	10X	1-17	1-22	824/	1-17	1-22	/////	1-17	1-22	11X	1-13	1-19	*****	1-19	2-2	8X	1-15	1-21	6X	1-16	1-25	6X
1-24	1-30	/////	1-24	1-30	824>/	1-24	1-30	/////	*****	*****	*****	1-24	1-30	11X	1-23	1-29	/////	1-23	1-29	/////	1-23	1-29	12X	1-20	1-26	*****				1-22	1-29	8X	1-26	2-2	7X
1-31	2-6	/////	1-31	2-6	825>/	1-31	2-6	/////	*****	*****	*****	No Date		12X	1-30	2-5	825L	1-30	2-5	9X	1-30	2-5	13X	1-27	2-2	*****	2-3	2-16	10X	1-30	2-4	*****	/////	/////	8
2-7	2-13	*****	2-7	2-13	826>/	2-7	2-13	9X	*****	*****	*****	No Date		13X	2-6	2-12	/////	2-6	2-12	/////	2-6	2-12	*****	2-3	2-9	*****				*****	*****	*****	2-10	2-16	9X
2-14	2-20	/////	2-14	2-20	827>/	2-14	2-20	/////	*****	*****	*****	2-14	2-20	*****	2-13	2-19	827L	2-13	2-19	/////	2-13	2-19	*****	2-10	2-16	*****	2-17	3-1	12X	*****	*****	*****	2-17	2-23	10X
2-21	2-27	/////	2-21	2-27	828>/	2-21	2-27	/////	*****	*****	*****	2-21	2-27	14X	2-20	2-26	828>	2-20	2-26	/////	2-20	2-26	14X	2-17	2-23	14X				*****	*****	*****	2-24	3-1	11X
2-28	3-5	*****	2-28	3-5	829>/	2-28	3-5	12X	*****	*****	*****	2-28	3-5	*****	2-27	3-4	829L	2-27	3-4	12X	2-27	3-4	*****	2-24	3-1	*****	3-2	3-14	13X	*****	*****	*****	3-2	3-7	12X
3-6	3-12	*****	3-6	3-12	830>/	3-6	3-12	13X	*****	*****	*****	3-6	3-12	15X	3-5	3-11	/////	3-5	3-11	13X	3-5	3-11	15X	3-2	3-8	15X				*****	*****	*****	No Date		13X
3-13	3-19	/////	3-13	3-19	831>/	3-13	3-19	/////	*****	*****	*****	3-13	3-19	16X	3-12	3-18	831L	3-12	3-18	/////	3-12	3-18	16X	3-9	3-17	17X	3-15	3-21	14X	*****	*****	*****	/////	/////	14
3-20	3-26	*****	3-20	3-26	832>/	3-20	3-26	/////	*****	*****	*****	3-20	3-26	17X	3-19	3-25	832L	3-19	3-25	/////	3-19	3-25	*****	3-18	3-24	*****	3-22	3-28	15X	*****	*****	*****	3-22	3-31	15X
3-27	4-2	/////	3-27	4-2	833>/	3-27	4-23	/////	*****	*****	*****	3-27	4-23	*****	3-26	4-1	/////	3-26	4-1	17X	3-26	4-1	*****	3-25	3-31	*****	3-29	4-4	16X	3-30	4-5	*****	4-1	4-7	16X
4-3	4-9	17X	4-3	4-9	834>/	4-3	4-9	17X	*****	*****	*****	4-3	4-9	19X	4-2	4-7	834L	4-2	4-8	17X	4-2	4-8	18X	4-1	4-7	*****	4-5	4-11	17X	4-6	4-12	17/	4-8	4-14	17X
4-10	4-16	/////	4-10	4-16	836>/	4-10	4-16	/////	*****	*****	*****	4-10	4-16	*****	4-8	4-11	835>	4-9	4-15	/////	4-9	4-15	*****	4-8	4-14	*****	4-12	4-18	18X	4-13	4-19	*****	4-15	4-21	18X
4-17	4-23	19X	4-17	4-23	838>/	4-17	4-23	19X	*****	*****	*****	4-17	4-23	20X	4-12	4-15	838>	4-16	4-22	19X	4-16	4-22	20X	4-15	4-22	20X	4-19	4-23	19X	*****	*****	*****	4-22	4-28	19X
4-24	4-30	*****	4-24	4-30	839>/	4-24	4-30	/////	*****	*****	*****	4-24	4-30	*****	4-16	4-19	838>	4-23	4-28	/////	4-23	4-28	*****	4-23	4-29	S45/	4-24	5-2	20X	*****	*****	*****	4-29	5-5	20X
5-1	5-7	*****	5-1	5-7	841>/	5-1	5-7	21X	*****	*****	*****	5-1	5-7	23X	4-20	4-29	839L	4-29	5-5	21X	4-29	5-5	*****	4-30	5-6	S45/	5-3	5-9	21X	*****	*****	*****	5-6	5-12	21X
5-8	5-14	22X	5-8	5-14	842>/	5-8	5-14	22X	*****	*****	*****	5-8	5-14	*****	4-30	5-6	841L	5-6	5-12	22X	5-6	5-12	*****	5-7	5-13	*****	5-10	5-16	22X	*****	*****	*****	5-13	5-19	22X
5-15	5-21	24X	5-15	5-21	844>	5-15	5-21	23X	*****	*****	*****	5-15	5-21	*****	5-7	5-11	/////	5-13	5-20	23X	5-13	5-20	*****	5-14	5-20	S45/	5-17	5-23	23X	*****	*****	*****	5-20	5-26	23X
5-22	5-28	*****	5-22	5-28	845>	5-22	5-28	24X	*****	*****	*****	5-22	5-28	*****	5-12	5-16	843>I	5-21	5-27	/////	5-21	5-27	*****	5-21	5-27	S45/	5-24	5-30	24X	*****	*****	*****	5-27	6-1	24X
5-29	6-4	/////	5-29	6-4	846>/	5-29	6-4	/////	*****	*****	*****	5-29	6-4	26X	5-17	5-20	844>I	5-28	6-3	/////	5-28	6-3	*****	5-28	6-3	S45/	6-1	6-6	25X	*****	*****	*****	6-2	6-9	25X
6-5	6-11	/////	6-5	6-11	848>/	6-5	6-11	/////	*****	*****	*****	6-5	6-11	*****	/////	/////	/////	6-4	6-10	27>	6-4	6-10	*****	6-4	6-10	*****	6-7	6-13	26X	*****	*****	*****	6-10	6-16	26X
6-12	6-18	27>	6-12	6-18	849>/	6-12	6-18	27>	*****	*****	*****	6-12	6-18	*****	6-11	6-17	/////	6-11	6-17	/////	6-11	6-17	*****	6-11	6-17	*****	6-14	6-20	27X	*****	*****	*****	6-17	6-23	27X
6-19	6-25	28>	6-19	6-25	850>/	6-19	6-25	28>	*****	*****	*****	6-19	6-25	29>	6-18	6-24	850L	6-18	6-24	/////	6-18	6-24	*****	6-18	6-24	*****	6-21	6-27	28X	*****	*****	*****	6-24	6-30	28X
6-26	7-2	/////	6-26	7-2	851>/	6-26	7-2	/////	*****	*****	*****	6-26	7-2	*****	6-25	7-1	/////	6-25	7-1	/////	6-25	7-1	*****	6-25	7-1	*****	6-28	7-4	29X	*****	*****	*****	7-1	7-7	29X
7-3	7-9	*****	7-3	7-9	852>/	7-3	7-9	30>	*****	*****	*****	7-3	7-9	*****	7-2	7-7	852L	7-2	7-8	/////	7-2	7-8	*****	7-2	7-8	*****	7-5	7-11	30X	*****	*****	*****	7-8	7-14	30X
7-10	7-16	*****	7-10	7-16	853>/	7-10	7-16	31>	*****	*****	*****	7-10	7-16	*****	7-9	7-15	/////	7-9	7-15	/////	7-9	7-15	*****	7-9	7-15	*****	7-12	7-18	31X	*****	*****	*****	7-15	7-21	31X
7-17	7-23	/////	7-17	7-23	854>/	7-17	7-23	/////	*****	*****	*****	7-17	7-23	*****	7-16	7-22	/////	7-16	7-22	/////	7-16	7-22	*****	7-16	7-22	*****	7-19	7-25	32X	*****	*****	*****	7-22	7-28	32X
7-24	7-30	*****	7-24	7-30	855>/	7-24	7-30	33>	*****	*****	*****	7-24	7-30	*****	7-23	7-29	/////	7-23	7-29	33>	7-23	7-29	*****	7-23	7-29	*****	7-26	8-1	33X	*****	*****	*****	7-29	8-4	33X
7-31	8-6	/////	7-31	8-6	856>/	7-31	8-6	/////	*****	*****	*****	7-31	8-6	*****	7-30	8-5	/////	7-30	8-5	/////	7-30	8-5	35/	7-30	8-5	S45/	8-2	8-8	34X	*****	*****	*****	8-5	8-11	34X
8-7	8-13	/////	8-7	8-13	857>/	8-7	8-13	/////	*****	*****	*****	8-7	8-13	*****	8-6	8-12	/////	8-6	8-12	/////	8-6	8-12	*****	8-6	8-12	*****	8-9	8-15	35X	*****	*****	*****	8-12	8-18	35X
8-14	8-20	36X	8-14	8-20	858>/	8-14	8-20	36>/	*****	*****	*****	8-14	8-20	*****	8-13	8-19	/////	8-13	8-19	36X	8-13	8-19	*****	8-13	8-19	S45/	8-16	8-22	36X	*****	*****	*****	8-19	8-25	36X
8-21	8-27	*****	8-21	8-27	859>/	8-21	8-27	37>/	*****	*****	*****	8-21	8-27	38/	8-20	8-26	/////	8-20	8-26	/////	8-20	8-26	*****	8-20	8-26	*****	8-23	8-29	37X	*****	*****	*****	8-26	9-1	37X
8-28	9-3	38X	8-28	9-3	860>/	8-28	9-3	38>/	*****	*****	*****	8-28	9-3	39X	8-27	9-2	/////	8-27	9-2	38>	8-27	9-2	*****	8-27	9-2	S45/	8-30	9-5	38X	*****	*****	*****	9-2	9-8	38X
9-4	9-10	39X	9-4	9-10	861>/	9-4	9-10	39>/	*****	*****	*****	9-4	9-10	*****	9-3	9-9	/////	9-3	9-9	39>	9-3	9-9	*****	9-3	9-9	*****	9-6	9-12	39X	*****	*****	*****	9-9	9-15	39X
9-11	9-17	40X	9-11	9-17	862>	9-11	9-17	40>/	*****	*****	*****	9-11	9-17	41X	9-10	9-15	/////	9-10	9-15	/////	9-10	9-15	*****	9-10	9-16	*****	9-13	9-19	40X	*****	*****	*****	9-16	9-22	40X
9-18	9-24	41X	9-18	9-24	863>	9-18	9-24	41>/	*****	*****	*****	9-18	9-24	*****	9-16	9-22	/////	9-16	9-22	41>	9-16	9-22	*****	9-17	9-23	*****	9-20	9-26	41X	*****	*****	*****	9-23	9-29	41X
9-25	10-1	42>	9-25	10-1	864>/	9-25	10-1	42>/	*****	*****	*****	9-25	10-1	*****	9-23	9-30	864>	9-23	9-30	42>	9-23	9-30	*****	9-24	9-30	*****	9-27	10-3	42X	*****	*****	*****	9-30	10-6	42X
10-2	10-8	43>	10-2	10-8	865>	10-2	10-8	43>/	*****	*****	*****	10-2	10-8	*****	10-1	10-7	/////	10-1	10-7	43>	10-1	10-7	*****	10-1	10-7	*****	10-4	10-10	43X	*****	*****	*****	10-7	10-13	43X
10-9	10-15	44X	10-9	10-15	866>/	10-9	10-15	44>/	*****	*****	*****	10-9	10-15	*****	10-8	10-14	/////	10-8	10-14	44>	10-8	10-14	*****	10-8	10-14	*****	10-11	10-17	44X	*****	*****	*****	10-14	10-20	44X
10-16	10-22	*****	10-16	10-22	867>/	10-16	10-22	45>/	*****	*****	*****	10-16	10-22	46X	10-15	10-20	/////	10-15	10-20	45>	10-15	10-20	*****	10-15	10-21	*****	10-18	10-24	45X	*****	*****	*****	10-21	10-27	45X
10-23	10-29	*****	10-23	10-29	868>/	10-23	10-29	46>/	*****	*****	*****	10-23	10-29	*****	10-21	10-28	/////	10-21	10-28	46>	10-21	10-28	*****	10-22	10-28	*****	10-25	10-31	46X	*****	*****	*****	10-28	11-3	46X
10-30	11-5	47>	10-30	11-5	869>/	10-30	11-5	47>/	*****	*****	*****	10-30	11-5	*****	10-29	11-4	/////	10-29	11-4	47>	10-29	11-4	*****	10-29	11-4	*****	11-1	11-7	47X	*****	*****	*****	11-4	11-10	47X
11-6	11-12	48>	11-6	11-12	870>/	11-6	11-12	48>/	*****	*****	*****	11-6	11-12	*****	11-5	11-11	/////	11-5	11-11	/////	11-5	11-11	*****	11-5	11-11	*****	11-8	11-14	48X	*****	*****	*****	11-11	11-17	48X
11-13	11-19	49>	11-13	11-19	871>/	11-13	11-19	49>/	*****	*****	*****	11-13	11-19	*****	11-12	11-18	/////	11-12	11-18	49>	11-12	11-18	*****	11-12	11-18	*****	11-15	11-21	49X	*****	*****	*****	11-18	11-24	49X
11-20	11-26	*****	11-20	11-26	872X	11-20	11-26	50>/	*****	*****	*****	11-20	11-26	*****	11-19	11-25	/////	11-19	11-25	50>	11-19	11-25	*****	11-19	11-25	*****	11-22	11-28	50X	*****	*****	*****	11-25	12-1	50X
11-27	12-3	51>/	11-27	12-3	873>/	11-27	12-3	51>/	*****	*****	*****	11-27	12-3	*****	11-26	12-2	/////	11-26	12-2	51>	11-26	12-2	*****	11-26	12-2	*****	11-29	12-5	52X	*****	*****	*****	12-2	12-8	51X
12-4	12-10	52>/	12-4	12-10	874>/	12-4	12-10	52>/	*****	*****	*****	12-4	12-10	*****	12-3	12-9	874L	12-3	12-8	52>	12-3	12-8	*****	12-3	12-9	S45/	12-6	12-19	54X	*****	*****	*****	12-9	12-13	52X
12-11	12-17	53>	12-11	12-17	875>/	12-11	12-17	53>	*****	*****	*****	12-11	12-17	56X	12-10	12-15	/////	12-9	12-15	53>	12-9	12-15	*****	12-10	12-16	*****				*****	*****	*****	12-14	12-20	53X

The data in this chart is the information used for the reconstruction of both the Philadelphia & New York Custom Houses, and supplementary data for Salem, Boston, Rhode Island, Connecticut & New Jersey Ports to fill in data from the Philadelphia & New York ships that interacted with them. This is not all the available data, this is only the data I was able to acqurie to date. These dates are the coverage for the shipping news not the issue dates.

***** - No Data Available / When you see this, it is only for the current newspaper, it has already been searched and no data was found for that week for that port.

Legend							
///	Data May Be Available	/	Partial Data Available	>	Captains Only	L	Local Only
X	Complete Data Available	*	No Data Available	S#	Check Sources	I	Inbound Only
Complete Data	Captain Names & Ship Names & Arrival, Departure Ports						
Partial Data	Captain Names & Arrival, Departure Ports and with or without Ship Names						
Captains Only	Captain Names Only & Arrival, Departure Ports no Ship Names						
Local Only	Captain Names Only & Arrival, Departure Ports no Ship Names / No Outbound Besides Local						

Boston Gazette			Boston News Letter			Boston Gazette			New England Courant			American Weekly Mercury			Boston News Letter			Boston Gazette			American Weekly Mercury			American Weekly Mercury & Source 45			American Weekly Mercury			American Weekly Mercury			American Weekly Mercury		
1721																																			
Salem – MA			Boston – MA												Newport – RI									New London – CT			New York – NY			Perth Amboy – NJ			Philadelphia – PA		
1-1	1-7	/////	1-1	1-7	878>/	1-1	1-7	/////	*****	*****	*****	1-1	1-7	*****	12-31	1-6	/////	12-31	1-6	/////	12-31	1-6	*****	12-31	1-6	S45/	1-3	1-16	58X	*****	*****	*****	1-4	1-10	56X
1-8	1-14	57>/	1-8	1-14	879>/	1-8	1-14	57>/	*****	*****	*****	1-8	1-14	*****	1-7	1-13	/////	1-7	1-13	57>	1-7	1-13	*****	1-7	1-13	*****				*****	*****	*****	1-11	1-17	57X
1-15	1-21	58X	1-15	1-21	880>/	1-15	1-21	58>/	*****	*****	*****	1-15	1-21	*****	1-14	1-19	/////	1-14	1-19	58>	1-14	1-19	*****	1-14	1-20	*****	1-17	1-31	60X	*****	*****	*****	1-18	1-24	58X
1-22	1-28	*****	1-22	1-28	881>/	1-22	1-28	59>/	*****	*****	*****	1-22	1-28	*****	1-20	1-27	/////	1-20	1-27	59>	1-20	1-27	*****	1-21	1-27	*****				*****	*****	*****	1-25	1-31	59X
1-29	2-4	*****	1-29	2-4	882>/	1-29	2-4	60X	*****	*****	*****	1-29	2-4	*****	1-28	2-3	/////	1-28	2-3	60>	1-28	2-1	*****	1-28	2-3	*****	2-1	2-13	62X	*****	*****	*****	2-1	2-7	60X
2-5	2-11	*****	2-5	2-11	883>/	2-5	2-11	61X	*****	*****	*****	2-5	2-11	*****	2-4	2-10	/////	2-4	2-10	/////	2-2	2-8	64/	2-4	2-10	*****				*****	*****	*****	2-8	2-14	61X
2-12	2-18	*****	2-12	2-18	884X	2-12	2-18	62X	*****	*****	*****	2-12	2-18	*****	2-11	2-17	/////	2-11	2-17	62>	2-9	2-17	*****	2-11	2-17	*****	2-14	2-27	63X	*****	*****	*****	2-15	2-21	62X
2-19	2-25	63X	2-19	2-25	/////	2-19	2-25	63X	*****	*****	*****	2-19	2-25	*****	2-18	2-24	/////	2-18	2-24	63>	2-18	2-24	*****	2-18	2-24	*****				*****	*****	*****	2-22	3-2	63X
2-26	3-4	*****	2-26	3-4	886>/	2-26	3-4	64>/	*****	*****	*****	2-26	3-4	*****	2-25	3-3	/////	2-25	3-3	/////	2-25	3-3	*****	2-25	3-3	*****	2-28	3-6	65X	*****	*****	*****	3-3	3-9	64X
3-5	3-11	65X	3-5	3-11	887>/	3-5	3-11	65X	*****	*****	*****	3-5	3-11	*****	3-4	3-10	/////	3-4	3-10	/////	3-4	3-10	*****	3-4	3-10	*****	3-7	3-13	65X	*****	*****	*****	3-10	3-16	65X
3-12	3-18	*****	3-12	3-18	888>/	3-12	3-18	66>/	*****	*****	*****	3-12	3-18	*****	3-11	3-17	/////	3-11	3-17	66>	3-11	3-17	*****	3-11	3-17	*****	3-14	3-20	66X	*****	*****	*****	3-17	3-23	66X
3-19	3-25	/////	3-19	3-25	889>/	3-19	3-25	/////	*****	*****	*****	3-19	3-25	*****	3-18	3-24	/////	3-18	3-24	/////	3-18	3-24	*****	3-18	3-24	S45/	3-21	3-27	67X	*****	*****	*****	3-24	3-30	67X
3-26	4-1	68>/	3-26	4-1	890>/	3-26	4-1	68>/	*****	*****	*****	3-26	4-1	*****	3-25	3-31	/////	3-25	3-31	68>	3-25	3-31	*****	3-25	3-31	*****	3-30	4-3	68X	*****	*****	*****	3-31	4-6	68X
4-2	4-8	*****	4-2	4-8	891>	4-2	4-8	69>/	*****	*****	*****	4-2	4-8	*****	4-1	4-7	/////	4-1	4-7	69>	4-1	4-7	*****	4-1	4-7	*****	4-4	4-10	69X	*****	*****	*****	4-7	4-13	69X
4-9	4-15	*****	4-9	4-15	893>/	4-9	4-15	70>	*****	*****	*****	4-9	4-15	*****	4-8	4-14	/////	4-8	4-14	70>	4-8	4-14	*****	4-8	4-14	*****	4-11	4-17	70X	*****	*****	*****	4-14	4-20	70X
4-16	4-22	71>/	4-16	4-22	894>/	4-16	4-22	71>/	*****	*****	*****	4-16	4-22	*****	4-15	4-21	/////	4-15	4-21	71>	4-15	4-21	*****	4-15	4-21	*****	4-18	4-24	71X	*****	*****	*****	4-21	4-27	71X
4-23	4-29	73>/	4-23	4-29	895>/	4-23	4-29	73>/	*****	*****	*****	4-23	4-29	*****	4-22	4-28	/////	4-22	4-28	/////	4-22	4-28	*****	4-22	4-28	S45/	4-25	5-1	72X	*****	*****	*****	4-28	5-4	72X
4-30	5-6	74>	4-30	5-6	896>/	4-30	5-6	74>/	*****	*****	*****	4-30	5-6	*****	4-29	5-5	/////	4-29	5-5	/////	4-29	5-5	*****	4-29	5-5	*****	5-2	5-7	73X	*****	*****	*****	5-5	5-11	73X
5-7	5-13	/////	5-7	5-13	897>/	5-7	5-13	/////	*****	*****	*****	5-7	5-13	*****	5-6	5-12	/////	5-6	5-12	/////	5-6	5-12	*****	5-6	5-12	*****	5-8	5-15	74X	*****	*****	*****	5-12	5-18	74X
5-14	5-20	/////	5-14	5-20	898>/	5-14	5-20	/////	*****	*****	*****	5-14	5-20	*****	5-13	5-19	898>I	5-13	5-19	/////	5-13	5-19	*****	5-13	5-19	*****	5-16	5-22	75X	*****	*****	*****	5-19	5-25	75X
5-21	5-27	77>	5-21	5-27	899>/	5-21	5-27	77>/	*****	*****	*****	5-21	5-27	*****	5-20	5-26	/////	5-20	5-26	77>	5-20	5-26	*****	5-20	5-26	*****	5-23	5-29	76X	*****	*****	*****	5-26	6-1	76X
5-28	6-3	/////	5-28	6-3	900>/	5-28	6-3	/////	*****	*****	*****	5-28	6-3	*****	5-27	6-2	/////	5-27	6-2	/////	5-27	6-2	*****	5-27	6-2	S45/	5-30	6-5	77X	5-31	6-6	*****	6-2	6-8	77X
6-4	6-10	/////	6-4	6-10	902>/	6-4	6-10	/////	*****	*****	*****	6-4	6-10	*****	6-3	6-9	902>	6-3	6-9	/////	6-3	6-9	*****	6-3	6-9	*****	6-6	6-12	78X	6-7	6-13	78X	6-9	6-15	78X
6-11	6-17	/////	6-11	6-17	904>/	6-11	6-17	80>/	*****	*****	*****	6-11	6-17	*****	6-10	6-16	/////	6-10	6-16	80>	6-10	6-16	*****	6-10	6-16	S45/	6-13	6-19	79X	6-14	6-20	*****	6-16	6-21	79X
6-18	6-24	/////	6-18	6-24	906>/	6-18	6-24	/////	*****	*****	*****	6-18	6-24	*****	6-17	6-23	906>I	6-17	6-24	/////	6-17	6-24	*****	6-17	6-23	*****	6-20	6-26	80X	*****	*****	*****	6-22	6-29	80X
6-25	7-1	83>	6-25	7-1	908>/	6-25	7-1	83>	*****	*****	*****	6-25	7-1	*****	6-24	6-30	908>I	6-25	7-1	/////	6-25	7-1	*****	6-24	6-30	S45/	6-27	7-3	81X	*****	*****	*****	6-30	7-6	81X
7-2	7-8	/////	7-2	7-8	910>/	7-2	7-8	/////	*****	*****	*****	7-2	7-8	*****	7-1	7-7	910>	7-2	7-8	/////	7-2	7-8	*****	7-1	7-7	*****	7-4	7-10	82X	*****	*****	*****	7-7	7-13	82X
7-9	7-15	85>	7-9	7-15	/////	7-9	7-15	85>/	*****	*****	*****	7-9	7-15	85X	7-8	7-14	/////	7-9	7-15	85>	7-9	7-15	*****	7-8	7-14	*****	7-11	7-17	83X	*****	*****	*****	7-14	7-20	83X
7-16	7-22	/////	7-16	7-22	/////	7-16	7-22	/////	*****	*****	*****	7-16	7-22	*****	7-15	7-21	/////	7-16	7-21	/////	7-16	7-21	*****	7-15	7-21	*****	7-18	7-24	84X	*****	*****	*****	7-21	7-27	84X
7-21	7-29	88>	7-21	7-29	913>/	7-21	7-29	88>/	*****	*****	*****	7-23	7-29	*****	7-22	7-28	913>/	7-22	7-28	88>	7-22	7-28	*****	7-20	7-28	S45/	7-25	7-31	85X	*****	*****	*****	7-28	8-3	85X
7-30	8-5	/////	7-30	8-5	914>/	7-30	8-5	/////	7-30	8-5	1X	7-30	8-5	*****	7-29	8-4	914>I	7-29	8-4	/////	7-29	8-4	*****	7-29	8-4	*****	8-1	8-7	86X	*****	*****	*****	8-4	8-10	86X
8-6	8-12	/////	8-6	8-12	915>/	8-6	8-12	/////	8-6	8-12	2>	8-8	8-12	88/	8-5	8-11	915>I	8-5	8-11	/////	8-5	8-11	*****	8-5	8-11	*****	8-8	8-14	87X	*****	*****	*****	8-11	8-17	87X
8-13	8-19	/////	8-13	8-19	/////	8-13	8-19	91>/	8-13	8-19	3X	8-15	8-19	*****	8-12	8-18	*****	8-12	8-18	91>	8-12	8-18	*****	8-12	8-18	*****	8-15	8-21	88X	*****	*****	*****	8-18	8-24	88X
8-20	8-26	92>	8-20	8-26	917>/	8-20	8-26	92>/	8-20	8-26	4X	8-20	8-26	*****	8-19	8-25	*****	8-19	8-25	/////	8-19	8-25	*****	8-19	8-25	*****	8-22	8-28	89X	*****	*****	*****	8-25	8-31	89X
8-27	9-2	93>	8-27	9-2	918>/	8-27	9-2	93>/	8-27	9-2	5X	8-27	9-2	*****	8-26	9-1	*****	8-26	9-1	93>	8-26	9-1	*****	8-26	9-1	*****	8-29	9-4	90X	*****	*****	*****	9-1	9-7	90X
9-3	9-9	/////	9-3	9-9	919>/	9-3	9-9	/////	9-3	9-8	6>	9-3	9-9	*****	9-2	9-8	919>I	9-2	9-8	/////	9-2	9-8	*****	9-2	9-8	*****	9-5	9-11	91X	*****	*****	*****	9-8	9-14	91X
9-10	9-16	/////	9-10	9-16	/////	9-10	9-16	/////	9-10	9-16	/////	9-10	9-16	*****	9-9	9-15	/////	9-9	9-15	/////	9-9	9-15	*****	9-9	9-15	*****	9-12	9-18	92X	*****	*****	*****	9-15	9-21	92X
9-17	9-23	/////	9-17	9-23	921>/	9-17	9-23	96>/	9-17	9-23	8>	9-17	9-23	*****	9-16	9-22	921>I	9-16	9-21	96>	9-16	9-21	*****	9-16	9-22	*****	9-19	9-25	93X	*****	*****	*****	9-22	9-28	93X
9-24	9-30	/////	9-24	9-30	922>/	9-24	9-30	97>/	9-24	9-30	*****	9-24	9-30	*****	9-23	9-29	*****	9-22	9-29	97>	9-22	9-29	*****	9-23	9-29	*****	9-26	10-2	94X	*****	*****	*****	9-29	10-5	94X
10-1	10-7	/////	10-1	10-7	923>/	10-1	10-7	98>/	10-1	10-7	*****	10-1	10-7	*****	9-30	10-6	923>	9-30	10-5	98>	9-30	10-5	*****	9-30	10-6	*****	10-3	10-9	95X	*****	*****	*****	10-6	10-12	95X
10-8	10-14	/////	10-8	10-14	924>/	10-8	10-14	/////	10-8	10-14	11>	10-8	10-14	*****	10-7	10-13	*****	10-6	10-13	/////	10-6	10-13	*****	10-7	10-13	*****	10-10	10-16	96X	10-11	10-17	*****	10-13	10-19	96X
10-15	10-21	100>	10-15	10-21	925/	10-15	10-21	100>/	10-15	10-21	12>	10-15	10-21	*****	10-14	10-20	925L	10-14	10-20	100>	10-14	10-20	*****	10-14	10-20	*****	10-17	10-23	97X	10-18	10-24	97/	10-20	10-26	97X
10-22	10-28	101>	10-22	10-28	926>/	10-22	10-28	101>/	10-22	10-28	13>	10-22	10-28	*****	10-21	10-27	926>I	10-21	10-27	/////	10-21	10-27	*****	10-21	10-27	*****	10-24	10-30	98X	10-25	10-31	*****	10-27	11-2	98X
10-29	11-4	/////	10-29	11-4	927>/	10-29	11-4	/////	10-29	11-4	14>	10-29	11-4	*****	10-28	11-3	*****	10-28	11-3	/////	10-28	11-3	*****	10-28	11-3	*****	10-31	11-6	99X	*****	*****	*****	11-3	11-9	99X
11-5	11-11	/////	11-5	11-11	928>/	11-5	11-11	/////	11-3	11-11	15>	11-5	11-11	*****	11-4	11-10	928>	11-4	11-10	/////	11-4	11-10	*****	11-4	11-10	S45/	11-7	11-13	100X	*****	*****	*****	11-10	11-16	100X
11-12	11-18	/////	11-12	11-18	929>/	11-12	11-18	/////	11-10	11-18	16>	11-12	11-18	*****	/////	/////	*****	11-11	11-17	/////	11-11	11-17	*****	11-11	11-17	*****	11-14	11-20	102X	*****	*****	*****	11-17	11-23	101X
11-17	11-25	/////	11-17	11-25	930>	11-17	11-25	/////	11-17	11-25	17>	11-17	11-25	*****	11-18	11-24	931>	11-18	11-23	/////	11-18	11-23	*****	11-18	11-24	*****	11-21	11-28	102X	*****	*****	*****	11-24	11-30	102X
11-26	12-2	106>	11-26	12-2	931>	11-26	12-2	106>/	11-26	12-2	18>/	11-26	12-2	*****	11-25	11-30	*****	11-24	11-30	106>	11-24	11-30	*****	11-25	12-1	S45/	11-29	12-5	104X	*****	*****	*****	12-1	12-7	103X
12-3	12-9	/////	12-3	12-9	932>	12-3	12-9	/////	12-3	12-9	19>/	12-3	12-9	*****	12-1	12-7	*****	12-1	12-7	/////	12-1	12-7	*****	12-2	12-8	*****	12-6	12-19	106X	*****	*****	*****	12-8	12-12	104X
12-10	12-16	/////	12-10	12-16	933>	12-10	12-16	/////	12-10	12-16	20>	12-10	12-16	*****	12-8	12-14	*****	12-8	12-14	/////	12-8	12-14	*****	12-9	12-15	*****				*****	*****	*****	12-13	12-19	105X
12-17	12-23	/////	12-17	12-23	/////	12-17	12-23	/////	12-17	12-23	21>	12-17	12-23	*****	12-15	12-21	/////	12-15	12-21	/////	12-15	12-21	*****	12-16	12-22	*****	12-20	1-1	108X	*****	*****	*****	12-20	12-26	106X
12-24	12-30	110>	12-24	12-30	935>	12-24	12-30	110>	12-24	12-30	22>	12-24	12-30	*****	12-22	12-29	*****	12-22	12-29	110>	12-22	12-29	*****	12-23	12-29	*****				*****	*****	*****	12-27	1-2	107X

Data Coverage / 9 Dec 1719 – 31 Dec 1723

The data in this chart is the information used for the reconstruction of both the Philadelphia & New York Custom Houses, and supplementary data for Salem, Boston, Rhode Island, Connecticut & New Jersey Ports to fill in data from the Philadelphia & New York ships that interacted with them. This is not all the available data, this is only the data I was able to acqurie to date. These dates are the coverage for the shipping news not the issue dates.

***** - No Data Available / When you see this, it is only for the current newspaper, it has already been searched and no data was found for that week for that port.

Legend							
/////	Data May Be Available	/	Partial Data Available	>	Captains Only	L	Local Only
X	Complete Data Available	*	No Data Available	S#	Check Sources	I	Inbound Only

Complete Data	Captain Names & Ship Names & Arrival, Departure Ports
Partial Data	Captain Names & Arrival, Departure Ports and with or without Ship Names
Captains Only	Captain Names Only & Arrival, Departure Ports no Ship Names
Local Only	Captain Names Only & Arrival, Departure Ports no Ship Names / No Outbound Besides Local

Boston Gazette			Boston News Letter			Boston Gazette			New England Courant			American Weekly Mercury			Boston News Letter			Boston Gazette			American Weekly Mercury			American Weekly Mercury & Source 45			American Weekly Mercury			American Weekly Mercury			American Weekly Mercury		
1722																																			
Salem – MA			Boston – MA												Newport – RI									New London – CT			New York – NY			Perth Amboy – NJ			Philadelphia – PA		
/////	/////	/////	12-31	1-6	936>/	12-31	1-6	111>/	12-31	1-6	23>	12-31	1-6	*****	12-30	1-5	*****	12-30	1-5	/////	12-30	1-5	*****	12-30	1-5	*****	1-2	1-15	110X	*****	*****	*****	1-3	1-9	108X
/////	/////	/////	1-7	1-13	937>/	1-7	1-13	112>/	1-7	1-13	24>	1-7	1-13	*****	1-6	1-12	/////	1-6	1-12	/////	1-6	1-12	*****	1-6	1-12	*****				*****	*****	*****	1-10	1-16	109X
/////	/////	/////	1-14	1-20	/////	1-14	1-20	/////	1-14	1-20	25>/	1-14	1-20	*****	1-13	1-19	/////	1-13	1-19	/////	1-13	1-19	*****	1-13	1-19	*****	1-16	1-29	112X	*****	*****	*****	1-17	1-22	110X
/////	/////	/////	1-21	1-27	/////	1-21	1-27	114>/	1-21	1-27	26>/	1-21	1-27	*****	1-20	1-26	/////	1-20	1-26	114>	1-20	1-26	*****	1-20	1-26	*****				*****	*****	*****	1-23	1-29	/////
1-28	2-3	115>	1-28	2-3	/////	1-28	2-3	115>/	1-28	2-3	27>	1-28	2-3	*****	1-27	2-2	/////	1-27	2-2	115>	1-27	2-2	*****	1-27	2-2	*****	1-30	2-12	114X	*****	*****	*****	1-30	2-6	112X
2-4	2-10	/////	2-4	2-10	941>/	2-4	2-10	116>/	2-4	2-10	28>	2-4	2-10	*****	2-3	2-9	*****	2-3	2-9	116>/	2-3	2-9	*****	2-3	2-9	*****				*****	*****	*****	2-7	2-13	113X
2-12	2-17	/////	2-12	2-17	/////	2-12	2-17	117>/	2-11	2-17	29>	2-11	2-17	*****	2-10	2-16	/////	2-10	2-16	/////	2-10	2-16	*****	2-10	2-16	*****	2-13	2-26	116X	*****	*****	*****	2-12	2-20	114X
2-18	2-24	/////	2-18	2-24	/////	2-18	2-24	/////	2-18	2-24	30>	2-18	2-24	*****	2-17	2-23	/////	2-17	2-23	/////	2-17	2-23	116/	2-17	2-23	*****				*****	*****	*****	2-21	2-27	115X
2-25	3-3	/////	2-25	3-3	/////	2-25	3-3	/////	2-25	3-3	31>	2-25	3-3	*****	2-24	3-2	/////	2-24	3-2	/////	2-24	3-2	*****	2-24	3-2	*****	2-27	3-12	118X	*****	*****	*****	2-28	3-2	116X
3-4	3-10	120>	3-4	3-10	/////	3-4	3-10	120>	3-4	3-10	32>	3-4	3-10	*****	3-3	3-9	/////	3-3	3-9	120>	3-3	3-9	*****	3-3	3-9	*****				*****	*****	*****	3-3	3-10	117X
3-11	3-17	/////	3-11	3-17	/////	3-11	3-17	121>	3-11	3-17	33>	3-11	3-17	*****	3-10	3-16	/////	3-10	3-16	121>	3-10	3-16	*****	3-10	3-16	*****	3-13	3-19	119X	*****	*****	*****	3-11	3-15	118X
3-18	3-24	/////	3-18	3-24	/////	3-18	3-24	/////	3-18	3-24	34>	3-18	3-24	*****	3-17	3-23	/////	3-17	3-23	/////	3-17	3-23	*****	3-17	3-23	*****	3-20	3-27	120X	*****	*****	*****	3-16	3-22	119X
3-25	3-31	/////	3-25	3-31	/////	3-25	3-31	/////	3-25	3-31	35>	3-25	3-31	*****	3-24	3-30	/////	3-24	3-30	/////	3-24	3-30	*****	3-24	3-30	*****	3-28	4-2	121X	*****	*****	*****	3-23	3-29	120X
4-1	4-7	/////	4-1	4-7	/////	4-1	4-7	/////	4-1	4-7	36>	4-1	4-7	*****	3-31	4-6	/////	3-31	4-6	/////	3-31	4-6	*****	3-31	4-6	*****	4-3	4-9	122X	3-30	4-5	*****	3-30	4-5	121X
4-8	4-14	/////	4-8	4-14	950>/	4-8	4-14	/////	4-8	4-14	37>	4-8	4-14	*****	4-7	4-13	*****	4-7	4-13	/////	4-7	4-13	*****	4-7	4-13	S45/	4-10	4-16	123X	4-4	4-10	122/	4-6	4-12	122X
4-15	4-21	/////	4-15	4-21	951>	4-15	4-21	/////	4-15	4-21	38>	4-15	4-21	*****	4-14	4-20	*****	4-14	4-20	/////	4-14	4-20	*****	4-14	4-20	S45/	4-17	4-23	124X	4-11	4-17	*****	4-13	4-19	123X
4-22	4-28	127>	4-22	4-28	952>	4-22	4-28	127>/	4-22	4-28	39>	4-22	4-28	*****	4-21	4-27	*****	4-21	4-27	127>	4-21	4-27	*****	4-21	4-27	S45/	4-24	4-30	125X	*****	*****	*****	4-20	4-26	124X
4-29	5-5	128>	4-29	5-5	/////	4-29	5-5	128>	4-29	5-5	40>	4-29	5-5	*****	4-28	5-4	/////	4-28	5-4	128>	4-28	5-4	*****	4-28	5-4	*****	5-1	5-7	126X	*****	*****	*****	4-27	5-3	125X
5-6	5-12	129>	5-6	5-12	/////	5-6	5-12	129>/	5-6	5-12	41>	5-6	5-12	*****	5-5	5-11	/////	5-5	5-11	129>	5-5	5-11	*****	5-5	5-11	*****	5-8	5-14	127X	*****	*****	*****	5-4	5-10	126X
5-13	5-19	130>	5-13	5-19	955>	5-13	5-19	130>/	5-13	5-19	42>	5-13	5-19	*****	5-12	5-18	*****	5-12	5-18	130>	5-12	5-18	*****	5-12	5-18	*****	5-15	5-21	128X	*****	*****	*****	5-11	5-17	127X
5-20	5-26	/////	5-20	5-26	956>	5-20	5-26	131>/	5-20	5-26	43>	5-20	5-26	*****	5-19	5-25	*****	5-19	5-25	131>	5-19	5-25	*****	5-19	5-25	*****	5-22	5-28	129X	*****	*****	*****	5-18	5-24	128X
5-27	6-2	/////	5-27	6-2	/////	5-27	6-2	/////	5-27	6-2	44>	5-27	6-2	*****	5-26	6-1	/////	5-26	6-1	/////	5-26	6-1	*****	5-26	6-1	S45/	5-29	6-4	130X	*****	*****	*****	5-25	5-31	129X
6-24	6-9	/////	6-24	6-9	958>/	6-24	6-9	/////	6-24	6-9	45>	6-24	6-9	*****	6-2	6-8	*****	6-2	6-8	/////	6-2	6-8	132/	6-2	6-8	*****	6-5	6-11	131X	*****	*****	*****	6-1	6-7	130X
6-10	6-16	/////	6-10	6-16	959>	6-10	6-16	/////	6-10	6-16	46>/	6-10	6-16	*****	6-9	6-15	*****	6-9	6-15	/////	6-9	6-15	*****	6-9	6-15	*****	6-12	6-18	132X	*****	*****	*****	6-8	6-14	131X
6-17	6-23	/////	6-17	6-23	960>/	6-17	6-23	/////	6-17	6-23	47>	6-17	6-23	134/	6-16	6-22	*****	6-16	6-22	/////	6-16	6-22	*****	6-16	6-22	*****	6-19	6-25	133X	*****	*****	*****	6-15	6-21	132X
6-24	6-30	136>	6-24	6-30	/////	6-24	6-30	136>	6-24	6-30	48>	6-24	6-30	*****	6-23	6-29	/////	6-23	6-29	136>	6-23	6-29	*****	6-23	6-29	*****	6-26	7-2	134X	*****	*****	*****	6-22	6-28	133X
7-1	7-7	/////	7-1	7-7	962>/	7-1	7-7	137>/	7-1	7-7	49>	7-1	7-7	*****	6-30	7-6	*****	6-30	7-6	137>	6-30	7-6	*****	6-30	7-6	*****	7-3	7-9	135X	*****	*****	*****	6-29	7-5	134X
7-8	7-14	140>	7-8	7-14	963>/	7-8	7-14	/////	7-8	7-14	50>/	7-8	7-14	*****	7-7	7-13	*****	7-7	7-13	/////	7-7	7-13	*****	7-7	7-13	*****	7-10	7-16	136X	*****	*****	*****	7-6	7-12	135X
7-15	7-21	/////	7-15	7-21	964>	7-15	7-21	139>/	7-15	7-21	51>	7-15	7-21	*****	7-14	7-20	*****	7-14	7-20	139>	7-14	7-20	*****	7-14	7-20	S45/	7-17	7-23	137X	*****	*****	*****	7-13	7-19	136X
7-22	7-28	/////	7-22	7-28	965>	7-22	7-28	140>	7-22	7-28	52>	7-22	7-28	*****	7-21	7-28	*****	7-21	7-28	140>	7-21	7-28	*****	7-21	7-27	S45/	7-24	7-30	138X	*****	*****	*****	7-20	7-26	137X
7-29	8-4	/////	7-29	8-4	966>	7-29	8-4	/////	7-29	8-4	53>	7-29	8-4	*****	7-28	8-3	*****	7-28	8-3	/////	7-28	8-3	*****	7-28	8-3	S45/	7-31	8-6	139X	*****	*****	*****	7-27	8-2	138X
8-5	8-11	142>	8-5	8-11	967>	8-5	8-11	142>/	8-5	8-11	54>	8-5	8-11	*****	8-4	8-10	967>	8-4	8-10	142>	8-4	8-10	*****	8-4	8-10	*****	8-7	8-13	140X	8-8	8-14	*****	8-3	8-9	139X
8-12	8-18	/////	8-12	8-18	968>	8-12	8-18	/////	8-12	8-18	55>	8-12	8-18	*****	8-11	8-17	968>	8-11	8-17	/////	8-11	8-17	*****	8-11	8-17	*****	8-14	8-20	141X	8-15	8-21	141/	8-10	8-16	140X
8-19	8-25	/////	8-19	8-25	969>	8-19	8-25	/////	8-19	8-25	56>	8-19	8-25	*****	8-18	8-24	969>	8-18	8-24	/////	8-18	8-24	*****	8-18	8-24	*****	8-21	8-27	142X	8-22	8-28	*****	8-17	8-23	141X
8-26	9-1	145>	8-26	9-1	970>	8-26	9-1	145>	8-26	9-1	57>/	8-26	9-1	*****	8-25	8-31	971>	8-25	8-31	145>	8-25	8-31	*****	8-25	8-31	*****	8-28	9-3	143X	8-29	9-4	143/	8-24	8-30	142X
9-2	9-8	146>	9-2	9-8	971>	9-2	9-8	146>/	9-2	9-8	58>	9-2	9-8	*****	9-1	9-7	971>	9-1	9-7	146>	9-1	9-7	*****	9-1	9-7	*****	9-4	9-10	144X	9-5	9-11	*****	8-31	9-6	143X
9-9	9-15	/////	9-9	9-15	972>	9-9	9-15	/////	9-9	9-15	59>	9-9	9-15	*****	9-8	9-14	*****	9-8	9-14	/////	9-8	9-14	*****	9-8	9-14	*****	9-11	9-17	145X	9-12	9-18	145X	9-7	9-13	144X
9-16	9-22	148>	9-16	9-22	973>	9-16	9-22	148>	9-16	9-22	60>	9-16	9-22	*****	9-15	9-21	*****	9-15	9-21	/////	9-15	9-21	*****	9-15	9-21	*****	9-18	9-24	146X	9-19	9-25	*****	9-14	9-20	145X
9-23	9-29	/////	9-23	9-29	974>	9-23	9-29	/////	9-23	9-29	61>	9-23	9-29	*****	9-22	9-28	*****	9-22	9-28	/////	9-22	9-28	*****	9-22	9-28	*****	9-25	10-1	147X	9-26	10-2	*****	9-21	9-27	146X
9-3	10-6	/////	9-3	10-6	975>	9-3	10-6	/////	9-3	10-6	62>	9-3	10-6	*****	9-29	10-5	*****	9-29	10-5	/////	9-29	10-5	*****	9-29	10-5	*****	10-2	10-8	148X	10-3	10-9	*****	9-28	10-3	147X
10-7	10-13	151>	10-7	10-13	976>/	10-7	10-13	151>/	10-7	10-13	63>	10-7	10-13	*****	10-6	10-12	*****	10-6	10-12	*****	10-6	10-12	*****	10-6	10-12	*****	10-9	10-15	149X	10-10	10-16	150/	10-4	10-10	148X
10-14	10-20	/////	10-14	10-20	977>	10-14	10-20	/////	10-14	10-20	64>	10-14	10-20	*****	10-13	10-19	*****	10-13	10-19	/////	10-13	10-19	*****	10-13	10-19	*****	10-16	10-21	150X	10-17	10-22	*****	10-11	10-18	149X
10-21	10-27	/////	10-21	10-27	978>	10-21	10-27	/////	10-21	10-27	65>	10-21	10-27	*****	10-20	10-26	*****	10-20	10-26	/////	10-20	10-26	*****	10-20	10-26	*****	10-22	10-29	151X	10-23	10-29	*****	10-19	10-25	150X
10-28	11-3	/////	10-28	11-3	979>	10-28	11-3	/////	10-28	11-3	66>	10-28	11-3	*****	10-27	11-2	*****	10-27	11-2	/////	10-27	11-2	*****	10-27	11-2	*****	10-30	11-5	152X	10-30	11-5	153/	10-26	11-1	151X
11-4	11-10	/////	11-4	11-10	980>	11-4	11-10	155>	11-4	11-10	67>	11-4	11-10	*****	11-3	11-9	*****	11-3	11-9	156>	11-3	11-9	*****	11-3	11-9	*****	11-6	11-12	153X	11-6	11-12	*****	11-2	11-8	152X
11-11	11-17	156>	11-11	11-17	981>	11-11	11-17	156>	11-11	11-17	68>	11-11	11-17	*****	11-10	11-16	*****	11-10	11-16	/////	11-10	11-16	*****	11-10	11-16	S45/	11-13	11-19	154X	*****	*****	*****	11-9	11-15	153X
11-18	11-24	157>	11-18	11-24	982>	11-18	11-24	157>	11-18	11-24	69>	11-18	11-24	*****	11-17	11-23	*****	11-17	11-23	158>	11-17	11-23	*****	11-17	11-23	*****	11-20	11-26	155X	*****	*****	*****	11-16	11-23	154X
11-25	12-1	158>	11-25	12-1	983>	11-25	12-1	158>	11-25	12-1	70>	11-25	12-1	*****	11-24	11-30	*****	11-24	11-30	158>	11-24	11-30	*****	11-24	11-30	*****	11-27	12-3	156X	*****	*****	*****	11-24	11-29	155X
12-22	12-8	159>	12-22	12-8	984>	12-22	12-8	159>	12-22	12-8	71>	12-22	12-8	*****	12-1	12-7	*****	12-1	12-7	160>	12-1	12-7	*****	12-1	12-7	*****	12-4	12-10	157X	*****	*****	*****	11-30	12-11	156X
12-9	12-15	160>	12-9	12-15	985>	12-9	12-15	160>	12-9	12-15	72>	12-9	12-15	*****	12-8	12-14	*****	12-8	12-14	/////	12-8	12-14	*****	12-8	12-14	*****	12-11	12-24	159X	*****	*****	*****	12-12	12-18	157X
12-16	12-22	/////	12-16	12-22	986>	12-16	12-22	/////	12-16	12-22	73>	12-16	12-22	*****	12-15	12-21	*****	12-15	12-21	/////	12-15	12-21	*****	12-15	12-21	S45/				*****	*****	*****	12-19	12-26	158X
12-23	12-29	162>	12-23	12-29	987>	12-23	12-29	162>	12-23	12-29	74>	12-23	12-29	*****	12-22	12-28	*****	12-22	12-28	/////	12-22	12-28	*****	12-22	12-28	*****				*****	*****	*****	12-27	1-1	159X

Data Coverage: 01 Dec 1722 – 31 Dec 1723

The data in this chart is the information used for the reconstruction of both the Philadelphia & New York Custom Houses, and supplementary data for Salem, Boston, Rhode Island, Connecticut & New Jersey Ports to fill in data from the Philadelphia & New York ships that interacted with them. This is not all the available data, this is only the data I was able to acquire to date. These dates are the coverage for the shipping news not the issue dates.

***** - No Data Available / When you see this, it is only for the current newspaper, it has already been searched and no data was found for that week for that port.

Legend

////	Data May Be Available	/	Partial Data Available	>	Captains Only	L	Local Only
X	Complete Data Available	*	No Data Available	S#	Check Sources	I	Inbound Only

Complete Data	Captain Names & Ship Names & Arrival, Departure Ports
Partial Data	Captain Names & Arrival, Departure Ports and with or without Ship Names
Captains Only	Captain Names Only & Arrival, Departure Ports no Ship Names
Local Only	Captain Names Only & Arrival, Departure Ports no Ship Names / No Outbound Besides Local

1723

Boston Gazette	Boston News Letter	Boston Gazette	New England Courant	American Weekly Mercury	Boston News Letter	Boston Gazette	American Weekly Mercury	American Weekly Mercury & Source 45	American Weekly Mercury	American Weekly Mercury	American Weekly Mercury
Salem – MA		Boston – MA						Newport – RI		New London – CT	New York – NY	Perth Amboy – NJ	Philadelphia – PA

Salem–MA			Boston–MA											Newport–RI						New London–CT			New York–NY			Perth Amboy–NJ			Philadelphia–PA		
////	////	////	////	////	////	12-30	1-5	75>	12-30	1-5	*****	12-29	1-4	*****	12-29	1-4	////	12-29	1-4	*****	////	////	////	1-2	1-8	160X
1-6	1-12	164>	1-6	1-12	989>	1-6	1-12	164>	1-6	1-12	76>	1-6	1-12	*****	1-5	1-11	*****	1-5	1-11	*****	1-5	1-11	*****	12-25	1-8	161X	*****	*****	*****	1-9	1-14	161X
1-13	1-19	////	1-13	1-19	890>/	1-13	1-19	////	1-13	1-19	77>	1-13	1-19	*****	1-12	1-18	*****	1-12	1-18	*****	1-12	1-19	*****				*****	*****	*****	1-15	1-21	162X
1-20	1-26	////	1-20	1-26	991>	1-20	1-26	////	1-20	1-26	////	1-20	1-26	*****	1-19	1-25	991>	1-19	1-25	////	1-19	1-25	*****	1-9	1-22	163X	*****	*****	*****	1-22	1-29	163X
1-27	2-2	////	1-27	2-2	992>	1-27	2-2	////	1-27	2-2	79>	1-27	2-2	*****	1-26	2-1	992>	1-26	2-1	////	1-26	2-1	167/	1-27	2-2	////	*****	*****	*****	1-30	2-5	164X
2-3	2-9	////	//// SEE NOTES ////			2-3	2-9	////	2-3	2-9	80>	2-3	2-9	*****	2-2	2-8	994>	2-2	2-8	////	2-2	2-8	*****	2-3	2-9	*****	1-23	2-5	165X	2-6	2-12	165X
2-10	2-16	////	2-7	2-13	994>	2-10	2-16	////	2-10	2-16	81>	2-10	2-16	*****	2-9	2-15	*****	2-9	2-15	////	2-9	2-15	*****	2-10	2-16	*****				2-13	2-19	166X
2-17	2-23	////	2-14	2-20	995>	2-17	2-23	////	2-17	2-23	82>	2-17	2-23	*****	2-16	2-21	996>	2-16	2-21	////	2-16	2-21	*****	2-17	2-23	*****	2-6	2-18	167X	2-20	2-26	167X
2-24	3-2	171>	2-21	2-27	996>	2-24	3-2	171>	2-24	3-2	83>	2-24	3-2	*****	2-22	2-28	997>	2-22	2-28	171>	2-22	2-28	*****	2-24	3-2	*****				2-27	3-7	168X
3-3	3-9	172>	2-28	3-6	997>	3-3	3-9	172>	3-3	3-9	84>	3-3	3-9	*****	3-1	3-7	998>	3-1	3-7	*****	3-1	3-7	171/	3-3	3-9	*****	2-26	3-4	168X	3-8	3-14	169X
3-10	3-16	////	3-7	3-13	998>	3-10	3-16	////	3-10	3-16	85>	3-10	3-16	*****	3-8	3-14	999>	3-8	3-14	////	3-8	3-14	*****	3-10	3-16	*****	3-5	3-11	169X	3-15	3-21	170X
3-17	3-23	////	3-14	3-20	999>	3-17	3-23	////	3-17	3-23	86>	3-17	3-23	*****	3-15	3-21	1000>	3-15	3-21	////	3-17	3-23	*****	3-17	3-23	*****	3-12	3-18	170X	3-22	3-28	////
3-24	3-30	175>	3-21	3-27	1000>	3-24	3-30	175>	3-24	3-30	87>	3-24	3-30	*****	3-22	3-28	1001>	3-22	3-28	175>	3-22	3-28	*****	3-24	3-30	*****	3-19	3-25	171X	3-29	4-4	172X
3-31	4-6	////	3-28	4-3	1001>/	3-31	4-6	////	3-31	4-6	88>	3-31	4-6	*****	3-29	4-4	////	3-29	4-4	////	3-29	4-4	*****	3-31	4-6	*****	3-26	4-1	172X	4-5	4-11	////
4-7	4-13	////	4-4	4-10	1002>	4-7	4-13	177>	4-7	4-13	89>	4-7	4-13	*****	4-5	4-11	1003>	4-5	4-11	*****	4-5	4-11	*****	4-7	4-13	*****	4-2	4-8	////	4-12	4-18	174X
4-12	4-20	////	4-11	4-17	1003>	4-12	4-20	////	4-12	4-20	90>	4-12	4-20	*****	4-12	4-18	1004>	4-12	4-18	////	4-12	4-18	*****	4-14	4-20	*****	4-9	4-15	174X	4-19	4-25	175X
4-19	4-27	////	4-18	4-24	1004>	4-19	4-27	////	4-19	4-27	91>	4-19	4-27	*****	4-19	4-25	1005>	4-19	4-25	////	4-19	4-25	*****	4-21	4-27	*****	4-16	4-22	175X	4-26	5-2	176X
4-28	5-4	////	4-25	5-1	1005>	4-28	5-4	////	4-28	5-4	92>	4-28	5-4	*****	4-26	5-2	1006>	4-26	5-2	////	4-26	5-2	*****	4-28	5-4	*****	4-22	4-28	176X	5-2	5-8	178X	5-3	5-9	177X
5-5	5-11	181>	5-2	5-8	1006>	5-5	5-11	181>	5-5	5-11	93>	5-5	5-11	*****	5-3	5-9	1007>	5-3	5-9	181>	5-3	5-9	*****	5-5	5-11	*****	4-29	5-6	177X	5-9	5-12	////	5-10	5-16	178X
5-12	5-18	////	5-9	5-15	1007>/	5-12	5-18	////	5-12	5-18	94>	5-12	5-18	*****	5-10	5-16	1008>	5-10	5-16	////	5-10	5-16	*****	5-12	5-18	*****	5-7	5-13	178X	5-13	5-19	179X	5-17	5-23	179X
5-19	5-25	////	5-16	5-22	1008>	5-19	5-25	////	5-19	5-25	95>	5-19	5-25	*****	5-17	5-23	1009>	5-17	5-23	////	5-17	5-23	*****	5-19	5-25	*****	5-14	5-20	179X	5-20	5-30	*****	5-24	5-30	180X
5-26	6-1	184>	5-23	5-29	////	5-26	6-1	184>	5-26	6-1	96>	5-26	6-1	*****	5-24	5-30	1010>	5-24	5-30	////	5-24	5-30	*****	5-26	6-1	*****	5-21	5-27	180X	5-31	6-6	182/	5-31	6-6	181X
6-2	6-8	////	5-30	6-5	1010>	6-2	6-8	////	6-2	6-8	97>	6-2	6-8	*****	5-31	6-6	1011>	5-31	6-6	////	5-31	6-6	*****	6-2	6-8	*****	5-28	6-3	181X	6-7	6-11	*****	6-7	6-13	182X
6-9	6-15	////	6-6	6-12	1011>	6-9	6-15	////	6-9	6-15	98>	6-9	6-15	*****	6-7	6-13	1012>	6-7	6-13	////	6-7	6-13	*****	6-9	6-15	*****	6-4	6-10	182X	6-12	6-17	*****	6-14	6-20	183X
6-16	6-22	187>	6-13	6-19	1012>	6-16	6-22	187>	6-16	6-22	99>	6-16	6-22	*****	6-14	6-20	1013>	6-14	6-20	187>	6-14	6-20	*****	6-16	6-22	*****	6-11	6-17	183X	6-18	6-24	184/	6-21	6-27	184X
6-23	6-29	////	6-20	6-26	1013>	6-23	6-29	////	6-23	6-29	100>	6-23	6-29	*****	6-21	6-28	1014>	6-21	6-28	////	6-21	6-28	*****	6-23	6-29	S45/	6-18	6-24	184X	6-25	7-1	*****	6-28	7-4	185X
6-30	7-6	////	6-26	7-2	1014>	6-30	7-6	////	6-30	7-6	101>	6-30	7-6	*****	6-29	7-5	1015>	6-29	7-5	////	6-29	7-5	*****	6-30	7-6	*****	6-25	7-1	185X	7-2	7-8	*****	7-5	7-11	186X
7-7	7-13	190>	7-3	7-10	1015>	7-7	7-13	190>	7-7	7-13	102>	7-7	7-13	*****	7-6	7-12	1016>	7-6	7-12	*****	7-6	7-12	*****	7-7	7-13	S45/	7-2	7-8	186X	7-9	7-15	*****	7-12	7-18	187X
7-14	7-20	////	7-11	7-17	1016>	7-14	7-20	////	7-14	7-20	103>	7-14	7-20	*****	7-13	7-19	1017>	7-13	7-19	////	7-13	7-19	*****	7-14	7-20	S45/	7-9	7-15	187X	7-16	7-22	*****	7-19	7-25	188X
7-21	7-27	////	7-18	7-24	1017>	7-21	7-27	////	7-21	7-27	104>	7-21	7-27	190/	7-20	7-26	1018>	7-20	7-26	////	7-20	7-26	*****	7-21	7-27	*****	7-16	7-22	188X	7-23	7-29	*****	7-26	7-29	189X
7-28	8-3	193>	7-25	7-31	1018>	7-28	8-3	193>	7-28	8-3	105>	7-28	8-3	*****	7-27	8-1	1019>	7-26	8-1	193/	7-27	8-1	*****	7-28	8-3	*****	7-23	7-29	////	7-30	8-5	*****	7-30	8-8	190X
8-4	8-10	////	8-1	8-7	1019>	8-4	8-10	////	8-4	8-10	106>	8-4	8-10	*****	8-2	8-8	1020>	8-2	8-8	////	8-2	8-8	*****	8-4	8-10	*****	7-30	8-5	190X	8-6	8-12	192X	8-9	8-15	191X
8-11	8-17	195>	8-8	8-14	1020>	8-11	8-17	195>	8-11	8-17	107>	8-11	8-17	*****	8-9	8-15	1021>	8-9	8-15	195/	8-9	8-15	*****	8-11	8-17	*****	8-6	8-12	191X	8-13	8-19	*****	8-16	8-22	192X
8-18	8-24	196>	8-15	8-21	1021>	8-18	8-24	196>/	8-18	8-24	108>	8-18	8-24	*****	8-16	8-22	1022>	8-16	8-22	196>	8-16	8-22	*****	8-18	8-24	*****	8-13	8-19	192X	*****	*****	*****	8-23	8-29	193X
8-25	8-31	197>	8-22	8-28	1022>	8-25	8-31	197>	8-25	8-31	109>	8-25	8-31	*****	8-23	8-29	1023>	8-23	8-29	197>	8-23	8-29	*****	8-25	8-31	*****	8-20	8-26	193X	*****	*****	*****	8-30	9-5	194X
9-1	9-7	198>	8-29	9-4	1023>	9-1	9-7	198>	9-1	9-7	110>	9-1	9-7	*****	8-30	9-5	1024>	8-30	9-5	198>	8-30	9-5	*****	9-1	9-7	*****	8-27	9-2	194X	*****	*****	*****	9-6	9-12	195X
9-8	9-14	199>	9-5	9-11	1024>	9-8	9-14	199>	9-8	9-14	111>	9-8	9-14	*****	9-6	9-12	1025>	9-6	9-12	199>	9-6	9-12	*****	9-8	9-14	*****	9-3	9-9	195X	*****	*****	*****	9-13	9-19	196X
9-15	9-21	200>	9-12	9-18	1025>	9-15	9-21	200>	9-15	9-21	112>	9-15	9-21	*****	9-13	9-19	1026>	9-13	9-19	200>	9-13	9-19	*****	9-15	9-21	*****	9-10	9-16	196X	*****	*****	*****	9-20	9-26	197X
9-22	9-28	201>	9-19	9-25	1026>	9-22	9-28	201>	9-22	9-28	113>	9-22	9-28	*****	9-20	9-26	1027>	9-20	9-26	*****	9-20	9-26	*****	9-22	9-28	*****	9-17	9-23	198X	*****	*****	*****	9-27	10-4	198X
9-29	10-5	202>	9-26	10-2	1027>	9-29	10-5	202>	9-29	10-5	114>	9-29	10-5	200>	9-27	10-3	1028>	9-27	10-3	202>	9-27	10-3	*****	9-29	10-5	*****	9-24	9-30	198X	*****	*****	*****	10-5	10-11	199X
10-6	10-12	203>	9-30	10-9	1028>	10-6	10-12	203>	10-6	10-12	115>	10-6	10-12	202/	10-4	10-10	1029>	10-4	10-10	203>	10-4	10-10	*****	10-6	10-12	*****	10-1	10-7	199X	*****	*****	*****	10-12	10-17	200X
10-13	10-19	204>	10-10	10-16	1029>	10-13	10-19	204>	10-13	10-19	116>	10-13	10-19	*****	10-11	10-17	1030>	10-11	10-17	204>	10-11	10-17	*****	10-13	10-19	*****	10-8	10-14	200X	*****	*****	*****	10-18	10-24	201X
10-20	10-26	////	10-17	10-23	1030>	10-20	10-26	////	10-20	10-26	117>	10-20	10-26	*****	10-18	10-24	1031>	10-18	10-24	////	10-18	10-24	*****	10-20	10-26	*****	10-15	10-21	201X	*****	*****	*****	10-25	10-31	202X
10-27	11-2	206>	10-24	10-30	1031>	10-27	11-2	206>	10-27	11-2	////	10-27	11-2	*****	10-25	10-31	1032>/	10-25	10-31	206>	10-25	10-31	*****	10-27	11-2	*****	10-22	10-28	202X	*****	*****	*****	11-1	11-7	203X
11-3	11-9	////	10-31	11-6	1032>/	11-3	11-9	////	11-3	11-9	////	11-3	11-9	*****	11-1	11-7	1033>	11-1	11-7	////	11-1	11-7	*****	11-3	11-9	*****	10-29	11-4	203X	*****	*****	*****	11-8	11-14	204X
11-10	11-16	////	11-7	11-13	1033>/	11-10	11-16	208>	11-10	11-16	////	11-10	11-16	*****	11-8	11-15	1034>	11-8	11-15	208>	11-8	11-15	*****	11-10	11-16	*****	11-5	11-11	204X	*****	*****	*****	11-15	11-21	205X
11-17	11-23	////	11-14	11-20	1034>	11-17	11-23	////	11-17	11-23	////	11-17	11-23	*****	11-16	11-22	1035>	11-16	11-22	////	11-16	11-22	*****	11-17	11-23	*****	11-12	11-18	205X	*****	*****	*****	11-22	11-28	206X
11-24	11-30	////	11-21	11-27	1035>	11-24	11-30	////	11-24	11-30	122>	11-24	11-30	*****	11-23	11-29	1036>	11-23	11-29	////	11-22	11-28	*****	11-24	11-30	*****	11-19	11-25	206X	*****	*****	*****	11-30	12-5	207X
12-1	12-7	211>	11-28	12-4	1036>	12-1	12-7	211>	12-1	12-7	123>	12-1	12-7	*****	11-30	12-6	1037>	11-30	12-5	211>	11-29	12-5	*****	12-1	12-7	*****	11-26	12-3	208X	*****	*****	*****	12-6	12-9	208X
12-8	12-14	213>	12-5	12-11	1037>	12-8	12-14	////	12-8	12-14	124>	12-8	12-14	*****	12-7	12-13	1038>	12-7	12-13	////	12-6	12-12	*****	12-8	12-14	S45/	12-4	12-17	210X	*****	*****	*****	12-12	12-17	209X
12-15	12-21	////	12-12	12-18	1038>	12-15	12-21	213>	12-15	12-21	125>	12-15	12-21	*****	12-14	12-20	1039>	12-14	12-20	////	12-13	12-19	*****	12-15	12-21	S45/				*****	*****	*****	12-18	12-24	210X
12-22	12-28	////	12-19	12-25	1039>	12-22	12-28	////	12-22	12-28	126>	12-22	12-28	*****	12-21	12-27	////	12-21	12-27	////	12-20	12-26	*****	12-22	12-28	S45/				*****	*****	*****	12-25	12-31	////
12-29	1-4	////	12-26	1-1	1040>	12-29	1-4	////	12-29	1-4	////				12-28	1-3	1041>	12-28	1-3	////	12-27	1-2	*****	12-29	1-4	*****	12-18	12-31	212X	*****	*****	*****			

Boston News Letter – NOTE: Date of Publication Changed From Monday to Thursday. You see a 3 day different in dates in the shipping news and it is no longer the same day as the other 3 newspapers.

Group	Year	Name	Type	Burden	First Name	Last Name	Length	Port	Arrival/Entered Inwards · Custom In/Entered Out · Custom Out/Cleared Out · Departure	Length	Port	Arrival/Entered Inwards · Custom In/Entered Out · Custom Out/Cleared Out · Departure	Page
?									(MSTR ID# / Registry Location / SHIP ID# / Source)			(Notes)	1
	1719					Mackintosh	Start	New York		>	Barbados		
	M-M-016							[New York]	(22 Dec 1719)		[Lesser Antilles]		
	S-?-019			5:4									
	1719					Brown	Start	New York		>	Antigua		
	M-B-038							[New York]	(22 Dec 1719)		[Leeward Islands]		
	S-?-020			5:4									
	1719					Payton	Start	New York	(22 Dec 1719)	>			
	M-P-022							[New York]	(22 Dec 1719)		Maryland		
	S-?-021			5:4									
	1721		Sloop			Burrough	Start	Boston		>	New York	(16 Jan 1721)	
	M-B-039							[Massachusetts]			[New York]		
	S-?-022			6:12									
	1720		Sloop		Joseph	Jacobs	Start	Jamaica		>	Pettiguavis		
	M-J-008							[Greater Antilles]			[Location Unkn]		
	S-?-023						>	Rhode Island	[18 Mar 1720]	>	New York	1 Apr 1720	
				5:34							[New York]		
									Passage Length: Jamaica → Pettiguavis → New York / Took 8 Weeks Total				
	1720		Sloop			Savage	Start	North Carolina		>	New York	5 Apr 1720	
	M-S-033										[New York]		
	S-?-024			5:36									
	1720		Sloop			Eustace	Start	Bermuda		>	New York	8 Apr 1720	
	M-E-004										[New York]		
	S-?-025			5:36									
	1720		Sloop		John	Tibbe	Start	Tortuga		>	New York	[2 May 1720]	
	M-T-013							[Haiti]			[New York]		
	S-?-026			5:45									
	1720		Brigantine			Thatcher	Start	Suriname		>	Barbados		
	M-T-014							[South America]			[Lesser Antilles]		
	S-?-027						>	New York	5 May 1720				
				5:50				[New York]					
	1720		Sloop			Miller	Start			>		14 May 1720	
	M-M-017	New York, New York									South Carolina		
	S-?-028												

MSTR ID# / SHIP ID#	Registry Location / Source	Type	Burden	First Name	Last Name	Length	Port / State / Country	Custom In / Entered Out / Custom Out / Cleared Out / Departure	Length	Port / State / Country	Custom In / Entered Out / Custom Out / Cleared Out / Departure
1720 / M-R-018 / S-?-029	5:63	Sloop			Roach	Start	Jamaica / [Greater Antilles]		>	New York / [New York]	13 Jun 1720
1720 / M-W-026 / S-?-030	5:63	Sloop			Wells	Start	Bermuda		>	New York / [New York]	13 Jun 1720
1720 / M-V-006 / S-?-031	5:70	Sloop			Van Heese	Start	South Carolina		>	Philadelphia / [Pennsylvania]	Never Reached Port / Chased Off
						>	Capes of Delaware	[? Jun 1720] / Chased Off / 2 Sloops	>	Sandy Hook / [New Jersey]	26 Jun 1720 / Chased Off / Ship
						>	New York / [New York]	27 Jun 1720			
1720 / M-M-018 / S-?-032	5:82	Sloop			Mosse	Start	Jamaica / [Greater Antilles]	[? Jun 1720]	>	New York / [New York]	19 Jul 1720
1720 / M-S-034 / S-?-033	5:88	Sloop			Scuse / Scufe	Start	North Carolina		>	New York / [New York]	2 Aug 1720
1720 / M-B-040 / S-?-034	5:92	Sloop			Buston	Start	Bermuda		10 Days	New York / [New York]	19 Aug 1720
1720 / M-S-035 / S-?-035	5:92	Sloop			Smith	Start	Curacao / [Leeward Antilles]		>	New York / [New York]	21 Aug 1720
1720 / M-M-019 / S-?-036	5:115 / 26:43	Brigantine		David	Minviele	Start	[Newport] / Rhode Island	[7 Oct 1720]	>	New York / [New York]	11 Oct 1720
1720 / M-U-001 / S-?-037	5:126	Sloop			Unran	Start	Curacao / [Leeward Antilles]		>	New York / [New York]	4 Nov 1720

Group	Ship				Captain / Master		Passage	Arrival / Departure 1		Passage	Arrival / Departure 2		Page
	Year	Name	Type	Burden	First Name	Last Name	Length	Port	Arrival / Entered Inwards / Custom In / Entered Out	Length	Port	Arrival / Entered Inwards / Custom In / Entered Out	
?	MSTR ID# / SHIP ID#	Registry Location						State / Country	Custom Out / Cleared Out / Departure		State / Country	Custom Out / Cleared Out / Departure	3
	Source							Notes					

	1720		Scallop			Shadden	Start			>	New York	11 Nov 1720	
	M-S-036 / S-?-038							Pennsylvania			[New York]		
	5:129												

	1720		Sloop			Leicester	Start	Jamaica		>	New York	22 Nov 1720	
	M-L-013 / S-?-039							[Greater Antilles]			[New York]		
	5:136												

	1721					Pitmore	Start			>	Suriname	2 Feb 1721	
	M-P-023 / S-?-040	New York, New York									[South America]		
	6:32												

	1721				Jacob	Soliel	Start			>	Suriname	2 Feb 1721	
	M-S-037 / S-?-041	New York, New York									[South America]		
	6:32												

	1721		Brigantine				Start	Terceira Island		>	New York	6 May 1721	
	M-?-004 / S-?-042							[Portugal]			[New York]		
	6:46												

	1721					Landy	Start	Bermuda		>	New York	1 Jun 1721	
	M-L-014 / S-?-043										[New York]		
	6:58												

	1721					Marston	Start	Jamaica		>	New York	3 Jul 1721	
	M-M-020 / S-?-044							[Greater Antilles]			[New York]		
	6:71,76												

	1721		Sloop			Marshall	Start	Havanna		>	New York	[14 Aug 1721]	
	M-M-021 / S-?-045							[Cuba]			[New York]		
	6:92												

	1721		Sloop			Jennings	Start	Bermuda		>	New York	17 Oct 1721	
	M-J-009 / S-?-046										[New York]		
	6:122												

	1721		Sloop		Richard	Vantile / Vantyle	Start	Boston		>	New York	[6 Nov 1721]	
	M-V-007 / S-?-047							[Massachusetts]	[21 Oct 1721]		[New York]		
	6:130 / 21:925												

	1721		Sloop			Geering	Start	Jamaica		>	New York	7 Nov 1721	
	M-G-018 / S-?-048							[Greater Antilles]			[New York]		
	6:132												

Year	Name	Type	Burden	First Name	Last Name	Length	Port	Custom In / Entered Out	Length	Port	Custom In / Entered Out
MSTR ID#	Registry Location						State / Country	Custom Out / Cleared Out		State / Country	Custom Out / Cleared Out
SHIP ID#								Departure			Departure
	Source							Notes			
1721		Sloop			Owen	Start	St Martin		>	New York	10 Nov 1721
M-O-004							[Leeward Islands]			[New York]	
S-?-049											
	6:132										
1722		Sloop			Burch	Start	Bermuda		>	New York	4 Apr 1722
M-B-041										[New York]	
S-?-050											
	7:42										
1722		Schooner			Burchen	Start	Cape Catoche		>	New York	[16 Apr 1722]
M-B-042							[Mexico]			[New York]	
S-?-051											
	7:45										
1722		Brigantine			Moses	Start	Jamaica		>	New York	22 Jun 1722
M-M-022							[Greater Antilles]			[New York]	
S-?-052											
						>	London				
							[England]				
	7:76							Sprung her main mast at sea, put into New York for repairs			
1722					Highinton	Start			>	New York	19 Jul 1722
M-H-028							Virginia			[New York]	
S-?-053											
	7:89										
1722		Sloop			Gilbert	Start	Bermuda		>	New York	14 Aug 1722
M-G-019										[New York]	
S-?-054											
	7:98										
1722		Sloop				Start	St Christopher		>	New York	8 Oct 1722
M-?-005							[Leeward Islands]			[New York]	
S-?-055											
	7:118										
1722		Sloop			Tregoe	Start	Anguilla		>	New York	[15 Oct 1722]
M-T-015							[Leeward Islands]			[New York]	
S-?-056											
	7:122										
1722		Sloop				Start	Bermuda		>	New York	11 Nov 1722
M-?-006										[New York]	
S-?-057											
	7:132										
1722		Sloop			Tret	Start	Bay of Honduras		>	New York	[12 Nov 1722]
M-T-016										[New York]	
S-?-058											
	7:132										

Group		Ship			Captain / Master		Passage	Arrival / Departure 1		Passage	Arrival / Departure 2		Page
?	Year	Name	Type	Burden	First Name	Last Name	Length	Port	Arrival / Entered Inwards / Custom In / Entered Out	Length	Port	Arrival / Entered Inwards / Custom In / Entered Out	5
	MSTR ID# SHIP ID#	Registry Location						State / Country	Custom Out / Cleared Out / Departure		State / Country	Custom Out / Cleared Out / Departure	
		Source							Notes				
	1722		Sloop			Paymer	Start			>	New York	[12 Nov 1722]	
	M-P-024 S-?-059							North Carolina			[New York]		
		7:132											
	1722		Brigantine			Holmes	Start			>	Manasquan	? Dec 1722	
	M-H-029 S-?-060							Ireland			[New Jersey]	Drove on Shore	
							&	Ships Crew & Passengers Saved		>	New York	Never Reached Port	
								Ship Was Lost			[New York]	Lost Before Arrival	
							>	New London	Never Reached Port				
								[Connecticut]	Lost Before Arrival				
		7:144,151						(Known Passengers / Passengers & Servants) New Jersey / Inward – ? Dec 1722 – Count 100+					
	1723		Sloop			Lancolet	Start	New London		>	New York	(4 Mar 1723)	
	M-L-015 S-?-061							[Connecticut]			[New York]		
		8:24											
	1723					Albin	Start	Barbados		>	New York		
	M-A-014 S-?-062							[Lesser Antilles]			[New York]		
		8:32						Source 8:32 - Has not arrived by 23 Mar 1723					
	1723		Sloop			Dodge	Start			>	New London		
	M-D-014 S-?-063							Rhode Island			[Connecticut]		
							>	New York	4 May 1723				
								[New York]					
		8:50											
	1723		Sloop			Cozens	Start	New Castle		>	New York	14 May 1723	
	M-C-018 S-?-064							[Delaware]			[New York]		
		8:58											
	1723		Sloop			Bush	Start	Curacao		>	New York	24 May 1723	
	M-B-043 S-?-065							[Leeward Antilles]			[New York]		
		8:60											
	1723		Sloop			Phillips	Start	New Castle		>	New York	4 May 1723	
	M-P-025 S-?-066							[Delaware]			[New York]		
							[>]	New Castle		>	New York	[22 Jul 1723]	
								[Delaware]			[New York]		
		8:50,81											

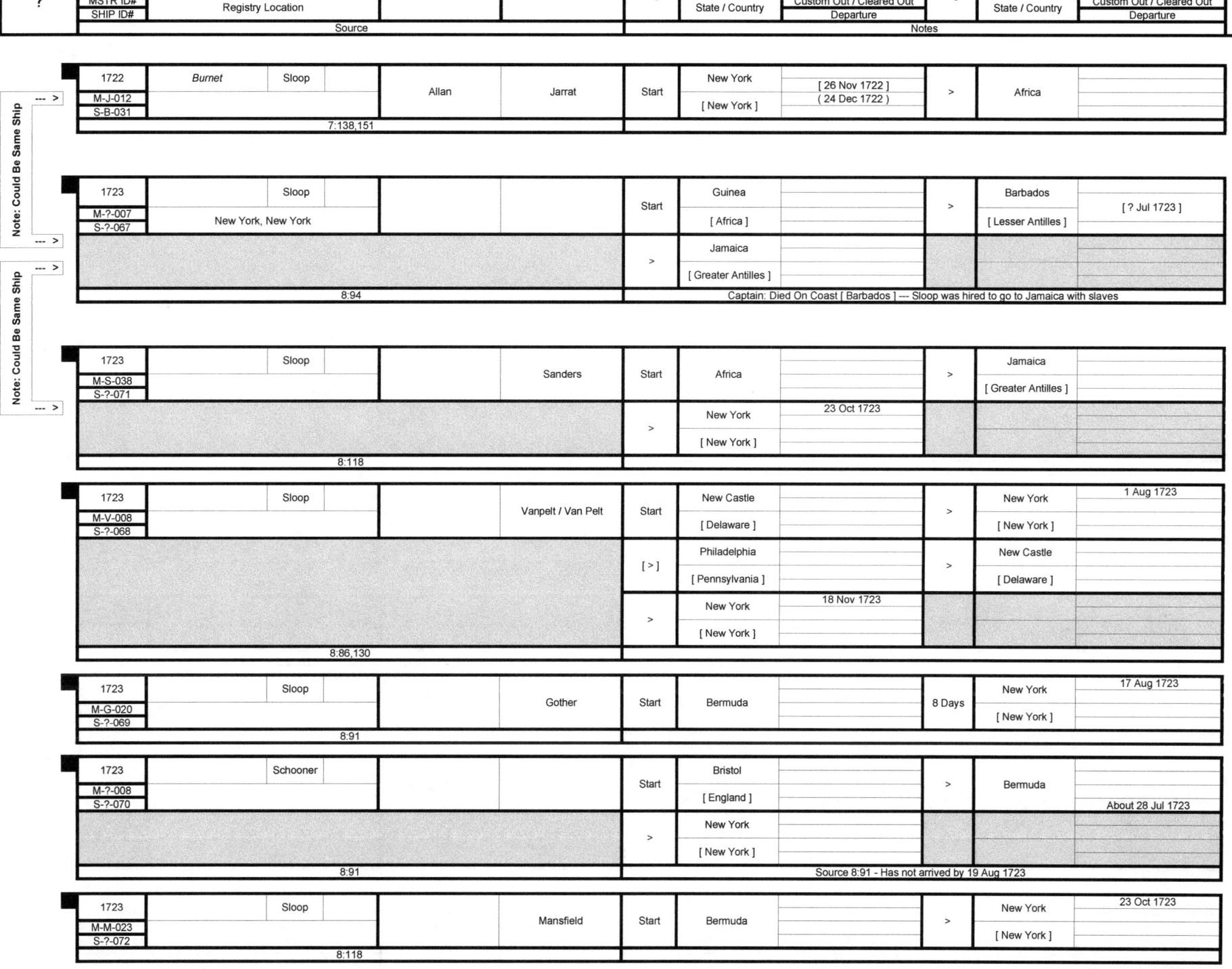

Year	MSTR ID# / SHIP ID#	Name	Type	Burden	First Name	Last Name	Length	Port / State / Country	Custom In / Entered Out / Custom Out / Cleared Out / Departure	Length	Port / State / Country	Custom In / Entered Out / Custom Out / Cleared Out / Departure
		Registry Location										
		Source							Notes			
1722	M-J-012 / S-B-031	*Burnet*	Sloop		Allan	Jarrat	Start	New York [New York]	[26 Nov 1722] (24 Dec 1722)	>	Africa	
		7:138,151										
1723	M-?-007 / S-?-067		Sloop				Start	Guinea [Africa]		>	Barbados [Lesser Antilles]	[? Jul 1723]
		New York, New York					>	Jamaica [Greater Antilles]				
		8:94						Captain: Died On Coast [Barbados] --- Sloop was hired to go to Jamaica with slaves				
1723	M-S-038 / S-?-071		Sloop			Sanders	Start	Africa		>	Jamaica [Greater Antilles]	
							>	New York [New York]	23 Oct 1723			
		8:118										
1723	M-V-008 / S-?-068		Sloop			Vanpelt / Van Pelt	Start	New Castle [Delaware]		>	New York [New York]	1 Aug 1723
							[>]	Philadelphia [Pennsylvania]		>	New Castle [Delaware]	
							>	New York [New York]	18 Nov 1723			
		8:86,130										
1723	M-G-020 / S-?-069		Sloop			Gother	Start	Bermuda		8 Days	New York [New York]	17 Aug 1723
		8:91										
1723	M-?-008 / S-?-070		Schooner				Start	Bristol [England]		>	Bermuda	About 28 Jul 1723
							>	New York [New York]				
		8:91						Source 8:91 - Has not arrived by 19 Aug 1723				
1723	M-M-023 / S-?-072		Sloop			Mansfield	Start	Bermuda		>	New York [New York]	23 Oct 1723
		8:118										

Note: Could Be Same Ship --->
Note: Could Be Same Ship --->

Group	Ship				Captain / Master		Passage	Arrival / Departure 1		Passage	Arrival / Departure 2		Page
	Year	Name	Type	Burden	First Name	Last Name	Length	Port	Arrival / Entered Inwards	Length	Port	Arrival / Entered Inwards	7
?									Custom In / Entered Out			Custom In / Entered Out	
	MSTR ID#	Registry Location						State / Country	Custom Out / Cleared Out		State / Country	Custom Out / Cleared Out	
	SHIP ID#								Departure			Departure	
	Source							Notes					

	1721 – 1723				John	Drummay / Druramey / Drumey	Start	Boston	[21 Oct 1721]	>		
	M-D-015								[21 Oct 1721]		New Jersey	
	S-?-073							[Massachusetts]				
	NO SUPPORTING DATA TO LINK TIMELINE											
							Start	Martinique		>	New York	[29 Oct 1722]
								[Lesser Antilles]			[New York]	
	NO SUPPORTING DATA TO LINK TIMELINE											
							Start			>	New York	[18 Mar 1723]
								Virginia			[New York]	
	7:126 / 8:28 / 23:59											

	1723		Sloop		John	Clock	Start			>	Boston	[27 Apr 1723]
	M-C-019											[27 Apr 1723]
	S-?-074							Connecticut			[Massachusetts]	[4 May 1723]
							>	New York	17 May 1723			
								[New York]				
	NO SUPPORTING DATA TO LINK TIMELINE											
							Start	Boston		>		
								[Massachusetts]	[13 Jul 1723]		Connecticut	
	NO SUPPORTING DATA TO LINK TIMELINE											
							Start	Boston		>	New York	[3 Dec 1723]
								[Massachusetts]			[New York]	
	8:58,134 / 20:91,92,102											

Year	Name	Type	Burden	First Name	Last Name	Length	Port	Custom In / Entered Out	Length	Port	Custom In / Entered Out
MSTR ID#	Registry Location						State / Country	Custom Out / Cleared Out		State / Country	Custom Out / Cleared Out
SHIP ID#								Departure			Departure
Source							Notes				
1719 – 1723	Abigail	Sloop		William	Jarrett / Jarrat / Jarratt	Start	New York	(22 Dec 1719)	>	Barbados	
M-J-010							[New York]	(2 Feb 1720)		[Lesser Antilles]	
S-A-020											
						[>]	Jamaica		25 Days	New York	13 Apr 1720
											[23 Apr 1720]
							[Greater Antilles]			[New York]	[16 May 1720]
						>	Jamaica		[>]	Curacao	
							[Greater Antilles]			[Leeward Antilles]	
						>	New York	16 Jul 1720	>	Jamaica	
								[8 Aug 1720]			
							[New York]	[29 Aug 1720]		[Greater Antilles]	
						[>]	Curacao		>	New York	2 Nov 1720
											[28 Nov 1720]
							[Leeward Antilles]			[New York]	
						>	Curacao		7 Weeks	New York	17 Mar 1721
											[24 Apr 1720]
							[Leeward Antilles]			[New York]	[15 May 1721]
						>	Barbados		>	New York	16 Jul 1721
											[31 Jul 1721]
							[Lesser Antilles]			[New York]	[7 Aug 1721]
						>	Barbados		>	New York	16 Oct 1721
											[5 Dec 1721]
							[Lesser Antilles]			[New York]	(19 Dec 1721)
						>	Curacao		[>]	New York	[16 Apr 1722]
							[Leeward Antilles]			[New York]	
						>	Jamaica		[>]	Barbados	
							[Greater Antilles]			[Lesser Antilles]	
						>	New York	28 Jun 1722	>	Curacao	
								[9 Jul 1722]			
							[New York]	[23 Jul 1722]		[Leeward Antilles]	
						>	New York	17 Sept 1722	>	Suriname	
								[29 Oct 1722]			4 Mar 1723
							[New York]	(24 Dec 1722)		[South America]	
						>	New York	14 May 1723	>	Curacao	
								[3 Jun 1723]			
							[New York]	[17 Jun 1723]		[Leeward Antilles]	
						>	New York	15 Sept 1723	>	Barbados	
								[11 Nov 1723]			
							[New York]	[25 Nov 1723]		[Lesser Antilles]	

5:4,16,38,41,53,78,88,94,125,136 / 6:32,42,49,79,87,90,122,144,148 / 7:45,79,82,89,110,126,151 / 8:34,58,62,68,100,126,130

Group					Captain / Master		Passage	Arrival / Departure 1		Passage	Arrival / Departure 2		Page
A	Year	Name	Type	Burden	First Name	Last Name	Length	Port	Arrival / Entered Inwards / Custom In / Entered Out / Custom Out / Cleared Out / Departure	Length	Port	Arrival / Entered Inwards / Custom In / Entered Out / Custom Out / Cleared Out / Departure	**9**
	MSTR ID#							State / Country			State / Country		
	SHIP ID#	Registry Location											
		Source							Notes				

Record 1

Year	Name	Type	Burden	MSTR ID#	SHIP ID#	First Name	Last Name	Passage Length	Port 1	Arr/Dep 1	Passage Length	Port 2	Arr/Dep 2
1722	*Abigail*	Sloop		M-D-016	S-A-021	John	Darkins / Daskins	Start	New York	[14 May 1722] [4 Jun 1722]	>	Boston	[23 Jun 1722]
									[New York]			[Massachusetts]	
								>			>	New York	22 Jul 1722
									Rhode Island			[New York]	

Source: 7:57,67,89 / 20:47

Record 2

Year	Name	Type	Burden	MSTR ID#	SHIP ID#	First Name	Last Name	Passage Length	Port 1	Arr/Dep 1	Passage Length	Port 2	Arr/Dep 2
1720	*Adventure*	Sloop		M-T-017	S-A-022	George	Tomlin / Tomlins	Start	New York	[18 Jul 1720] [25 Jul 1720]	>		
									[New York]			North Carolina	

Source: 5:78,82

Record 3

Year	Name	Type	Burden	MSTR ID#	SHIP ID#	First Name	Last Name	Passage Length	Port 1	Arr/Dep 1	Passage Length	Port 2	Arr/Dep 2
1720 – 1723	*Albany*	Brigantine		M-J-011	S-A-023	Isaac	Johnson	Start	Amsterdam		>	Cowes	
									[Holland]			[England]	31 Mar 1720
								>	New York	27 May 1720 [25 Jul 1720]	>	Madeira Island	
									[New York]			[Portugal]	
								5 Weeks	New York	14 Nov 1720 [28 Nov 1720] (19 Dec 1720)	>	Jamaica	
									[New York]			[Greater Antilles]	
								28 Days	New York	27 Apr 1721 [29 May 1721] [12 Jun 1721]	>	Holland	
									[New York]				
								>	Cowes		>	New York	10 Nov 1721 [5 Dec 1721] (19 Dec 1721)
									[England]	About 10 Sept 1721		[New York]	
								>	Barbados		[>]	Anguilla	
									[Lesser Antilles]			[Leeward Islands]	
								14 Days	New York	19 Feb 1722 [19 Mar 1722]	>	Holland	
									[New York]				
								[>]	Cowes		>	New York	[5 Nov 1722] [26 Nov 1722]
									[England]	[? Jul 1722]		[New York]	
								>	Barbados		>	New York	4 May 1723 [13 May 1723]
									[Lesser Antilles]			[New York]	
								>	Isle of Wight		>	Holland	
									[England]				
								[>]	Cowes		8 Weeks	New York	11 Dec 1723
									[England]			[New York]	

Source: 5:58,82,133,136 / 6:4,44,56,58,60,125,132,144,148 / 7:26,34,112,130,138 / 8:50,54,138

MSTR ID# / SHIP ID#	Year	Name	Type	Burden	First Name	Last Name	Length	Port / State / Country	Custom In / Entered Out / Custom Out / Cleared Out / Departure	Length	Port / State / Country	Custom In / Entered Out / Custom Out / Cleared Out / Departure
Registry Location												
Source								Notes				
M-S-039 / S-A-015	1720	Anne	Sloop		William	Smith	Start	New York / [New York]	[13 Jun 1720] / [20 Jun 1720]	>	Jamaica / [Greater Antilles]	
5:63,67												
M-B-044 / S-A-016	1720 – 1721	Anne	Sloop		Justus	Burch / Borch / Bosch	Start	Nevis / [Leeward Islands]		>	Bermuda	Docked For 15 Days / Chased In By Pirates
							8 Days	New York / [New York]	31 Jul 1720 / [12 Sept 1720] / [19 Sept 1720]	>	Rhode Island	
									NO SUPPORTING DATA TO LINK TIMELINE			
							Start	New York / [New York]	[15 May 1721] / [15 May 1721]	>	Rhode Island	
5:85,99,103 / 6:49												
M-B-045 / S-A-017	1720	Anne	Sloop		Isaac	Bedlow	Start	New York / [New York]	[12 Sept 1720] / [19 Sept 1720]	>	Jamaica / [Greater Antilles]	
5:99,103												
M-D-017 / S-A-018	1721	Anne	Sloop		Samuel	Dunscomb	Start	Bay of Honduras		>	New York / [New York]	23 Mar 1721
6:34												
M-H-002 / S-A-007	1723	Anne	Sloop		Robert	Holmes	Start	New York / [New York]	[25 Mar 1723] / [1 Apr 1723]	>	Boston / [Massachusetts]	[13 Apr 1723] / [4 May 1723]
							>	Pennsylvania		>	Boston / [Massachusetts]	[6 Jul 1723] / [13 Jul 1723]
							>	Pennsylvania				
8:32,34 / 20:89,92,101,102												
M-D-018 / S-A-019	1723	Anne	Sloop		Jonathan	Dunscomb / Dunicomb	Start	Bermuda		>	New York / [New York]	28 Aug 1723 / [2 Sept 1723] / [9 Sept 1723]
							>	Bermuda				
8:96,98												

Group	Year	Name	Type	Burden	First Name	Last Name	Passage Length	Port (A/D 1)	Arrival / Entered Inwards · Custom In / Entered Out · Custom Out / Cleared Out · Departure	Passage Length	Port (A/D 2)	Arrival / Entered Inwards · Custom In / Entered Out · Custom Out / Cleared Out · Departure	Page
A													11
								State / Country			State / Country		
								Source	Notes				

Row 1 (MSTR ID# M-C-020, SHIP ID# S-A-024)

Year	Name	Type	First Name	Last Name	Passage	Port 1	State/Country 1	Dates 1	Passage	Port 2	State/Country 2	Dates 2
1722	*Antelope*	Sloop	Joseph	Clarke	Start	Guadeloupe	[Leeward Islands]		>	New York	[New York]	[30 Apr 1722] / [7 May 1722] / [21 May 1722]
					>	Madeira Island	[Portugal]		[>]	Dublin	[Ireland]	
					>	New York	[New York]	[12 Nov 1722] / [26 Nov 1722] / (24 Dec 1722)	>	Jamaica	[Greater Antilles]	

Source: 7:51,54,60,132,138,151

Row 2 (MSTR ID# M-B-034, SHIP ID# S-A-010)

Left box: Philadelphia / M-J-007 / S-A-010 / Page # 71 / Book   <

Year	Name	Type	First Name	Last Name	Passage	Port 1	State/Country 1	Dates 1	Passage	Port 2	State/Country 2	Dates 2
1722 – 1723	*Antelope*	Sloop	Samuel	Bourdet	Start	Philadelphia	[Pennsylvania]	XX [17 May 1722] XX / XXXXXXXXXXXXXXX / [13 Sept 1722]		Antigua	[Leeward Islands]	
					>	Anguilla	[Leeward Islands]		>	New York	[New York]	31 Jul 1723 / [12 Aug 1723] / [26 Aug 1723]
					>	Antigua	[Leeward Islands]					

Source: 7:108 / 8:86,88,94

Year / MSTR ID# / SHIP ID#	Name / Registry Location	Type	Burden	First Name	Last Name	Length	Port / State / Country	Custom In / Entered Out / Custom Out / Cleared Out / Departure	Length	Port / State / Country	Custom In / Entered Out / Custom Out / Cleared Out / Departure
1720 – 1723 / M-S-040 / S-B-022	Beaver	Ship		Thomas	Smith	Start	London [England]	26 Feb 1720	>	Downs [England]	8 Mar 1720
						>	Isle of Wight [England]	18 Mar 1720	>	New York [New York]	2 May 1720 / [16 May 1720] / 14 Jun 1720 / 14 Jun 1720
						>	Sandy Hook [New Jersey]	19 Jun 1720	>	London [England]	24 – 25 Jul 1720
						>	Downs [England]	12 Sept 1720	>	New York [New York]	8 Nov 1720 / [21 Nov 1720] / (19 Dec 1720) / 17 Dec 1720
						>	London [England]	26 Jan 1721	2 Weeks	Torbay England	
						8 Weeks	New York [New York]	5 Jun 1721 / [12 Jun 1721] / [26 Jun 1721] / 28 Jun 1721	>	London [England]	10 Sept 1721
						>	Land's End [England]		5 Weeks	New York [New York]	2 Nov 1721 / [13 Nov 1721] / [5 Dec 1721] / 4 Dec 1721
						>	London [England]	10 Mar 1722	>	New York [New York]	7 May 1722 / [14 May 1722] / [28 May 1722] / 26 May 1722
						>	London [England]	30 Jun 1722	>	Gravesend [England]	17 Aug 1722
						>	Plymouth [England]	1 Sept 1722	>	New York [New York]	19 Oct 1722 / [29 Oct 1722] / [26 Nov 1722] / 27 Nov 1722
						>	London [England]	10 Mar 1723	>	Downs [England]	17 Mar 1723
						>	New York [New York]	25 Apr 1723 / [6 May 1723] / [27 May 1723]	>	London [England]	13 Sept 1723
						>	New York [New York]	26 Oct 1723 / [4 Nov 1723] / [25 Nov 1723]	>	London [England]	

Source: 5:40,50,53,56,58,60,63,67,123,129,133,141 / 6:4,40,58,60,67,71,125,130,132,137,138,144 / 7:48,54,57,60,112,122,126,132,138 / 8:44,45,50,58,60,109,112,118,122,126,130

Year / MSTR ID# / SHIP ID#	Name / Registry Location	Type	Burden	First Name	Last Name	Length	Port / State / Country	Custom In / Out	Length	Port / State / Country	Custom In / Out
1723 / M-H-030 / S-B-023	Benjamin	Sloop		Benjamin	Hinson	Start	Jamaica [Greater Antilles]		>	New York [New York]	23 Aug 1723 / [16 Sept 1723] / [30 Sept 1723]
						>	Jamaica [Greater Antilles]				

Source: 8:94,100,106

Group	Year	Name	Type	Burden	First Name	Last Name	Length	Port	Arrival / Entered Inwards / Custom In / Entered Out / Custom Out / Cleared Out / Departure	Length	Port	Arrival / Entered Inwards / Custom In / Entered Out / Custom Out / Cleared Out / Departure	Page
B								State / Country	Notes		State / Country		13

Benjamin (Ship) — MSTR ID# M-H-031 / SHIP ID# S-B-024

	Year	Name	Type	First Name	Last Name	Length	Port	Dates	Length	Port	Dates
	1719 – 1720	Benjamin	Ship	Robert	Hays / Hayes	Start	Barbados [Lesser Antilles]		>	New York [New York]	13 Dec 1719 / (22 Dec 1719) / (18 Jan 1720)
						>	Barbados [Lesser Antilles]	[? Feb 1720] / Taken / Pirates	>	Barbados [Lesser Antilles]	Taken / In Fight of the Island / 6 Tons of Goods
						>	Barbados [Lesser Antilles]	[? Feb 1720] / Released / Pirates			

Source: 5:4,12,34

Benjamin (Sloop) — MSTR ID# M-G-002 / SHIP ID# M-B-002

	Year	Name	Type	First Name	Last Name	Length	Port	Dates	Length	Port	Dates
	1719 – 1721	Benjamin	Sloop	Ephraim	Gilbert	Start	Madeira Island [Portugal]	18 Nov 1719	>	Bermuda	Dec 1719 – Jan 1720
						28 Days	New York [New York]	20 Feb 1720	[>]	Jamaica [Greater Antilles]	
						>	Philadelphia [Pennsylvania]	3 Oct 1720 / [27 Oct 1720]	>	Barbados [Lesser Antilles]	
						[>]	Bermuda		>	Philadelphia [Pennsylvania]	[20 Apr 1721] / [27 Apr 1721] / [11 May 1721]
						>	Jamaica [Greater Antilles]				

Source: 5:24,110,120 / 6:40,42,46

Notes: (Ship) Bermuda / Infected Small Pox – Dec 1719

Beginning (Sloop) — MSTR ID# M-R-013 / SHIP ID# S-B-016

	Year	Name	Type	First Name	Last Name	Length	Port	Dates	Length	Port	Dates
	1720	Beginning	Sloop	Joseph	Royal	Start	New York [New York]	[6 Jun 1720] / [6 Jun 1720]	>	Pennsylvania	[? ? 1720] / XX [10 Nov 1720] XX / XXXXXXXXXXXXXX / XXXXXXXXXXXXXX

Source: 5:60

Philadelphia — M-G-013 / S-B-016 / Page # 58 / Book

Bersheba (Sloop) — MSTR ID# M-M-024 / SHIP ID# S-B-025

	Year	Name	Type	First Name	Last Name	Length	Port	Dates	Length	Port	Dates
	1720	Bersheba	Sloop	William	Manning	Start	New York [New York]	[10 Oct 1720] / [31 Oct 1720]	>	Barbados [Lesser Antilles]	

Source: 5:112,123

Notes: Could be the same Manning from Philadelphia Book - (M-M-015)

Bersheba (Sloop) — MSTR ID# M-F-009 / SHIP ID# S-B-026

	Year	Name	Type	First Name	Last Name	Length	Port	Dates	Length	Port	Dates
	1721	Bersheba	Sloop	Samuel	Fox	Start	New York [New York]	[13 Nov 1721] / [5 Dec 1721]	>	Barbados [Lesser Antilles]	

Source: 6:132,144

Bersheba & Mary (Sloop) — MSTR ID# M-D-019 / SHIP ID# S-B-027

	Year	Name	Type	First Name	Last Name	Length	Port	Dates	Length	Port	Dates
	1722	Bersheba & Mary	Sloop	Henry	Dewilde / de Wilde	Start	New York [New York]	[7 May 1722] / [14 May 1722]	>	New Providence [Bahamas]	

Year	Name	Type	Burden	First Name	Last Name	Length	Port / State / Country	Custom In / Entered Out / Custom Out / Cleared Out / Departure	Length	Port / State / Country	Custom In / Entered Out / Custom Out / Cleared Out / Departure
MSTR ID# / SHIP ID#	Registry Location										
	Source							Notes			
1722 – 1723	Blessing	Pink		John	Moorsom	Start	Rotterdam [Holland]		>	Harwich [England]	
M-M-025 / S-B-028						>	New York [New York]	[29 Oct 1722] (8 Jan 1723) (8 Jan 1723)	>	Perth Amboy New Jersey	[26 Mar 1723] [8 May 1723]
						>	London [England]				
	7:125,126 / 8:5,32 / 23:69,70						(Known Passengers / Palatines) New York / Inward – 29 Oct 1722 – Count 200+				
1723	Blessing	Sloop		John	Onterbridge / Outerbridge	Start	Bermuda		>	New York [New York]	[29 Jul 1723] [5 Aug 1723] [19 Aug 1723]
M-O-005 / S-B-029						>	Jamaica [Greater Antilles]				
	8:86,91 / 26:193										
1720	Boneta	Sloop		James	Banbury	Start	South Carolina		>	New York [New York]	17 Aug 1720 [5 Sept 1720] [12 Sept 1720]
M-B-046 / S-B-030						>	South Carolina				
	5:92,96,99										
1722 – 1723	Burnet	Pink		Silvanus	Furse	Start	Bristol [England]		>	New York [New York]	16 May 1722 [28 May 1722] [11 Jun 1722]
M-F-010 / S-B-032						>	Bristol [England]		>	New York [New York]	19 Nov 1722
						[>]	Rhode Island		>	New York [New York]	(8 Jan 1723) (8 Jan 1723) (8 Jan 1723)
						>	Bristol [England]				
	7:60,63,70,136 / 8:5										

Group					Ship					Captain / Master		Passage	Arrival / Departure 1		Passage	Arrival / Departure 2		Page
		Year	Name	Type	Burden	First Name	Last Name	Length	Port	Arrival / Entered Inwards	Length	Port	Arrival / Entered Inwards	
C		MSTR ID#								Custom In / Entered Out			Custom In / Entered Out	15
		SHIP ID#	Registry Location						State / Country	Custom Out / Cleared Out		State / Country	Custom Out / Cleared Out	
		Source								Departure		Notes	Departure	

	1722	Catherine	Sloop		Jonathan	Woodberry / Woodbury	Start	Antigua		>		Never Reached Port	
	M-W-027							[Leeward Islands]			Virginia	Distress of Weather	
	S-C-018						>	Perth Amboy	[5 Nov 1722]	>	New York	vv Transfer vv	
									vv Transfer vv			[26 Nov 1722]	
								[New Jersey]	vv Transfer vv		[New York]	[26 Nov 1722]	
									vv Transfer vv				
							>			>			
								Rhode Island					
	7:138 / 23:66												

	1721 – 1722	Catherine & Mary	Sloop		Benjamin	Applebe / Appleby	Start	New Castle		>	New York	[20 Nov 1721]	
	M-A-015											(12 Mar 1722)	
	S-C-019							[Delaware]			[New York]	[19 Mar 1722]	
							>			>	New York	[14 May 1722]	
								Virginia			[New York]		
	6:137 / 7:32,34,57												

	1722 – 1723	Catherine & Mary	Sloop		Cornelius	Vanscise	Start	New York	[27 Aug 1722]	>	Boston	
	M-V-009								[3 Sept 1722]			
	S-C-020							[New York]			[Massachusetts]	
							>	New York	[8 Oct 1722]	>	Boston	
									[15 Oct 1722]			
								[New York]	[29 Oct 1722]		[Massachusetts]	
							>	New York	[10 Dec 1722]	>	Boston	[2 Mar 1723]
									(18 Feb 1723)			[16 Mar 1723]
								[New York]	(18 Feb 1723)		[Massachusetts]	[23 Mar 1723]
							>	New York	[15 Apr 1723]	>	Curacao	
									[29 Jul 1723]			
								[New York]	[5 Aug 1723]		[Leeward Antilles]	
	7:102,105,118,122,126,144 / 8:21,39,84,86 / 20:82,85,86 / 26:193											

	1720 – 1721	Content	Sloop		William	Lyford	Start	New York	[14 Nov 1720]	>	New Providence	
	M-L-016								[21 Nov 1720]			
	S-C-021							[New York]			[Bahamas]	
							12 Days	New York	3 Apr 1721	>	New Providence	
									[15 May 1721]			
								[New York]	[22 May 1721]		[Bahamas]	
							[>]			>	Cape Charles	22 Nov 1721
								South Carolina			[Virginia]	Lost
							&	Ships Crew Saved		>	New York	Never Reached Port
								Ship & Cargo Lost			[New York]	Lost
	5:129,133 / 6:36,49,52 / 7:4											

Year	Name	Type	Burden	First Name	Last Name	Length	Port	Custom In / Entered Out	Length	Port	Custom In / Entered Out
MSTR ID#	Registry Location						State / Country	Custom Out / Cleared Out		State / Country	Custom Out / Cleared Out
SHIP ID#								Departure			Departure
	Source							Notes			
1721	*Content*	Sloop		William	Cook / Cooke	Start	Jamaica		>	Hispaniola	
M-C-021							[Greater Antilles]			[Greater Antilles]	
S-C-022											
						>	New York	20 Sept 1721	>	Jamaica	Kept 3 Weeks
								[6 Nov 1721]			
							[New York]	[20 Nov 1721]		[Greater Antilles]	Taken / Pirates
	6:108,130,137 / 7:40										
1720	*Crane / Crean*	Snow			Jandine	Start	New York	[29 Aug 1720]	>	Bristol	
M-J-013							[New York]			[England]	
S-C-023											
	5:94										
1720	*Crane / Crean*	Snow		Owen	Carty	Start	New York		>	Bristol	
M-C-022							[New York]	[3 Oct 1720]		[England]	
S-C-024											
	5:110										
1721	*Crane / Crean*	Snow		John	Margeson	>	Jamaica	28 May 1721	>	New York	[19 Jun 1721]
M-M-026											
S-C-025							[Greater Antilles]			[New York]	[24 Jul 1721]
						>	Curacao	16 Oct 1721	>	New York	[23 Oct 1721]
							[Leeward Antilles]			[New York]	[20 Nov 1721]
						>	Curacao		>	Hispaniola	?? ??? 1722
							[Leeward Antilles]			[Greater Antilles]	Taken / Pirates
						>	Some Men – Marooned / Pirates		>	New York	Never Reached Port
							Some Men – Murdered / Pirates			[New York]	Taken / Pirates
						>		Snow Taken Into	>	St Domingo	Snow Taken Into
							Porto Rico	Refused to Condemn		Hispaniola	Left
	6:56,63,84,122,137 / 7:74						Source 6:74 – Captain Margeson papers were found on board the Spanish Sloop / Pirates were captured and executed.				
1721	*Crown Galley*	Ship			Downing	>	Africa		>	New York	3 Jun 1721
M-D-020										[New York]	
S-C-026											
	6:58						(Known Passengers / Slaves) New York / Inward – 3 Jun 1721 – Count 117+				
1722	*Cutwater*	Sloop		John	Price	Start	Bath Town		>	Philadelphia	[26 Apr 1722]
M-P-002											[3 May 1722]
S-C-010							North Carolina			[Pennsylvania]	[3 May 1722]
						>	Lewes		>	New York	[27 Aug 1722]
											[10 Sept 1722]
							[Delaware]			[New York]	[10 Sept 1722]
						>	Lewes				
							Delaware				
	7:48,52,102,108										

Group	Year	Name	Type	Burden	First Name	Last Name	Length (Passage)	Port	State/Country	Arrival/Entered Inwards — Custom In/Entered Out — Custom Out/Cleared Out — Departure	Length (Passage)	Port	State/Country	Arrival/Entered Inwards — Custom In/Entered Out — Custom Out/Cleared Out — Departure	Page
D															17

D | 1723 | Devonshire | Sloop
MSTR ID# M-M-027 — SHIP ID# S-D-013
Captain: William Martindale / Marsindale — Passage: Start
Arrival/Departure 1: Nevis [Leeward Islands]
Passage: > — Arrival/Departure 2: New York [New York] — 5 Jun 1723 / [17 Jun 1723] / [1 Jul 1723]
(second row) Passage: > — Nevis [Leeward Islands]
Source: 8:65,68,73

D | 1720 | Devonshire | Ship
MSTR ID# M-B-047 — SHIP ID# S-D-014
Captain: Elisha Bennett — Passage: Start
Arrival/Departure 1: New York [New York] — [21 Mar 1720] / [21 Mar 1720]
Passage: > — Arrival/Departure 2: Rhode Island
Source: 5:30

D | 1721 | Devonshire | Sloop
MSTR ID# M-G-021 — SHIP ID# S-D-015
Captain: Richard Gilbert — Passage: Start
Arrival/Departure 1: New York [New York] — [19 Jun 1721] / [26 Jun 1721]
Passage: > — Arrival/Departure 2: Madeira Island [Portugal]
Source: 6:63,67

D | 1720 | Diamond | Sloop
MSTR ID# M-D-021 — SHIP ID# S-D-016
Captain: Benjamin Dill — Passage: Start
Arrival/Departure 1: New York [New York] — [5 Sept 1720] / [19 Sept 1720]
Passage: > — Arrival/Departure 2: Jamaica [Greater Antilles]
Source: 5:96,103

D | 1721 | Diamond | Sloop
MSTR ID# M-B-048 — SHIP ID# S-D-017
Captain: John Birch — Passage: Start
Arrival/Departure 1: New York [New York] — [22 May 1721] / [29 May 1721]
Passage: > — Arrival/Departure 2: St Thomas [Virgin Islands]
Source: 6:52,56

D | 1723 | Dolphin | Schooner
MSTR ID# M-B-049 — SHIP ID# S-D-018
Captain: James Brown — Passage: Start
Arrival/Departure 1: Rhode Island — [1 Aug 1723]
Passage: > — Arrival/Departure 2: Perth Amboy [New Jersey] — [12 Aug 1723] / vv Transfer vv / vv Transfer vv / vv Transfer vv
(second row) Passage: [>] — New York [New York] — vv Transfer vv / [16 Aug 1723] / [16 Aug 1723] — Passage: > — Arrival/Departure 2: Rhode Island
Source: 8:91,94 / 23:73

D | 1720 | Dolphin | Snow
MSTR ID# M-T-018 — SHIP ID# S-D-019
Captain: Thomas Tannatt / Tannett — Passage: Start
Arrival/Departure 1: New York [New York] — [9 May 1720] / [11 Jul 1720] / 15 Jul 1720
Passage: > — Arrival/Departure 2: Sandy Hook [New Jersey] — 17 Jul 1720
(second row) Passage: > — Bristol [England]
Source: 5:50,70,72,75,78

D | 1722 | Dolphin | Sloop
MSTR ID# M-V-010 — SHIP ID# S-D-020
Captain: Richard Vantuyl / Vantuyle — Passage: Start
Arrival/Departure 1: New York [New York] — [4 Jun 1722] / [2 Jul 1722]
Passage: > — Arrival/Departure 2: Curacao [Leeward Antilles]
Source: 7:67,79

D | 1722 | Dolphin | Sloop
MSTR ID# M-P-026 — SHIP ID# S-D-021
Captain: John Painter / Paynter — Passage: Start
Arrival/Departure 1: New York [New York] — [3 Dec 1722] / [3 Dec 1722]
Passage: > — Arrival/Departure 2: Lewes [Delaware]
Source: 7:144

	Year	Name	Type	Burden	First Name	Last Name	Length	Port	Custom In / Entered Out	Length	Port	Custom In / Entered Out	
D	MSTR ID#							State / Country	Custom Out / Cleared Out		State / Country	Custom Out / Cleared Out	18
	SHIP ID#	Registry Location							Departure			Departure	
				Source						Notes			

	1723	Dolphin	Schooner		Mayes	Nicholls	Start	New London	(18 Feb 1723)	>	New York	(18 Feb 1723)
	M-N-007							[Connecticut]			[New York]	(18 Feb 1723)
	S-D-022								(18 Feb 1723)			
							>	Rhode Island				
				8:21								

	1723	Dreadnought	Sloop		Thomas	Lea	Start	Madeira Island		>	Bermuda	
	M-L-017							[Portugal]				
	S-D-023											
							>	New York	[8 Apr 1723]	>	Bermuda	
									[15 Apr 1723]			
								[New York]	[22 Apr 1723]			
				8:39,42 / 26:177								

Group	Year / MSTR ID# / SHIP ID#	Ship Name	Type	Burden	First Name	Last Name	Passage Length	Port / State-Country (Arr/Dep 1)	Arrival / Custom In / Custom Out / Departure	Passage Length	Port / State-Country (Arr/Dep 2)	Arrival / Custom In / Custom Out / Departure	Page
E		Name	Type	Burden	First Name	Last Name	Length	Port	Arrival / Entered Inwards; Custom In / Entered Out	Length	Port	Arrival / Entered Inwards; Custom In / Entered Out	**19**
	MSTR ID# / SHIP ID#	Registry Location						State / Country	Custom Out / Cleared Out; Departure		State / Country	Custom Out / Cleared Out; Departure	
		Source							Notes				

1720 — Eagle — Snow — M-?-009 / S-E-014
Start	New York	>	Barbados
	[New York]		[Lesser Antilles]

Source: 5:26

1720 – 1721 — Easter — Sloop — John Hall — M-H-019 / S-E-015
Start	New York — [8 Aug 1720] / [15 Aug 1720]	>	South Carolina
	[New York]		

NO SUPPORTING DATA TO LINK TIMELINE
Start	Maryland	>	New York — 8 Oct 1721 / [5 Dec 1721] / (19 Dec 1721) / [New York]
>	Barbados — [Lesser Antilles]		

Source: 5:88,90 / 6:114,144,148

1722 — Elizabeth — Sloop — Joseph Young — M-Y-001 / S-E-016
Start	Jamaica — [Greater Antilles]	>	New York — 20 Aug 1722 / [3 Sept 1722] / [3 Sept 1722] / [New York]
>	Bermuda		

Source: 7:98,105

1720 — Elizabeth — Sloop — John Gibs — M-G-022 / S-E-017
Start	New York — [27 Jun 1720] / [4 Jul 1720]	>	Jamaica
	[New York]		[Greater Antilles]

Source: 5:70,72

1720 — Elizabeth — Sloop — William Carlisle — M-C-023 / S-E-018
Start	New York — [18 Jul 1720] / [25 Jul 1720] / [New York]	>	South Carolina
[>]	New York — [21 Nov 1720] / [28 Nov 1720] / [New York]	>	New Providence — [Bahamas]

Source: 5:78,82,133

1721 — Elizabeth — Sloop — Daniel Lasher / Lusher — M-L-018 / S-E-019
Start	Leogand — [Location Unkn]	>	New York — 8 Oct 1721 / [16 Oct 1721] / [23 Oct 1721] / [New York]
>	Jamaica — [Greater Antilles]		

Source: 6:114,119,122

1720 — Elizabeth — Brigantine — Phillip Rawlings / Rawings — M-R-019 / S-E-020
Start	St Christopher — [Leeward Islands]	20 Days	New York — 30 Jun 1720 / [18 Jul 1720] / [25 Jul 1720] / [New York]
>	Boston — [Massachusetts]		

Source: 5:72,78,82

Year	Name	Type	Burden	First Name	Last Name	Length	Port	Custom In / Entered Out	Length	Port	Custom In / Entered Out
MSTR ID#	Registry Location						State / Country	Custom Out / Cleared Out		State / Country	Custom Out / Cleared Out
SHIP ID#								Departure			Departure
	Source							Notes			
1720 – 1722	*Elizabeth*	Sloop		Thomas	Birch	Start	Bermuda		>	New York	4 Nov 1720
M-B-050											[21 Nov 1720]
S-E-021										[New York]	[28 Nov 1720]
						>	Barbados		[>]	Bermuda	
							[Lesser Antilles]				
						>	New York	29 Apr 1721	[>]	St Martin	
							[New York]			[Leeward Islands]	
						>	Bermuda		16 Days	New York	9 Sept 1721
										[New York]	[16 Apr 1722]
						>	Curacao				
							[Leeward Antilles]				
	5:126,133,136 / 6:44,103 / 7:45										
1721	*Elizabeth*	Sloop		Richard	Mathelin	Start	New York	[19 Jun 1721]	>	St Eustatius	
M-M-028								[26 Jun 1721]			
S-E-022							[New York]			[Leeward Islands]	
	6:63,67										
1720	*Elizabeth & Anne*	Ship		John	Meredith	Start	Liverpool		>	Cork	
M-M-029											
S-E-023							[England]			[Ireland]	
						10 Weeks	New York	9 Jun 1720	>	Barbados	
								[18 Jul 1720]			
							[New York]	[12 Sept 1720]		[Lesser Antilles]	
	5:62,63,78,99										
1721	*Elizabeth & Anne*	Sloop		Henry	Morgan	Start	Cape Catoche		>	New York	[22 May 1721]
M-M-030											[5 Jun 1721]
S-E-024							[Mexico]			[New York]	[19 Jun 1721]
						>	Bermuda				
	6:52,58,63										
1723	*Elizabeth & Anne*	Sloop		Richard	Leacraft	Start	Turks Island		>	Bermuda	
M-L-019											
S-E-025											
						>	New York	[1 Jul 1723]	>	Jamaica	
								[15 Jul 1723]			
							[New York]	[29 Jul 1723]		[Greater Antilles]	
	8:73,78,84										

Group													Page
	Ship				**Captain / Master**		**Passage**	**Arrival / Departure 1**		**Passage**	**Arrival / Departure 2**		
	Year	Name	Type	Burden	First Name	Last Name	Length	Port	Arrival / Entered Inwards / Custom In / Entered Out / Custom Out / Cleared Out / Departure	Length	Port	Arrival / Entered Inwards / Custom In / Entered Out / Custom Out / Cleared Out / Departure	
	MSTR ID# / SHIP ID#	Registry Location						State / Country			State / Country		
		Source							Notes				

Group E — Page 21

1721 – 1722 — Elizabeth & Martha — Sloop
MSTR ID# M-G-005 / SHIP ID# S-E-004 — Captain: John Gibbs

Passage	Port	State / Country	Dates		Passage	Port	State / Country	Dates
Start	Bermuda			>		Philadelphia	[Pennsylvania]	7 Aug 1721 / [24 Aug 1721] / [7 Sept 1721]
>	Barbados	[Lesser Antilles]						
	NO SUPPORTING DATA TO LINK TIMELINE							
Start	Turks Island			>		New York	[New York]	[3 Sept 1722] / [10 Sept 1722]
>	Curacao	[Leeward Antilles]						

Source: 6:90,94,100 / 7:105,108

1721 — Endeavor — Sloop
MSTR ID# M-H-033 / SHIP ID# S-E-026 — Captain: Nathaniel Hall

Passage	Port	State / Country	Dates		Passage	Port	State / Country
Start	New York	[New York]	[16 Oct 1721] / [23 Oct 1721]	>		Lewes	Delaware

Source: 6:119,122

1720 — Endeavor — Sloop
MSTR ID# M-C-024 / SHIP ID# S-E-027 — Captain: Jonathan Clarke

Passage	Port	State / Country	Dates		Passage	Port	State / Country
Start	New York	[New York]	[23 May 1720] / [6 Jun 1720]	>		Nevis	[Leeward Islands]

Source: 5:56,60

1719 – 1720 — Endeavor — Sloop
MSTR ID# M-B-051 / SHIP ID# S-E-028 — Captain: Richard Brasse / Brask

Passage	Port	State / Country	Dates		Passage	Port	State / Country
Start	New York	[New York]	(22 Dec 1719) / (5 Jan 1720)	>		Curacao	[Leeward Antilles]

Source: 5:4,8

1720 – 1721 — Endeavor — Sloop
MSTR ID# M-S-041 / SHIP ID# S-E-029 — Captain: James Studley

Passage	Port	State / Country	Dates		Passage	Port	State / Country
Start	London	[England]	24 Jul 1720	>		Sandy Hook	[New Jersey]
>	New York	[New York]	8 Dec 1720 / (31 Jan 1721) / (27 Feb 1721)	>		Barbados	[Lesser Antilles]

Source: 5:129, 6:4,16,23

1722 — Endeavor — Sloop
MSTR ID# M-T-019 / SHIP ID# S-E-030 — Captain: Edward Todd

Passage	Port	State / Country	Dates		Passage	Port	State / Country	Dates
Start	Bermuda			>		New York	[New York]	22 Jun 1722 / [2 Jul 1722] / [16 Jul 1722]
>	Barbados	[Lesser Antilles]						

Source: 7:75,79,85

1722 – 1723 — Endeavor — Sloop
MSTR ID# M-H-034 / SHIP ID# S-E-031 — Captain: James Hodsol / Hodsoll

Passage	Port	State / Country		Passage	Port	State / Country	Dates
Start	Rhode Island		>		New York	[New York]	(24 Dec 1722) / (8 Jan 1723) / (8 Jan 1723)
>	New London	[Connecticut]					

Source: 7:151 / 8:5

	MSTR ID#	Name	Type	Burden	First Name	Last Name	Length	Port	Custom In / Entered Out	Length	Port	Custom In / Entered Out	
E	SHIP ID#	Registry Location						State / Country	Custom Out / Cleared Out		State / Country	Custom Out / Cleared Out	22
		Source							Departure			Notes	
	1723	Endeavor	Sloop		Tiddman	Hull	Start	New York	[3 Jun 1723]	>			
	M-H-035							[New York]	[3 Jun 1723]		Rhode Island		
	S-E-032		8:62										

	MSTR ID#	Name	Type	Burden	First Name	Last Name	Length	Port	Custom In / Entered Out	Length	Port	Custom In / Entered Out
	1721 – 1723	Endeavor	Sloop		Richard	Robinson	Start			>	New York	[19 Jun 1721]
	M-R-020							Rhode Island			[New York]	[26 Jun 1721]
	S-E-033											[3 Jul 1721]
							>			>	New York	[17 Jul 1721]
								Rhode Island			[New York]	
							[>]			>	New York	15 Aug 1721
								Rhode Island			[New York]	
								NO SUPPORTING DATA TO LINK TIMELINE				
							Start			>	New York	(24 Dec 1722)
								Rhode Island			[New York]	(8 Jan 1723)
												(8 Jan 1723)
							>	New London		[>]		
								[Connecticut]			Rhode Island	
							>	New York	(18 Feb 1723)	>		
								[New York]	(18 Feb 1723)		Rhode Island	
									(4 Mar 1723)			
							[>]	Boston	[23 Mar 1723]	>		
								[Massachusetts]	[23 Mar 1723]		Rhode Island	
									[30 Mar 1723]			
							>	New York	17 Apr 1723	>		
								[New York]	[22 Apr 1723]		Rhode Island	
							>	New York	14 May 1723	>		
								[New York]	[20 May 1723]		Rhode Island	
									[3 Jun 1723]			
							>	New York	[1 Jul 1723]	>		
								[New York]	[8 Jul 1723]		Rhode Island	
							[>]			>	Boston	[31 Aug 1723]
								Connecticut			[Massachusetts]	[7 Sept 1723]
												[14 Sept 1723]
							>	Newport		>	New York	[30 Sept 1723]
								Rhode Island			[New York]	[14 Oct 1723]
												[21 Oct 1723]
							>	Boston		[>]		
								[Massachusetts]			Rhode Island	
							>	New York	(17 Dec 1723)			
								[New York]				

6:63,66,71,79,94 / 7:151 / 8:5,21,24,42,58,62,73,76,106,112,114,138 / 20:86,87,109,110,111

Group	Ship					Captain / Master			Passage	Arrival / Departure 1			Passage	Arrival / Departure 2			Page
E	Year	Name	Type	Burden	Registry Location	First Name	Last Name	Length	Length	Port	State / Country	Length	Port	State / Country		23
					SHIP ID#					Arrival / Entered Inwards	Custom In / Entered Out		Arrival / Entered Inwards	Custom In / Entered Out		
					MSTR ID#					Custom Out / Cleared Out	Departure		Custom Out / Cleared Out	Departure		
					Source								Notes			
	1720	Evelyn	Ship			Robert	Long	Start		London	[England]	<	Downs	[England]		
					M-L-020					About 19 Feb 1720						
					S-E-034											
					5.38,45,60			7 Weeks & 3 Days		New York	New York	<	Jamaica	[Greater Antilles]		
										16 Apr 1720						
										[2 May 1720]						
										[6 Jun 1720]						

Year	Name	Type	Burden	First Name	Last Name	Length	Port	Custom In / Entered Out	Length	Port	Custom In / Entered Out
MSTR ID#							State / Country	Custom Out / Cleared Out		State / Country	Custom Out / Cleared Out
SHIP ID#	Registry Location							Departure			Departure
	Source							Notes			
1723	*Fame*	Sloop		William	Garland	Start	Bristol		9 Weeks	New York	18 Jul 1723
M-G-023							[England]			[New York]	[5 Aug 1723]
S-F-012											[9 Sept 1723]
						>	Bristol				
							[England]				
	8:81,86,98										
1720 – 1721	*French Merchant*	Brigantine		Thomas	Hopper	Start	New York	[21 Nov 1720]	>	Barbados	
M-H-036							[New York]	(19 Dec 1720)		[Lesser Antilles]	
S-F-013											
						[>]	Martinique		>	New York	11 Jun 1721
							[Lesser Antilles]			[New York]	[10 Jul 1721]
											[31 Jul 1721]
						>	Barbados				
							[Lesser Antilles]				
	5:133 / 6:4,60,76,87										
1719 – 1720	*Friends Adventure*	Sloop		John	Jackson	Start	Boston		>	New York	16 Jan 1720
M-J-014							[Massachusetts]	[? Dec 1719]		[New York]	(2 Feb 1720)
S-F-014											(2 Feb 1720)
						>			>	Boston	[14 Mar 1720]
							Rhode Island	[26 Feb 1720]		[Massachusetts]	
	XXXXXXXXXX XXXXXXXXXX Captain / Master Changed Ships XXXXXXXXXX XXXXXXXXXX										
1720						Start	Boston		>	New York	
S-?-075							[Massachusetts]	[10 Sept 1720]		[New York]	
	5:2,12,16,30,32,106										

Group	Year	Name	Type	Burden	MSTR ID# / SHIP ID#	First Name	Last Name	Passage Length	Port 1 / State-Country 1	Arrival/Dep 1 dates	Passage	Port 2 / State-Country 2	Arrival/Dep 2 dates	Source	Page
G	1720	George	Sloop		M-A-016 / S-G-009	John	Ablin	Start	New York [New York]	(5 Jan 1720)	>	Antigua [Leeward Islands]		5:8	25
	1721 – 1722	George	Sloop		M-V-011 / S-G-010	John	Vear	Start	Jamaica [Greater Antilles]			New York [New York]	7 May 1721 / [14 Aug 1721] / (1 Jan 1722)	6:46,92 / 7:4	
								>	Jamaica [Greater Antilles]						
	1722	George	Sloop		M-B-028 / S-G-007	John	Burch	Start	Jamaica [Greater Antilles]		>	Philadelphia [Pennsylvania]	[12 Apr 1722] / [12 Apr 1722]	7:42,94,96,98	
								>	Jamaica [Greater Antilles]		[>]	Bermuda			
								>	New York [New York]	[6 Aug 1722] / [13 Aug 1722] / [20 Aug 1722]	>	Jamaica [Greater Antilles]			
	1723	George	Sloop		M-B-052 / S-G-011	Christopher	Bennet	Start	New York [New York]	(18 Feb 1723)	>	Barbados [Lesser Antilles]		8:21	
	1721	Good Intent	Boat		M-T-020 / S-G-012	Vincent	Tilion / Tillyon / Tuel	Start	Rhode Island		>	New York [New York]	[2 Oct 1721] / [9 Oct 1721] / [16 Oct 1721]	6:111,114,119,138	
								>	Boston [Massachusetts]		>	New York [New York]	[28 Nov 1721]		
	1722	Good Intent	Sloop		M-M-031 / S-G-013	Joseph	Misereau	Start	New York [New York]	(29 Jan 1722)	>	Jamaica [Greater Antilles]		7:13	

MSTR ID# / SHIP ID#	Registry Location	Name	Type		First Name	Last Name	Length	Port / State / Country	Custom In / Entered Out / Custom Out / Cleared Out / Departure	Length	Port / State / Country	Custom In / Entered Out / Custom Out / Cleared Out / Departure
1719 – 1720 M-J-015 S-G-014		Goodwill	Sloop		Joseph	Johnson	Start	Boston [Massachusetts]	[28 Nov 1719] [12 Dec 1719]	>	North Carolina	
							[>]	Boston [Massachusetts]	[14 May 1720]	>	North Carolina	
							[>]	Terceira Island [Portugal]		>	Boston [Massachusetts]	[3 Sept 1720] [1 Oct 1720]
							[>]	New York [New York]	[24 Oct 1720] [21 Nov 1720]	>	Boston [Massachusetts]	[17 Dec 1720]
Source: 5:2,99,120,133 / 6:8 / 21:815,817,864 / 26:22												
1722 – 1723 M-C-025 S-G-015		Greyhound	Snow		Richard	Cupitt / Cupittina	Start	Rotterdam [Holland]		>	Plymouth [England]	
							>	New York [New York]	(24 Dec 1722) (22 Jan 1723) (5 Feb 1723)	>	Plymouth [England]	
Source: 7:151,152 / 8:5,10								Notes: (Known Passengers / Palatines) New York / Inward – 24 Dec 1722 – Count ?+				

Group					Captain / Master		Passage	Arrival / Departure 1		Passage	Arrival / Departure 2		Page
	Year	Name	Type	Burden	First Name	Last Name	Length	Port	Arrival / Entered Inwards / Custom In / Entered Out	Length	Port	Arrival / Entered Inwards / Custom In / Entered Out	
H	MSTR ID# / SHIP ID#	Registry Location						State / Country	Custom Out / Cleared Out / Departure		State / Country	Custom Out / Cleared Out / Departure	27
	Source							Notes					

Hamilton Galley

1720 – 1723	Hamilton Galley	Snow		Andrew	Bisset / Bissett	Start	New York		>	Jamaica		
M-B-053 / S-H-018							[New York]	(22 Dec 1719)		[Greater Antilles]		
						>	Pettiguavis		>	New York	1 Apr 1720 / [18 Apr 1720] / [2 May 1720]	
							[Location Unkn]			[New York]		
						>	Barbados		>	New York	21 Jul 1720 / [21 Nov 1720] / (19 Dec 1720)	
							[Lesser Antilles]			[New York]		
						>	Barbados		>	Anguilla		
							[Lesser Antilles]			[Leeward Islands]	8 Feb 1721	
						>	New York	13 Mar 1721 / [27 Mar 1721] / [17 Apr 1721]	>	Barbados		
							[New York]			[Lesser Antilles]		
						[>]	New York	[31 Jul 1721] / [21 Aug 1721]	>	Jamaica		
							[New York]			[Greater Antilles]		
						[>]	Bristol		>	New York	16 May 1722 / [16 Jul 1722] / [27 Aug 1722]	
							[England]			[New York]		
						>	London		>	Madeira Island		
							[England]	6 Dec 1723		[Portugal]		
						>	New York	12 Mar 1723 / [1 Apr 1723] / [15 Apr 1723]	>	Barbados		
							[New York]			[Lesser Antilles]		
						4 Weeks	New York	13 Jul 1723 / [22 Jul 1723] / [12 Aug 1723]	>	Jamaica		
							[New York]			[Greater Antilles]		
						>	New York	6 Nov 1723 / [3 Dec 1723] / (17 Dec 1723)	>	Barbados		
							[New York]			[Lesser Antilles]		

Source: 5:4,34,38,45,82,133 / 6:4,28,32,34,40,87,94 / 7:60,85,94,102 / 8:28,34,39,78,81,88,126,134,138

Notes: Passage Length: Jamaica → Pettiguavis → New York / Took 8 Weeks Total

Hester & Sarah

1721 – 1722	Hester & Sarah	Sloop		Valentine	Robinson	Start	Boston		>	New York	[5 Dec 1721] / (1 Jan 1722) / (15 Jan 1722)	
M-R-021 / S-H-019							[Massachusetts]			[New York]		
						>	Antigua					
							[Leeward Islands]					

Source: 6:144 / 7:4,8

Year	Name	Type	Burden	First Name	Last Name	Length	Port	Custom In / Entered Out	Length	Port	Custom In / Entered Out
MSTR ID#	Registry Location						State / Country	Custom Out / Cleared Out		State / Country	Custom Out / Cleared Out
SHIP ID#								Departure			Departure
	Source							Notes			
1722 – 1723	Hope	Brigantine		Jacob	Sarly / Sarley / Sirly	Start	Bristol		>	New York	30 Jan 1723 (4 Mar 1723)
M-S-042							[England]	24 Nov 1722		[New York]	[18 Mar 1723]
S-H-020						>	South Carolina		[>]	Bristol [England]	
						9 Weeks	New York [New York]	16 Oct 1723 [4 Nov 1723] [25 Nov 1723]	>	Jamaica [Greater Antilles]	
	8:5,15,24,28,114,122,130										
1723	Happy Margaret	Sloop		Abraham	Watson	Start	New York [New York]	[5 Aug 1723] [5 Aug 1723]	>	Rhode Island	
M-W-028											
S-H-021	8:86										
1719 – 1722	Happy Return	Brigantine		Joseph	Gardiner	Start	New London [Connecticut]	Launch – 3 Oct 1719			
M-G-024											
S-H-022								NO SUPPORTING DATA TO LINK TIMELINE			
						Start	New London [Connecticut]	15 Apr 1720	>	Barbados [Lesser Antilles]	
								NO SUPPORTING DATA TO LINK TIMELINE			
						Start	Saltertuda [Location Unkn]		>	New London [Connecticut]	25 Apr 1721
								NO SUPPORTING DATA TO LINK TIMELINE			
						Start	New London [Connecticut]	25 Nov 1721	>	Barbados [Lesser Antilles]	
						[>]	New London [Connecticut]	21 Apr 1722	>	New York [New York]	[14 May 1722] [28 May 1722] [28 May 1722]
						>	New London [Connecticut]	20 Jul 1722	>	Jamaica [Greater Antilles]	
						>	Rhode Island		>	New London [Connecticut]	17 Dec 1722
	7:57,63 / 45:92,97,108,116,120,123,128						Source 45:128 – Stopped at Rhode Island to bury a passenger				
1720	Hopewell	Brigantine		John	Erwing	Start	New York [New York]	[6 Jun 1720]	>	Holland	
M-E-005											
S-H-023	5:60										

Group					Captain / Master		Passage	Arrival / Departure 1		Passage	Arrival / Departure 2		Page
	Year	Name	Type	Burden	First Name	Last Name	Length	Port	Arrival / Entered Inwards / Custom In / Entered Out / Custom Out / Cleared Out / Departure	Length	Port	Arrival / Entered Inwards / Custom In / Entered Out / Custom Out / Cleared Out / Departure	29
H	MSTR ID# / SHIP ID#	Registry Location						State / Country			State / Country		
	Source							Notes					

1723 — Hopewell — Sloop (M-J-016, S-H-024)
Caleb Jefferys — Passage: Start
- New York [15 Jul 1723] / [15 Jul 1723] — [New York] > Rhode Island
- Perth Amboy [12 Aug 1723] — [New Jersey]
Source: 8:78,91

1721 — Hopewell — Sloop (M-E-006, S-H-025)
John Ellwood — Passage: Start
- St Christopher — [Leeward Islands] > New York 10 Jul 1721 / [28 Aug 1721] / [4 Sept 1721] — [New York]
- Antigua — [Leeward Islands]
Source: 6:79,96,100

1720 — Humbird — Sloop (M-C-026, S-H-026)
Phillip Callender — Passage: Start
- Rhode Island [8 Apr 1720] > New York [2 May 1720] / [2 May 1720] — [New York]
- Rhode Island
Source: 5:38,45

1722 — Humbird — Sloop (M-C-027, S-H-027)
Ebenezer Cook — Passage: Start
- New York [19 Mar 1722] / [19 Mar 1722] — [New York] > Rhode Island
Source: 7:34

1720 — Hunter — Sloop (M-H-037, S-H-028)
Hickford — Passage: Start
- New York — [New York] > St Christopher — [Leeward Islands]
- New York 19 Jan 1720 — [New York] [>] Riohacha — Colombia
- New York 7 May 1720 — [New York]
Source: 5:16,32,50
Notes: Ship Mary Galley Retaken By: Captain Hickford at St Christopher's – Taken to New York 19 Jan 1720 for Salvage

1720 — Hunter Galley (M-C-028, S-H-029)
Coarten — Passage: Start
- New York — [New York] > Curacao — [Leeward Antilles]
- Jamaica — [Greater Antilles] [>] — 27 Days — New York 17 Apr 1720 — [New York]
Source: 5:24,38

MSTR ID#				First Name	Last Name	Length		Custom In / Entered Out	Length		Custom In / Entered Out	30
SHIP ID#	Registry Location						State / Country	Custom Out / Cleared Out		State / Country	Custom Out / Cleared Out	
Source								Departure		Notes	Departure	
1720	Industry	Sloop		Thomas	Walker Jr.	Start	New Providence		>	New York	9 Jun 1720 [4 Jul 1720]	
M-W-029							[Bahamas]			[New York]		
S-I-004						>	Jamaica					
							[Greater Antilles]					
5:63,72												

Group		Ship				Captain / Master		Passage	Arrival / Departure 1		Passage	Arrival / Departure 2		Page
	Year	Name	Type	Burden		First Name	Last Name	Length	Port	Arrival / Entered Inwards	Length	Port	Arrival / Entered Inwards	
J										Custom In / Entered Out			Custom In / Entered Out	31
	MSTR ID#								State / Country	Custom Out / Cleared Out		State / Country	Custom Out / Cleared Out	
	SHIP ID#	Registry Location								Departure			Departure	
		Source									Notes			

	1720 – 1723	John & Mary	Sloop			John	Clarke	Start	Delaware River		>	New York	27 Jun 1720	
													[10 Oct 1720]	
	M-C-003											[New York]	[17 Oct 1720]	
	S-J-007													

Passage	Port	Arrival / Entered Inwards	Passage	Port	Arrival / Entered Inwards
>	Boston		>		
	[Massachusetts]			Rhode Island	
>	New York	24 Nov 1720	[>]	New Castle	
	[New York]			[Delaware]	
>	New York	[3 Jul 1721]	[>]	Lewes	
	[New York]			[Delaware]	
>	New York	[14 Aug 1721]	[>]	New Castle	
	[New York]			[Delaware]	
>	New York	[19 Dec 1721]	[>] —	New Castle	
	[New York]			[Delaware]	
>	New York	[23 Apr 1722]	[>]	Lewes	
	[New York]			[Delaware]	
>	New York	13 Jul 1722	[>]	New Castle	
	[New York]			[Delaware]	
>	New York	10 Sept 1722	[>]	New Castle	
	[New York]			[Delaware]	
>	New York	[24 Dec 1722]	>	Philadelphia	[5 Feb 1723]
	[New York]			[Pennsylvania]	
>	Lewes		>	Curacao	
	[Delaware]			[Leeward Antilles]	
>	New York	4 Jun 1723	>	Placentia	
		[17 Jun 1723]			
	[New York]	[24 Jun 1723]		Newfoundland	
1 Month	New York	19 Sept 1723	>	Philadelphia	[11 Oct 1723]
	[New York]			[Pennsylvania]	[24 Oct 1723]
>	New Castle		>	New York	18 Nov 1723
	[Delaware]			[New York]	

5:70,112,115,136 / 6:71,92,148 / 7:48,85,108,151 / 8:12,16,65,68,70,106,109,114,130

Year	Name	Type	Burden	First Name	Last Name	Length	Port	Custom In / Entered Out	Length	Port	Custom In / Entered Out
MSTR ID#	Registry Location						State / Country	Custom Out / Cleared Out		State / Country	Custom Out / Cleared Out
SHIP ID#								Departure			Departure
	Source							Notes			
1721	Jenny	Sloop		David	Yeaman	Start	New York	[5 Dec 1721]		Jamaica	
M-Y-002							[New York]	(19 Dec 1721)		[Greater Antilles]	
S-J-015											
	XXXXXXXXXX XXXXXXXXXX Captain / Master Changed Ships XXXXXXXXXX XXXXXXXXXX										
1722		Sloop				Start	Boston		>	New York	[30 Jul 1722]
S-?-076							[Massachusetts]	[7 Jul 1722]		[New York]	
	6:138,144,148 / 7:92 / 20:49										
1722	John & Catherine	Sloop		John	Tuder / Tudor	Start	Barbados		31 Days	New York	24 May 1722
M-T-021											[11 Jun 1722]
S-J-016							[Lesser Antilles]			[New York]	[18 Jun 1722]
						>	Barbados		>	Perth Amboy	31 Aug 1722
											[4 Sept 1722]
							[Lesser Antilles]			[New Jersey]	
						>	New York	[17 Sept 1722]	>	Barbados	
							[New York]	[1 Oct 1722]		[Lesser Antilles]	
	7:63,70,74,105,110,114 / 23:64										
1720	John & Elizabeth	Sloop		Charles	Phelpes	Start			>	New York	[26 Sept 1720]
M-P-027											[26 Sept 1720]
S-J-017							Rhode Island			[New York]	[3 Oct 1720]
						>					
							Rhode Island				
	5:107,110										
1721	John & Elizabeth	Sloop		Tormut	Rose	Start			>	New York	[2 Oct 1721]
M-R-022											[2 Oct 1721]
S-J-018							Rhode Island			[New York]	
						>					
							Rhode Island				
	6:111										
1722	John & Rebekah	Ship		Jeremiah	Owen	Start	New York	(26 Feb 1722)	>	Boston	[31 Mar 1722]
M-O-006											
S-J-019							[New York]			[Massachusetts]	
	7:26 / 20:35										

Group	Ship				Captain / Master		Passage	Arrival / Departure 1		Passage	Arrival / Departure 2		Page
	Year	Name	Type	Burden	First Name	Last Name	Length	Port	Arrival / Entered Inwards	Length	Port	Arrival / Entered Inwards	33
J									Custom In / Entered Out			Custom In / Entered Out	
	MSTR ID#							State / Country	Custom Out / Cleared Out		State / Country	Custom Out / Cleared Out	
	SHIP ID#	Registry Location							Departure			Departure	
	Source							Notes					

	1723	*Joseph & Betty*	Ship		Robert	Willary	Start			>	New York	15 Nov 1723	
	M-W-030							Virginia			[New York]		
	S-J-020						>	Liverpool					
								[England]					
	8:128							Source 8:128 – Was forced into New York to stop her leaks					

	1720	*Jolly*	Sloop		George	Webb	Start	New York	(16 Feb 1720)	>		[18 Mar 1720]	
	M-W-031							[New York]	(14 Mar 1720)		Rhode Island		
	S-J-021						[>]	New York	[4 Apr 1720]	>		[22 Apr 1720]	
								[New York]	[18 Apr 1720]		Rhode Island		
							[>]	New York	[9 May 1720]	>			
								[New York]	[16 May 1720]		Rhode Island		
							>	New York	7 Jun 1720	>			
									[13 Jun 1720]				
								[New York]	[11 Jul 1720]		Rhode Island		
							[>]	New York	[8 Aug 1720]	>			
								[New York]	[8 Aug 1720]		Rhode Island		
							>	New York	[5 Sept 1720]				
								[New York]					
	5:20,27,34,36,38,45,50,53,62,63,75,88,96												

MSTR ID# / SHIP ID#	Registry Location		First Name	Last Name	Length	State / Country	Custom In / Entered Out / Custom Out / Cleared Out / Departure	Length	State / Country	Custom In / Entered Out / Custom Out / Cleared Out / Departure
	Source						Notes			
1722 / M-G-025 / S-K-002	*King Fisher / Kingfisher*	Sloop	Ebenezer	Gardner	Start	Rhode Island		>	New York / [New York]	8 Jul 1722 / [23 Jul 1722]
					>	Boston / [Massachusetts]		>	New York / [New York]	14 Sept 1722 / [17 Sept 1722] / [8 Oct 1722]
					>	Boston / [Massachusetts]				
	7:82,89,110,118									
1720 / M-G-026 / S-K-003	*King George*	Snow	Jacob	Goelet	Start	Holland		11 Weeks	New York / [New York]	2 Jan 1720
	5:8									
1720 – 1721 / M-L-021 / S-K-004	*King George*	Ship	Lawrance / Laurence	Lawrance / Laurence	Start	New York / [New York]	(14 Mar 1720) / (14 Mar 1720)	>	Maryland	
						NO SUPPORTING DATA TO LINK TIMELINE				
					Start	New York / [New York]	[22 May 1721] / [29 May 1721]	>	Maryland	
	5:27 / 6:52,56									
1721 / M-W-032 / S-K-005	*King George*	Snow		Waldron	Start	Cowes / [England]	[6 Feb 1721]	12 Weeks	New York / [New York]	29 Apr 1721
	6:44,46					(Known Passengers / Passengers) New York / Inward – 29 Apr 1721 – Count 1+				

Group		Ship			Captain / Master		Passage	Arrival / Departure 1		Passage	Arrival / Departure 2		Page
	Year	Name	Type	Burden	First Name	Last Name	Length	Port	Arrival / Entered Inwards / Custom In / Entered Out	Length	Port	Arrival / Entered Inwards / Custom In / Entered Out	35
L	MSTR ID#	Registry Location						State / Country	Custom Out / Cleared Out / Departure		State / Country	Custom Out / Cleared Out / Departure	
	SHIP ID#												
		Source							Notes				

	1722	Lark	Sloop		John	Burras	Start	New Castle		>	New York	[14 May 1722]	
M-B-054								[Delaware]			[New York]		
S-L-011													
		7:57											

	1722	Lark / Larke	Pink		John	Soley	Start	London		>	Gravesend		
M-S-043								[England]			[England]	
S-L-012							>	New York	24 Jun 1722 / [2 Jul 1722] / [23 Jul 1722]	>	Boston	
								[New York]			[Massachusetts]	[18 Aug 1722]
							>					
								New Hampshire				
		7:76,79,89 / 20:55										

	1720	Levett	Ship		Thomas	Lashbrook	Start	Bristol		>	New York	11 May 1720 / [6 Jun 1720] / [20 Jun 1720]
M-L-022								[England]	3 Mar 1720		[New York]	
S-L-013							>					
								Rhode Island				
		5:53,60,67										

	1723	Leve / Love	Sloop		John	Burgis	Start	Turks Island		>	New York	14 Sept 1723 / [23 Sept 1723] / [7 Oct 1723]
M-B-055											[New York]	
S-L-014							>	Curacao				
								[Leeward Antilles]				
		8:100,106,109										

	1722	Lydia	Brigantine		William	Williams	Start	Bristol		>	New York	8 Jun 1722 / [18 Jun 1722] / [9 Jul 1722]
M-W-033								[England]	8 Apr 1722		[New York]	
S-L-015							>	Bristol		>	New York	19 Nov 1722 / [10 Dec 1722] / (24 Dec 1722) / 24 Dec 1722
								[England]			[New York]	
							>	Bristol				
								[England]				
		7:70,74,82,136,144,151,152										

	1723	Lyon	Ship	160 Tons	John	Tempest	Start	Bay of Honduras		>	New York	[9 Sept 1723] / [11 Nov 1723]
M-T-022		London, England									[New York]	
S-L-016							>	West Indies				
		8:98,126										

Year	Name	Type	Burden	First Name	Last Name	Length	Port	Custom In / Entered Out	Length	Port	Custom In / Entered Out
MSTR ID#							State / Country	Custom Out / Cleared Out		State / Country	Custom Out / Cleared Out
SHIP ID#	Registry Location							Departure			Departure
Source							Notes				
1720 – 1723	Mary	Sloop		William	Beckman / Beekman	Start	New York	(14 Mar 1720)	>	Boston	
M-B-056							[New York]	[28 Mar 1720]		[Massachusetts]	
S-M-032											
						>	New York	[16 May 1720]	>	Boston	
								[27 Jun 1720]			
							[New York]	[4 Jul 1720]		[Massachusetts]	
						>	New York	12 Aug 1720	>	Boston	
								[22 Aug 1720]			
							[New York]	[3 Oct 1720]		[Massachusetts]	
						>	New York	11 Nov 1720	>	Boston	
								[7 May 1721]			
							[New York]	[22 May 1721]		[Massachusetts]	
						>	New York	[26 Jun 1721]	>	Boston	
								[26 Jun 1721]			
							[New York]	[3 Jul 1721]		[Massachusetts]	
						>	New York	[14 Aug 1721]	>	Boston	
								[11 Sept 1721]			
							[New York]	[25 Sept 1721]		[Massachusetts]	
						>	New York	[6 Nov 1721]	>	Boston	[31 Mar 1722]
								(12 Feb 1722)			[14 Apr 1722]
							[New York]	[19 Mar 1722]		[Massachusetts]	
						>	New York	[23 Apr 1722]	>	Boston	[26 May 1722]
								[23 Apr 1722]			[26 May 1722]
							[New York]	[14 May 1722]		[Massachusetts]	
						>	New York	[18 Jun 1722]	>	Boston	
								[18 Jun 1722]			[21 Jul 1722]
							[New York]	[9 Jul 1722]		[Massachusetts]	
						>	New York	[13 Aug 1722]	>	Boston	[6 Oct 1722]
								[10 Sept 1722]			
							[New York]	[24 Sept 1722]		[Massachusetts]	
						>	New York	4 Nov 1722	>	Boston	[16 Feb 1723]
								(5 Feb 1723)			[23 Feb 1723]
							[New York]	(18 Feb 1723)		[Massachusetts]	[2 Mar 1723]
						>	New York	[18 Mar 1723]	>	Boston	[27 Apr 1723]
								[18 Mar 1723]			[4 May 1723]
							[New York]	[15 Apr 1723]		[Massachusetts]	[11 May 1723]
						>	New York	17 May 1723	>	Boston	[15 Jun 1723]
								[27 May 1723]			[22 Jun 1723]
							[New York]	[10 Jun 1723]		[Massachusetts]	[29 Jun 1723]
						>	New York	[8 Jul 1723]	>	Boston	[31 Aug 1723]
								[15 Jul 1723]			
							[New York]	[19 Aug 1723]		[Massachusetts]	[14 Sept 1723]
						>	New York	[23 Sept 1723]	>	Boston	[19 Oct 1723]
								[23 Sept 1723]			[26 Oct 1723]
							[New York]	[7 Oct 1723]		[Massachusetts]	
						>	New York	18 Nov 1723			
							[New York]				

5:27,32,53,70,72,90,92,110,129 / 6:46,52,66,67,71,92,103,108,130 / 7:20,34,48,57,74,82,96,108,112,130 / 8:16,21,28,39,58,60,65,76,78,91,106,130 / 20:35,37,43,51,62,81,82,83,91,92,93,98,99,100,109,111,116,117

Group	Year	Ship Name	Type	Burden	First Name	Last Name	Passage Length	Port / State / Country	Arrival / Entered Inwards / Custom In / Entered Out / Custom Out / Cleared Out / Departure	Passage Length	Port / State / Country	Arrival / Entered Inwards / Custom In / Entered Out / Custom Out / Cleared Out / Departure	Page
M													37

M-B-057 / S-M-033 — Mary Anne (Schooner), 1723

	Year	Name	Type	First Name	Last Name	Passage	Port / State / Country	Dates	Passage	Port / State / Country	Dates
	1723	Mary Anne	Schooner	John	Bret / Brett	Start	Antigua / [Leeward Islands]		>	New York / [New York]	[1 Jul 1723] / [15 Jul 1723] / [5 Aug 1723]
						>	St John's / Antigua	20 Sept 1723 / Lost	&	Ship Was Lost / Or Deemed To Be Lost	
						>	St John's / Antigua	Lost In Harbor / Hurricane			

Source: 8:73,78,86,126

M-S-044 / S-M-034 — Martha & Jane (Sloop), 1720

	1720	Martha & Jane	Sloop	Charles	Strahan / Strachan	Start	Bermuda		>	New York / [New York]	28 Aug 1720 / [12 Sept 1720] / [19 Sept 1720]
						>	Antigua / [Leeward Islands]				

Source: 5:94,99,103

M-T-023 / S-M-035 — Mary & Martha (Sloop), 1720 & 1722

	1720 & 1722	Mary & Martha	Sloop	John	Tatem	Start	New York / [New York]	[3 Oct 1720] / [10 Oct 1720]	>	Barbados / [Lesser Antilles]	
							NO SUPPORTING DATA TO LINK TIMELINE				
						Start	Bermuda		>	New York / [New York]	[14 May 1722] / [21 May 1722] / [28 May 1722]
						>	Jamaica / [Greater Antilles]				

Source: 5:110,112 / 7:57,60,64

M-G-027 / S-M-036 — Mary & Martha (Sloop), 1722

	1722	Mary & Martha	Sloop	John	Giles	Start	New York / [New York]	[24 Sept 1722]	>	Curacao / [Leeward Antilles]	

Source: 7:112

M-B-058 / S-M-037 — Mary (Sloop), 1720

	1720	Mary	Sloop	Vincent	Beaudine	Start	New York / [New York]	[4 Apr 1720]	>	Suriname / [South America]	

Source: 5:34

M-B-059 / S-M-038 — Mary (Sloop), 1720

	1720	Mary	Sloop	Vincent	Bodin / Bodine	Start	New York / [New York]	[25 Jul 1720]	>	St Christopher / [Leeward Islands]	
						22 Days	New York / [New York]	21 Oct 1720 / [28 Nov 1720] / (19 Dec 1720)	>	Barbados / [Lesser Antilles]	

Source: 5:82,120,136 / 6:4

MSTR ID# / SHIP ID#	Year	Name	Type	Burden	First Name	Last Name	Length	Port / State / Country	Custom In/Entered Out / Custom Out/Cleared Out / Departure	Length	Port / State / Country	Custom In/Entered Out / Custom Out/Cleared Out / Departure
M-C-029 / S-M-039	1720	Mary	Sloop		Abel	Churchil	Start	New York / [New York]	[5 Sept 1720] / [12 Sept 1720]	>	Rhode Island	
							>	New York / [New York]	11 Oct 1720			
Source: 5:96,99,115												
M-K-004 / S-M-040	1721	Mary	Sloop		John	Kiersted	Start	New York / [New York]	(13 Feb 1721) / (27 Feb 1721)	>	Boston / [Massachusetts]	
							>	New York / [New York]	[7 May 1721]			
Source: 6:20,23,46												
M-D-022 / S-M-041	1720	Mary	Sloop		Stephen	Doick	Start	Rhode Island		>	New York / [New York]	[26 Sept 1720] / [24 Oct 1720] / [31 Oct 1720]
							>	Boston / [Massachusetts]				
Source: 5:107,120,123												
M-L-023 / S-M-042	1722	Mary	Sloop		Dennis	Laurance / Lawrence	Start	New York / [New York]	[18 Jun 1722] / [18 Jun 1722]	>	Virginia	
							>	New York / [New York]	15 Jul 1722 / [30 Jul 1722] / [6 Aug 1722]	>	Curacao / [Leeward Antilles]	
							>	New York / [New York]	[12 Nov 1722]			
Source: 7:74,85,92,94,132												
M-M-032 / S-M-043 Registry: Glasgow, Scotland	1721	Mary	Ship		Alexander	Mayne	Start	Glasgow / [Scotland]		>	Barbados / [Lesser Antilles]	
							6 Weeks	New York / [New York]	12 Feb 1721 / [20 Mar 1721]	>	Barbados / [Lesser Antilles]	
Source: 6:19,32 — Notes: Source 6:19 – Upwards of 16 Weeks from Glasgow, Scotland to New York, New York												
M-C-030 / S-M-044	1721	Mary	Sloop		Florentius	Cox	Start	Nevis / [Leeward Islands]		>	Bermuda	
							>	New York / [New York]	[26 Jun 1721] / [10 Jul 1721] / [17 Jul 1721]	>	Nevis / [Leeward Islands]	
Source: 6:66,76,79												

Group														Page
	Year	Name	Type	Burden	First Name	Last Name	Length	Port	Arrival / Entered Inwards		Length	Port	Arrival / Entered Inwards	
M		Ship			Captain / Master		Passage	Arrival / Departure 1	Custom In / Entered Out	Passage	Arrival / Departure 2		Custom In / Entered Out	39
	MSTR ID#							State / Country	Custom Out / Cleared Out			State / Country	Custom Out / Cleared Out	
	SHIP ID#	Registry Location							Departure				Departure	
			Source						Notes					

Year	Name	Type	Burden	First Name	Last Name	Length	Port / State	Arr. In / Custom / Out / Dep.	Length	Port / State	Arr. In / Custom / Out / Dep.
1723	*Mary*	Sloop		William	Pinfold	Start	New York		>	Jamaica	
M-P-028							[New York]	(5 Feb 1723)		[Greater Antilles]	
S-M-045											
			8:16								

1723	*Mary*	Sloop		Nicholas	Trot / Trott	Start	St Christopher		>	St Eustatius	
M-T-024							[Leeward Islands]			[Leeward Islands]	
S-M-046											
						>	New York	24 May 1723 / [24 Jun 1723] / [1 Jul 1723]	>	St Christopher	
							[New York]			[Leeward Islands]	
			8:60,70								

1723	*Mary*	Sloop		John	Satant	Start	New York	[5 Aug 1723]	>	Barbados	
M-S-045							[New York]			[Lesser Antilles]	
S-M-047											
			8:86								

1723	*Mary*	Schooner		Dugald / Dugalo	Campbell	Start	New York	[10 Jun 1723] / [1 Jul 1723]	>	Bristol	
M-C-031							[New York]			[England]	
S-M-048											
						>	New York	6 Nov 1723 / [25 Nov 1723] / (17 Dec 1723)	>	Bristol	
							[New York]			[England]	
			8:65,73,126,130,138								

1722	*Mary & Anne*	Sloop		Thomas	Noxon Jr	Start	New York	[19 Mar 1722]	>	Ships Crew Marooned / Pirates	
M-N-008							[New York]			Sloop & Cargo Taken / Pirates	
S-M-049											
						>	Ships Crew Saved By Bermudean Passing By		>	Jamaica [Greater Antilles]	Never Reached Port / Taken / Pirates
			7:34,75								

1723	*Mary & Anne*	Schooner		William	Smith	Start	New York	[3 Jun 1723] / [10 Jun 1723]	>	Jamaica	
M-S-046							[New York]			[Greater Antilles]	
S-M-050											
						>	New York	21 Aug 1723 / [26 Aug 1723] / [2 Sept 1723]	>	Curacao	
							[New York]			[Leeward Antilles]	
						>	New York	22 Nov 1723 / [3 Dec 1723] / (17 Dec 1723)	>	Curacao	
							[New York]			[Leeward Antilles]	
			8:62,65,94,96,130,134,138								

1720	*Mayflower*	Sloop		Benjamin	Lusher	Start	New York	[9 May 1720] / [16 May 1720]	>	Bermuda	
M-L-024							[New York]				
S-M-051											
			5:50,53								

Year	Name	Type	Burden	First Name	Last Name	Length	Port / State / Country	Custom In / Entered Out / Custom Out / Cleared Out / Departure	Length	Port / State / Country	Custom In / Entered Out / Custom Out / Cleared Out / Departure
1722	Mayflower	Sloop		William	Chamberlain	Start	Rhode Island		>	New York / [New York]	[8 Oct 1722] / [8 Oct 1722] / [29 Oct 1722]
M-C-032											
S-M-052											
						>	Rhode Island				
Source: 7:118,126											
1723	Mayflower	Brigantine		Edward	Coddington	Start	London / [England]	[? Aug 1723]	>	New York / [New York]	4 Oct 1723 / [14 Oct 1723] / [14 Oct 1723]
M-C-033											
S-M-053											
						>	Rhode Island				
Source: 8:109,112											
1723	Medara	Sloop		Ebenezer	Simmons	Start	South Carolina		>	New York / [New York]	17 May 1723 / [3 Jun 1723]
M-S-047											
S-M-054											
						>	South Carolina				
Source: 8:58,62											
1721	Miriam	Sloop		John	Hunt	Start	Bermuda		>	New York / [New York]	[1 May 1721] / [15 May 1721] / [29 May 1721]
M-H-038											
S-M-055											
						>	Curacao / [Leeward Antilles]				
Source: 6:44,49,56											
1721	Marianne	Sloop		John	Smith	Start	New York / [New York]	[22 May 1721] / [29 May 1721]	>	South Carolina	
M-S-048											
S-M-056											
Source: 6:52,56											

Group	Ship				Captain / Master		Passage	Arrival / Departure 1		Passage	Arrival / Departure 2		Page
	Year	Name	Type	Burden	First Name	Last Name	Length	Port	Arrival / Entered Inwards	Length	Port	Arrival / Entered Inwards	41
N									Custom In / Entered Out			Custom In / Entered Out	
	MSTR ID#							State / Country	Custom Out / Cleared Out		State / Country	Custom Out / Cleared Out	
	SHIP ID#	Registry Location							Departure			Departure	
		Source								Notes			

	1720	*New York*	Sloop							>	Bermuda		
	M-?-010												
	S-N-010												
		5:24						Retaken from the Spaniards by Capt Cracraft					

	1720	*New York*	Pink		William	Clarke	Start			>	Cowes		
	M-C-034							Holland			[England]		
	S-N-011											4 May 1720	
							>	New York	9 Jul 1720	>			
									[14 Nov 1720]				
								[New York]	[21 Nov 1720]		Maryland		
		5:75,129,133											

	1720	*Neut / Nut*	Ship		John	Richards	Start	New York		>	Boston		
	M-R-023								[9 May 1720]				
	S-N-012							[New York]	[13 Jun 1720]		[Massachusetts]		
		5:50,63											

MSTR ID# / SHIP ID#	Registry Location	First Name	Last Name	Length	State / Country	Custom In / Entered Out / Custom Out / Cleared Out / Departure	Length	State / Country	Custom In / Entered Out / Custom Out / Cleared Out / Departure
1720 – 1723 M-B-060 S-P-018		Peter	Sloop Middleton Billop	Start	Jamaica [Greater Antilles]		27 Days	New York [New York]	17 Apr 1720 [2 May 1720] [23 May 1720]
				>	Jamaica [Greater Antilles]		>	New York [New York]	5 Aug 1720 [22 Aug 1720] [29 Aug 1720]
				>	Curacao [Leeward Antilles]		21 Days	New York [New York]	8 Nov 1720 [14 Nov 1720] [21 Nov 1720]
				>	Jamaica [Greater Antilles]		>	Cape Catoche [Mexico]	
				>	New York [New York]	[7 May 1721] [12 Jun 1721] [26 Jun 1721]	>	Curacao [Leeward Antilles]	
				[>]	Jamaica [Greater Antilles]		>	New York [New York]	16 Oct 1721 (19 Dec 1721) (1 Jan 1722)
				>	Curacao [Leeward Antilles]		>	New York [New York]	16 Mar 1722 [9 Apr 1722] [23 Apr 1722]
				>	Barbados [Lesser Antilles]		>	New York [New York]	[13 Aug 1722] [26 Nov 1722] [10 Dec 1722]
				>	Curacao [Leeward Antilles]		>	New York [New York]	10 Mar 1723 [18 Mar 1723]
				>	Curacao [Leeward Antilles]		>	New York [New York]	20 May 1723 [3 Jun 1723] [17 Jun 1723]
				>	Curacao [Leeward Antilles]		[>]	Jamaica [Greater Antilles]	
				15 Days	New York [New York]	11 Aug 1723 [2 Sept 1723]	>	Curacao [Leeward Antilles]	
				>	New York [New York]	11 Nov 1723 [3 Dec 1723] (17 Dec 1723)	>	Curacao [Leeward Antilles]	

5:38,45,56,88,92,94,129,133 / 6:46,60,67,122,148 / 7:4,34,42,48,96,138,144 / 8:26,28,60,62,68,88,96,126,134,138

Group	Ship				Captain / Master		Passage	Arrival / Departure 1		Passage	Arrival / Departure 2		Page
	Year	Name	Type	Burden	First Name	Last Name	Length	Port	Arrival / Entered Inwards / Custom In / Entered Out	Length	Port	Arrival / Entered Inwards / Custom In / Entered Out	43
P	MSTR ID# / SHIP ID#	Registry Location						State / Country	Custom Out / Cleared Out / Departure		State / Country	Custom Out / Cleared Out / Departure	
	Source							Notes					

1722 – 1723 · Paddock / Padock · Sloop · M-T-025 · S-P-019 · John Thurman

Passage	Port	Dates	Passage	Port	Dates
Start	New York	(29 Jan 1722) (29 Jan 1722)	>	South Carolina	
	[New York]				
>	New York	13 Apr 1722 [23 Apr 1722]	>	Boston	
	[New York]			[Massachusetts]	[26 May 1722]
>	New York	[4 Jun 1722] (18 Feb 1723) (18 Feb 1723)	>	St Thomas	
	[New York]			[Virgin Islands]	
>	New York	23 Apr 1723 [27 May 1723] [3 Jun 1723]	>	Curacao	
	[New York]			[Leeward Antilles]	
>	New York	6 Aug 1723			
	[New York]				

Source: 7:13,45,48,67 / 8:21,45,60,62,88 / 20:43

1720 – 1721 · Phenix · Sloop · M-R-024 · S-P-020 · Robert Rivers

Passage	Port	Dates	Passage	Port	Dates
Start	Bermuda			New York	[5 Dec 1720] (19 Dec 1720)
				[New York]	
>	Barbados		[>]	Saltertuda	
	[Lesser Antilles]			[Location Unkn]	
>	New York	21 Apr 1721 [7 May 1721] [15 May 1721]	>	Barbados	
	[New York]			[Lesser Antilles]	

Source: 5:136,141 / 6:4,42,46,49

1721 · Postilion · Ship · M-D-023 · S-P-021 · Dennis Downing

Passage	Port	Dates	Passage	Port	Dates
Start	New York	[19 Jun 1721] [31 Jul 1721] 3 Aug 1721	>	London	
	[New York]			[England]	

Source: 6:63,76,87,90

1719 – 1720 · Pearl · Sloop · M-B-061 · S-P-022 · Samuel Bourdet Jr. · New York, New York

Passage	Port	Dates	Passage	Port	Dates
Start	New York	[9 Dec 1719] (22 Dec 1719)	>	Curacao	
	[New York]			[Leeward Antilles]	
>	New York	7 Mar 1720 (14 Mar 1720) [28 Mar 1720]	>	Curacao	
	[New York]			[Leeward Antilles]	
[>]	Jamaica		>		18 Jun 1720
	[Greater Antilles]	[? Jun 1720]		Cuba	Drove on Shore
&	Nothing Saved		>		Lost on Shore / Storm
	Ship & Ships Crew Were Lost			Cuba	

Source: 5:2,4,26,27,32,82,86

Notes: 20 Souls Lost in All / West End of Cuba – Source 5:86 Has detailed report of all 13 ships of the fleet lost in the storm.

Year / MSTR ID# / SHIP ID#	Name / Registry Location	Type	Burden	First Name	Last Name	Length	Port / State/Country	Arrival/Entered Inwards / Custom Out / Cleared Out / Departure	Length	Port / State/Country	Arrival/Entered Inwards / Custom Out / Cleared Out / Departure
1720 – 1721 / M-T-026 / S-P-023	Phillipsburgh	Ship		Michael	Thody / Thodie	Start	Perth Amboy [New Jersey]	[21 Jan 1720]	>	Madeira Island [Portugal]	
						6 Weeks & 5 Days	New York [New York]	7 Jun 1720 / [27 Jun 1720] / [22 Aug 1720]	>	Barbados [Lesser Antilles]	
						>	New York [New York]	11 Nov 1720 / (13 Feb 1721) / [13 Mar 1721] / 20-21 Mar 1721	>	Barbados [Lesser Antilles]	24 Apr 1721 / 21 May 1721
						21 Days	New York [New York]	10 Jun 1721 / [31 Jul 1721] / [4 Sept 1721]	>	Curacao [Leeward Antilles]	
						>	New York [New York]	(19 Dec 1721)			
							NO SUPPORTING DATA TO LINK TIMELINE				
1723 / / S-P-023						Start	Madeira Island [Portugal]		>	New York [New York]	21 Apr 1723 / [12 May 1723] / [3 Jun 1723]
						>	Barbados [Lesser Antilles]		>	?? ??? 1723 – Lost All Mast / Violent Storm few days out of Barbados	
						&	Ships Crew & Ship Saved / Ship bound for New York put into Antigua		>	Antigua [Leeward Islands]	
						>	New York [New York]	18 Nov 1723			
Source: 5:12,62,70,92,129 / 6:20,28,32,56,60,87,100,148 / 8:42,54,62,112,122,130 / 23:46											
1723 / M-M-033 / S-P-024	Peter	Sloop		John	Marston	Start	Jamaica [Greater Antilles]		15 Days	New York [New York]	11 Aug 1723 / [19 Aug 1723] / [2 Sept 1723]
						>	Jamaica [Greater Antilles]		>	New York [New York]	11 Nov 1723 / [3 Dec 1723] / XXXXXXXXXXXXXX / XXXXXXXXXXXXXX
						>	Barbados [Lesser Antilles]	Never Left For Port / See Next Ship Or Captain			
							XXXXXXXXX Changed Departure Location XXXXXXXXX				
						>	New York [New York]	XXXXXXXXXXXXXX / XXXXXXXXXXXXXX / (17 Dec 1723)	>	Jamaica [Greater Antilles]	
Source: 8:88,91,96,128,134,138											

Group	Ship				Captain / Master		Passage	Arrival / Departure 1		Passage	Arrival / Departure 2		Page
	Year	Name	Type	Burden	First Name	Last Name	Length	Port	Arrival / Entered Inwards	Length	Port	Arrival / Entered Inwards	
P									Custom In / Entered Out			Custom In / Entered Out	45
	MSTR ID#							State / Country	Custom Out / Cleared Out		State / Country	Custom Out / Cleared Out	
	SHIP ID#	Registry Location							Departure			Departure	
		Source							Notes				

	1723	Phenix Galley	Ship		James	Morine	Start	Bristol		8 Weeks	New York	[17 Jun 1723]	
	M-M-034											[1 Jul 1723]	
	S-P-025							[England]			[New York]	[8 Jul 1723]	
							>	Newfoundland					
		8:68,73,76						(Known Passengers / Passengers) New York / Inward – 17 Jun 1723 – Count 1+					

	1722	Phoebe & Mary	Sloop		Richard	Norwood	Start	New York	[15 Oct 1722]	>	Curacao		
	M-N-009							[New York]	[26 Nov 1722]		[Leeward Antilles]		
	S-P-026												
		7:122,138											

	1723	Providence	Sloop		Isaac	Singer	Start	Havanna		>	New York	19 Apr 1723	
	M-S-049											[6 May 1723]	
	S-P-027							[Cuba]			[New York]	[27 May 1723]	
							>	St Eustatius					
								[Leeward Antilles]					
		8:42,50,60											

	1721	Prudence	Sloop		John	Conyars	Start	Jamaica		>	Bermuda		
	M-C-035							[Greater Antilles]					
	S-P-028						>	New York	[6 Nov 1721]	>	Barbados		
									[13 Nov 1721]				
								[New York]	[28 Nov 1721]		[Lesser Antilles]		
		6:130,132,138											

	1723	Prudence	Sloop		James	Seymour / Saymare / Saymour	Start	Jamaica		>	Bermuda		
	M-S-050							[Greater Antilles]					
	S-P-029						>	New York	19 Jun 1723	>	Barbados		
									[1 Jul 1723]				
								[New York]	[1 Jul 1723]		[Lesser Antilles]		
							>	New York	5 Oct 1723	>	Barbados		
									[14 Oct 1723]				
								[New York]	[28 Oct 1723]		[Lesser Antilles]		
		8:70,73,109,112,118											

R	**1719 – 1723** M-L-025 S-R-011	*Rubie / Ruby*	Sloop		Peter	Low / Law / Louw	Start	New York [New York]	(22 Dec 1719) (5 Jan 1720)	>	Barbados [Lesser Antilles]
							[>]	Curacao [Leeward Antilles]		>	New York — 25 Mar 1720 [New York] [18 Apr 1720] [23 Apr 1720]
							>	Curacao [Leeward Antilles]		[>]	Jamaica [Greater Antilles]
							28 Days	New York [New York]	28 Sept 1720 (19 Dec 1720) (31 Jan 1721)	>	Curacao [Leeward Antilles]
							21 Days	New York [New York]	2 Apr 1721 [15 May 1721] [22 May 1721]	>	Curacao [Leeward Antilles]
							>	New York [New York]	25 Jul 1721 [4 Sept 1721] [18 Sept 1721]	>	Curacao [Leeward Antilles]
							>	New York [New York]	22 Nov 1721 (19 Dec 1721) (1 Jan 1722)	>	Curacao [Leeward Antilles]
							>	New York [New York]	22 Mar 1722 [9 Apr 1722] [23 Apr 1722]	>	Curacao [Leeward Antilles]
							20 Days	New York [New York]	22 Jun 1722 [6 Aug 1722] [3 Sept 1722]	>	Curacao [Leeward Antilles]
							>	New York [New York]	[12 Nov 1722] (24 Dec 1722) (22 Jan 1723)	>	Curacao [Leeward Antilles]
							21 Days	New York [New York]	9 Mar 1723 [25 Mar 1723] [1 Apr 1723]	>	Curacao [Leeward Antilles]
							>	New York [New York]	28 May 1723 [17 Jun 1723] [1 Jul 1723]	>	Curacao [Leeward Antilles]
							>	New York [New York]	14 Sept 1723 [30 Sept 1723] [21 Oct 1723]	>	Curacao [Leeward Antilles]

Source: 5:4,8,32,38,41,110 / 6:4,16,36,49,52,87,100,106,138,148 / 7:4,38,42,48,75,94,105,132,151 / 8:10,26,32,34,62,68,73,100,106,114

	1721 M-G-028 S-R-012	*Rubie / Ruby*	Sloop		Thomas	Gailaspy / Gallasoy	Start	Jamaica [Greater Antilles]		>	New York — 22 May 1721 [New York] [26 Jun 1721] [31 Jul 1721]
							>	Jamaica [Greater Antilles]			

Source: 6:52,66,87

Group	Ship				Captain / Master		Passage	Arrival / Departure 1		Passage	Arrival / Departure 2		Page
	Year	Name	Type	Burden	First Name	Last Name	Length	Port	Arrival / Entered Inwards / Custom In / Entered Out	Length	Port	Arrival / Entered Inwards / Custom In / Entered Out	47
R	MSTR ID#								Custom Out / Cleared Out			Custom Out / Cleared Out	
	SHIP ID#	Registry Location						State / Country	Departure		State / Country	Departure	
	Source							Notes					

Rose — Sloop — M-M-035 / S-R-017 — 1720 – 1721

	Captain	Passage	Port	Dates	Passage	Port	Dates
	John Martin	Start	New York [New York]	[21 Mar 1720] [4 Apr 1720]	>	Curacao [Leeward Antilles]	
		[>]	Jamaica [Greater Antilles]		>	New York [New York]	30 Nov 1720 (27 Feb 1721) [6 Mar 1721]
		>	Curacao [Leeward Antilles]				

Source: 5:30,34,141 / 6:23,28

Revenge — Sloop — M-M-036 / S-R-013 — 1720

	Captain	Passage	Port	Dates	Passage	Port	Dates
	Peter Margatt / Morgat	Start	New York [New York]	(2 Feb 1720)	>	Barbados [Lesser Antilles]	
		[>]	New York [New York]	[13 Jun 1720] [27 Jun 1720]	>	Holland	

Source: 5:8,16,63,70

Revenge — Sloop — M-Y-003 / S-R-014 — 1720

	Captain	Passage	Port	Dates	Passage	Port	Dates
	John Yeats / Yeates	Start	New York [New York]	[7 Nov 1720] [14 Nov 1720]	>	Rhode Island	

Source: 5:126,129

Revenge — Sloop — M-B-062 / S-R-015 — 1721

	Captain	Passage	Port	Dates	Passage	Port	Dates
	John Bradick / Braddick	Start	New York [New York]	[10 Jul 1721] [31 Jul 1721]	>	Boston [Massachusetts]	[26 Aug 1721]

Source: 6:76,87 / 20:4

Rubie / Ruby — Sloop — M-L-026 / S-R-016 — 1720 – 1721

	Captain	Passage	Port	Dates	Passage	Port	Dates
	Richard Leacraft	Start	Antigua [Leeward Islands]		>	Bermuda	
		>	New York [New York]	6 Jul 1720	[>]	Bermuda	
		>	New York [New York]	2 Nov 1720 [21 Nov 1720] [5 Dec 1720]	>	Jamaica [Greater Antilles]	
		[>]	Bermuda		>	New York [New York]	13 May 1721 [5 Jun 1721] [26 Jun 1721]
		>	Jamaica [Greater Antilles]				

Source: 5:75,125,133,141 / 6:48,58,67

S	Year	Name	Type	Burden	First Name	Last Name	Length	Port	Custom In / Entered Out	Length	Port	Custom In / Entered Out	48
	MSTR ID#	Registry Location						State / Country	Custom Out / Cleared Out		State / Country	Custom Out / Cleared Out	
	SHIP ID#								Departure			Departure	
		Source							Notes				

1723	St. Christophers	Snow		Richard	Thorpe	Start	St Christopher		>	New York	17 Jun 1723 [5 Aug 1723]
M-T-027							[Leeward Islands]			[New York]	[19 Aug 1723]
S-S-037						>	St Christopher				
							[Leeward Islands]				
	8:70,86,91										

1723	St. George	Sloop		Rupert / Ruport	Waring / Warring	Start	Vera Cruz		>	New York	8 Aug 1723 [11 Nov 1723]
M-W-034										[New York]	[18 Nov 1723]
S-S-038						>	Jamaica				
							[Greater Antilles]				
	8:88,126,128										

1720	Saint Michael	Sloop		Christopher	Dupler	Start	New York		>	Martinique	
M-D-024							[New York]	(5 Jan 1720)		[Lesser Antilles]	
S-S-039											
	5:8										

1720	Samuel	Sloop		Joseph	Vesey / Vezey	Start	New York	[22 Aug 1720]	>	St Christopher	
M-V-012							[New York]	[5 Sept 1720]		[Leeward Islands]	
S-S-040											
	5:92,96										

1722 – 1723	Samuel	Ship		Thomas	Fitch / Fitz	Start	New York	[9 Apr 1722]	>	London	
M-F-011							[New York]	[4 Jun 1722]		[England]	
S-S-041											2 Sept 1722
						>	New York	30 Oct 1722 [19 Nov 1722]	>	London	
							[New York]	[10 Dec 1722]		[England]	
						>	New York	30 May 1723 [10 Jun 1723]	>	London	
							[New York]	[1 Jul 1723]		[England]	
						7 Weeks	New York	24 Nov 1723 [3 Dec 1723]	>	London	
							[New York]	(17 Dec 1723)		[England]	
	7:42,60,63,67,122,130,136,144 / 8:62,65,73,112,130,134,138										

1720	Samuel & Elizabeth	Sloop		James	Camerford / Comerford	Start	New York	[17 Oct 1720]	>	Jamaica	
M-C-036							[New York]	[28 Nov 1720]		[Greater Antilles]	
S-S-042											
	5:115,136										

1720	Sarah	Sloop		Peter	Albony	Start	New York	(14 Mar 1720)	>	Jamaica	
M-A-017							[New York]	[21 Mar 1720]		[Greater Antilles]	
S-S-043											
	5:27,30										

1722	Sarah	Sloop		John	Harriot	Start	New York	(12 Mar 1722)	>	Jamaica	
M-H-039							[New York]	[27 Mar 1722]		[Greater Antilles]	
S-S-044											
	7:32,38										

Group	Year	Name	Type	Burden	First Name	Last Name	Passage Length	Port	Arr/Entered Inwards · Custom In/Entered Out · Custom Out/Cleared Out · Departure	Passage Length	Port	Arr/Entered Inwards · Custom In/Entered Out · Custom Out/Cleared Out · Departure	Page
S								State / Country	Notes		State / Country		49
	MSTR ID#		Registry Location										
	SHIP ID#												

Record S-S-045

Year	Name	Type	Burden	MSTR ID#	SHIP ID#	First Name	Last Name	Passage	Port 1	State/Country 1	Dates 1	Passage	Port 2	State/Country 2	Dates 2
1723	Sarah	Scallop		M-B-063	S-S-045	James	Bayles	Start	New Castle	[Delaware]	[18 Mar 1723] / [25 Mar 1723] / [1 Apr 1723]	>	New York	[New York]	
								>	New Castle	[Delaware]					

Source: 8:28,32,34

Record S-S-046

Year	Name	Type	MSTR ID#	SHIP ID#	First Name	Last Name	Passage	Port 1	State/Country 1	Dates 1	Passage	Port 2	State/Country 2	Dates 2
1721	Sarah	Sloop	M-C-037	S-S-046	Ebenezer	Coffin	Start	Nantucket	[Massachusetts]	20 Aug 1721 / [4 Sept 1721] / [4 Sept 1721]	>	New York	[New York]	
							>	Nantucket	[Massachusetts]		>	Newport	[Rhode Island]	[6 Oct 1721] / [6 Oct 1721]
							>	Nantucket	[Massachusetts]					

Source: 6:94,100 / 20:11

Record S-S-047

Year	Name	Type	MSTR ID#	SHIP ID#	First Name	Last Name	Passage	Port 1	State/Country 1	Dates 1	Passage	Port 2	State/Country 2
1723	Sarah	Sloop	M-B-064	S-S-047	Christopher	Burrows	Start	Barbados	[Lesser Antilles]		>	Anguilla	[Leeward Islands]
							>	New York	[New York]	21 Apr 1723 / [13 May 1723] / [3 Jun 1723]	>	Barbados	[Lesser Antilles]

Source: 8:42,54,62

Record S-S-048

Year	Name	Type	MSTR ID#	SHIP ID#	First Name	Last Name	Passage	Port 1	State/Country 1	Passage	Port 2	State/Country 2	Dates 2
1720	Sarah	Sloop	M-S-051	S-S-048	Josiah	Smith	Start	St Christopher	[Leeward Islands]	22 Days	New York	[New York]	15 Apr 1720 / [2 May 1720] / [6 Jun 1720]
							>	Madeira Island	[Portugal]				

Source: 5:38,45,60

Notes: Passenager: Captain John Moulton – 15 Apr 1720 / To Retake Command of the Ship Mary Galley

Record S-S-049

Year	Name	Type	MSTR ID#	SHIP ID#	First Name	Last Name	Passage	Port 1	State/Country 1	Dates 1	Passage	Port 2	State/Country 2	Dates 2
1722	Sarah & Elizabeth	Sloop	M-W-035	S-S-049	William	Wells	Start	Turks Island			>	New York	[New York]	[4 Jun 1722] / [11 Jun 1722] / [25 Jun 1722]
							>	Curacao	[Leeward Antilles]					
							NO SUPPORTING DATA TO LINK TIMELINE							
							Start	Tortuga	[Haiti]		>	New York	[New York]	[1 Apr 1723] / [15 Apr 1723] / [22 Apr 1723]
							>	Curacao	[Leeward Antilles]		[>]	Bermuda		
							New York	[New York]	[29 Jul 1723] / [5 Aug 1723] / [19 Aug 1723]		>	Curacao	[Leeward Antilles]	

Source: 7:67,70,76 / 8:34,39,42,86,91 / 26:193

MSTR ID# / SHIP ID#	Registry Location			First Name	Last Name	Length	State / Country	Custom In / Entered Out / Custom Out / Cleared Out / Departure	Length	State / Country	Custom In / Entered Out / Custom Out / Cleared Out / Departure
1722 / M-B-065 / S-S-050	Sarah & Mary	Sloop		Jos.	Burt	Start	Bay of Honduras		>	New York / [New York]	[14 May 1722]
			7:57								
1721 / M-C-038 / S-S-051	Sarah & Rebekah	Sloop		Daniel	Cogeshal	Start	New York / [New York]	[17 Jul 1721] / [17 Jul 1721]	>	Rhode Island	
			6:79								
1722 / M-C-039 / S-S-052	Seabrook	Sloop		John	Chamberlain / Chamberlaine	Start	New London / [Connecticut]		>	New York / [New York]	[14 May 1722] / [28 May 1722] / [28 May 1722]
						>	New London / [Connecticut]				
			7:57,63								
1720 / M-E-007 / S-S-053	Sea Flower	Sloop		Adrian	Erasmus	Start	New York / [New York]	[22 Aug 1720]	>	Curacao / [Leeward Antilles]	
			5:92								
1721 / M-D-025 / S-S-054	Sea Flower	Sloop		Samuel	Dunham	Start	North Carolina		18 Days	Perth Amboy / [New Jersey]	29 Mar 1721
						>	New York / [New York]	[10 Apr 1721]	>	Perth Amboy / [New Jersey]	[13 Jun 1721]
						>	North Carolina				
			6:36,38,60 / 23:56								
1722 / M-F-012 / S-S-055	Sea Flower	Schooner		Christopher	Fell	Start	New York / [New York]	[10 Dec 1722] / (24 Dec 1722)	>	Virginia	
						>	New York / [New York]	[8 Apr 1723] / [1 Jul 1723] / [1 Jul 1723]	>	St Eustatius / [Leeward Islands]	
			7:144,151 / 8:73 / 26:177								
1720 / M-B-066 / S-S-056	Swanswick	Ship			Brown	Start	London / [England]		>	Dartmouth / [England]	9 Oct 1720
						>	New York / [New York]	4 Dec 1720			
			5:129,141								

Group					Captain / Master		Passage	Arrival / Departure 1		Passage	Arrival / Departure 2		Page
	Ship								Arrival / Entered Inwards			Arrival / Entered Inwards	
	Year	Name	Type	Burden	First Name	Last Name	Length	Port	Custom In / Entered Out	Length	Port	Custom In / Entered Out	
S	MSTR ID#								Custom Out / Cleared Out			Custom Out / Cleared Out	51
	SHIP ID#	Registry Location						State / Country	Departure		State / Country	Departure	
	Source							Notes					

	Year	Name	Type	Burden	First Name	Last Name	Length	Port / State-Country	Dates	Length	Port / State-Country	Dates
	1720 – 1721	*Seneca*	Snow		John	Jones	Start	Bristol		>	New York	22 Apr 1720 / [9 May 1720]
	M-J-017							[England]	26 Feb 1720		[New York]	[6 Jun 1720]
	S-S-057											
							>	Barbados				
								[Lesser Antilles]				
								NO SUPPORTING DATA TO LINK TIMELINE				
							Start	Bristol		>	New York	11 Jun 1721 / [26 Jun 1721]
								[England]	3 Apr 1721		[New York]	[10 Jul 1721] / 12 Jul 1721
							>	Bristol				
								[England]				
								NO SUPPORTING DATA TO LINK TIMELINE				
	1723						Start	London		>	Lisbon	[2 Apr 1723]
	S-S-057							[England]			Portugal	
	5:40,50,60 / 6:60,66,67,71,76 / 8:77											

	Year	Name	Type	Burden	First Name	Last Name	Length	Port / State-Country	Dates	Length	Port / State-Country	Dates
	1723	*Shareham*	Sloop		William	Torsh	Start			29 Days	New York	7 Oct 1723 / [14 Oct 1723]
	M-T-028							South Carolina			[New York]	[14 Oct 1723]
	S-S-058											
							>					
								Rhode Island				
	8:109,112											

	Year	Name	Type	Burden	First Name	Last Name	Length	Port / State-Country	Dates	Length	Port / State-Country	Dates
	1719 – 1720	*Shepherd*	Pink		Richard	Barrington	Start	New York	(22 Dec 1719)	>	London	
	M-B-067							[New York]	(2 Feb 1720) / 12 Mar 1720		[England]	
	S-S-059											
	5:4,8,12,16,20,24,27											

	Year	Name	Type	Burden	First Name	Last Name	Length	Port / State-Country	Dates	Length	Port / State-Country	Dates
	1723	*Sparrow*	Sloop		John	Davis	Start			>	New York	[4 Nov 1723] / [11 Nov 1723]
	M-D-026							Rhode Island			[New York]	[11 Nov 1723]
	S-S-060											
							>			>	New York	24 Nov 1723 / [3 Dec 1723]
								Rhode Island			[New York]	[3 Dec 1723]
							>					
								Rhode Island				
	8:122,126,130,134											

S	Year	Name	Type	Burden	First Name	Last Name	Length	Port	Arrival / Entered Inwards	Length	Port	Arrival / Entered Inwards	52
	MSTR ID#								Custom In / Entered Out			Custom In / Entered Out	
	SHIP ID#	Registry Location						State / Country	Custom Out / Cleared Out		State / Country	Custom Out / Cleared Out	
		Source							Departure		Notes	Departure	

1721 – 1722	*Speedwell*	Sloop		James	Cahoone	Start	Boston		>	Newport	
M-C-006							[Massachusetts]	[5 Aug 1721]		[Rhode Island]	[1 Sept 1721]
S-S-010											
						>	Salem		>	Philadelphia	[28 Sept 1721] / [28 Sept 1721]
							[New Jersey]			[Pennsylvania]	[5 Oct 1721]
						>	Salem		[>]		
							[New Jersey]			Rhode Island	
						>	New York	(19 Dec 1721) / (19 Dec 1721)	>		
							[New York]	(19 Dec 1721)		Rhode Island	
						[>]	New London		>	New York	[2 Apr 1722]
							[Connecticut]			[New York]	
						[>]	Block Island	[? Jun 1722]			
							[Rhode Island]	Taken / Pirates			
6:108,112,148 / 7:40,73 / 20:1 / 20:45 / 23:58							Source 7:73 - Full report on pirates / Source 20:45 – Also has report on how sloop was taken				

1723	*Speedwell*	Scallop		Samuel	Pound	Start	New Castle		>	New York	4 Jun 1723 / [10 Jun 1723]
M-P-029							[Delaware]			[New York]	[10 Jun 1723]
S-S-061						>	New Castle				
							[Delaware]				
8:65											

1722	*Speedwell*	Sloop		Maletier / Meletier	Hatch	Start			>	New York	[12 Nov 1722] / [26 Nov 1722]
M-H-040							Rhode Island			[New York]	[3 Dec 1722]
S-S-062						>					
							Rhode Island				
7:132,138,144											

1721	*Speedwell*	Sloop		John	Barber	Start			>	Philadelphia	[30 Mar 1721] / [13 Apr 1721]
M-B-026							Rhode Island			[Pennsylvania]	[20 Apr 1721]
S-S-008						>					
							Rhode Island				
							NO SUPPORTING DATA TO LINK TIMELINE				
						Start			>	New York	[2 Oct 1721] / [9 Oct 1721]
							Rhode Island			[New York]	[16 Oct 1721]
						>					
							Rhode Island				
6:34,38,40,111,114,119											

Group		Ship			Captain / Master		Passage	Arrival / Departure 1		Passage	Arrival / Departure 2		Page
	Year	Name	Type	Burden	First Name	Last Name	Length	Port	Arrival / Entered Inwards	Length	Port	Arrival / Entered Inwards	53
S									Custom In / Entered Out			Custom In / Entered Out	
	MSTR ID#							State / Country	Custom Out / Cleared Out		State / Country	Custom Out / Cleared Out	
	SHIP ID#	Registry Location							Departure			Departure	
		Source							Notes				
	1723	*Stanhope*	Snow		John	Delap / Dalap	Start	New York	[11 Mar 1723]	>	Antigua		
	M-D-027								[8 Apr 1723]				
	S-S-063							[New York]			[Leeward Islands]		
							>	New York	21 Aug 1723	>	Bristol		
									[2 Sept 1723]				
								[New York]	[4 Nov 1723]		[England]		
		8:26,94,96,112,122 / 26:177											
	1720	*Success*	Sloop		James	Whippo	Start	New Providence		14 Days	New York	22 Apr 1720	
	M-W-036											[16 May 1720]	
	S-S-064							[Bahamas]			[New York]	[6 Jun 1720]	
							>	Antigua		20 Days	New York	29 Aug 1720	
												[5 Sept 1720]	
								[Leeward Islands]			[New York]	[12 Sept 1720]	
							>	New Providence		25 Days	New York	8 Nov 1720	
												[5 Dec 1720]	
								[Bahamas]			[New York]	(19 Dec 1720)	
							>	St Thomas					
								[Virgin Islands]					
		5:40,41,53,60,94,96,99,129,141 / 6:4											
	1720 – 1722	*Success*	Sloop		Percinet / Percint	Spofforth	Start	Barbados		>	New York	7 Jul 1720	
	M-S-052											[18 Jul 1720]	
	S-S-065							[Lesser Antilles]			[New York]	[25 Jul 1720]	
							>	Jamaica		[>]	Curacao		
								[Greater Antilles]			[Leeward Antilles]		
							>	New York	15 Oct 1720	>	Barbados		
									[31 Oct 1720]				
								[New York]	[14 Nov 1720]		[Lesser Antilles]		
							[>]	Bermuda		>	New York	27 Apr 1721	
												[15 May 1721]	
											[New York]	[29 May 1721]	
							>	Bermuda					
								NO SUPPORTING DATA TO LINK TIMELINE					
							Start	New York	[26 Nov 1722]	>	Jamaica		
								[New York]	[10 Dec 1722]		[Greater Antilles]		
		5:75,78,82,115,123,129 / 6:44,49,56 / 7:134,144											
	1720	*Susanna / Susannah*	Sloop		Jehoshaphat	Welman / Welmon	Start	Bermuda		>	New York	[21 Nov 1720]	
	M-W-037											[5 Dec 1720]	
	S-S-066										[New York]	(19 Dec 1720)	
							>	Barbados					
								[Lesser Antilles]					
		5:133,141 / 6:4											

	MSTR ID#			First Name	Last Name	Length	Port	Custom In / Entered Out	Length	Port	Custom In / Entered Out	
T	SHIP ID#	Registry Location					State / Country	Custom Out / Cleared Out Departure		State / Country	Custom Out / Cleared Out Departure	54
		Source						Notes				

	1720	Three Brothers	Sloop		John	Styles	Start	Philadelphia	XX [28 Apr 1720] XX [5 May 1720]	>	Jamaica	
Philadelphia	M-S-025							[Pennsylvania]	[26 May 1720]		[Greater Antilles]	
M-D-010 < S-T-008 Page # 49 Book	S-T-008				[>]	Turks Island				>	New York	28 Sept 1720 [10 Oct 1720] [24 Oct 1720]
											[New York]	
					>	Antigua						
						[Leeward Islands]						
		5:45,56,110,112,120										

	1719 – 1720	Three Sisters	Sloop		Nicholas	Webb	Start	New York	(9 Dec 1719) (5 Jan 1720)	>	Barbados	
	M-W-017							[New York]			[Lesser Antilles]	
	S-T-009				>	Philadelphia			[28 Apr 1720] [19 May 1720]	>	Barbados	
						[Pennsylvania]					[Lesser Antilles]	Philadelphia > M-B-030 S-T-009 Page # 52 Book
					>	Philadelphia			3 Aug 1720 [11 Aug 1720] [18 Aug 1720]	>	Barbados	
						[Pennsylvania]					[Lesser Antilles]	
					>	Philadelphia			15 Nov 1720 [24 Nov 1720] [1 Dec 1720]	>	Barbados	XXXXXXXXXXXXXX XXXXXXXXXXXXXX XXXXXXXXXXXXXX
						[Pennsylvania]					[Lesser Antilles]	
		5:2,8,41,53,85,88,90,129,133,136										

	1720	Tempest	Brigantine		William	Tempest	Start	New York	[14 Nov 1720]	>	Jamaica	
	M-T-029							[New York]			[Greater Antilles]	
	S-T-010	5:129										

	1720	Two Brothers	Sloop		Henry	Feaver	Start	New York	(16 Feb 1720) (1 Mar 1720)	>	Bermuda	
	M-F-013							[New York]				
	S-T-011	5:20,24										

	1720	Two Brothers	Sloop		Thomas	Ware	Start	New York	[4 Jul 1720] [11 Jul 1720]	>	Jamaica	
	M-W-038							[New York]			[Greater Antilles]	
	S-T-012	5:72,75										

	1723	Trampoose	Sloop		John	Steed / Sreed	Start	Nevis		>	New York	21 Apr 1723 [28 Apr 1723] [6 May 1723]
	M-S-053							[Leeward Islands]			[New York]	
	S-T-013				>	Nevis						
						[Leeward Islands]						
		8:42,45,50										

Group	Ship				Captain / Master		Passage	Arrival / Departure 1		Passage	Arrival / Departure 2		Page
	Year	Name	Type	Burden	First Name	Last Name	Length	Port	Arrival / Entered Inwards	Length	Port	Arrival / Entered Inwards	55
T									Custom In / Entered Out			Custom In / Entered Out	
	MSTR ID#							State / Country	Custom Out / Cleared Out		State / Country	Custom Out / Cleared Out	
	SHIP ID#	Registry Location							Departure			Departure	
	Source							Notes					

Group T — Record 1

1721 – 1723	Trial / Tryal / Tryall	Sloop		Francis	Vandick / Vanduck / Vandyck	Start	New York	[17 Jul 1721]	>	Boston	[12 Aug 1721]
M-V-013											[19 Aug 1721]
S-T-014							[New York]	[24 Jul 1721]		[Massachusetts]	[2 Sept 1721]
						>	New York	[11 Sept 1721]	>	Boston	
							[New York]	[16 Oct 1721]		[Massachusetts]	
						>	New York	20 Nov 1721			
							[New York]				
						NO SUPPORTING DATA TO LINK TIMELINE					
						Start	New York	[30 Jul 1722]	>	Philadelphia	
							[New York]	[30 Jul 1722]		[Pennsylvania]	
						NO SUPPORTING DATA TO LINK TIMELINE					
						Start	New York	(5 Feb 1723)	>	Boston	[16 Feb 1723]
											[23 Feb 1723]
							[New York]	(18 Feb 1723)		[Massachusetts]	[2 Mar 1723]
						>	New York	[18 Mar 1723]	>	Boston	[27 Apr 1723]
								[25 Mar 1723]			
							[New York]	[8 Apr 1723]		[Massachusetts]	[11 May 1723]
						>	New York	20 May 1723	>	Boston	[13 Jul 1723]
								[24 Jun 1723]			[13 Jul 1723]
							[New York]	[8 Jul 1723]		[Massachusetts]	[27 Jul 1723]
						>	New York	6 Aug 1723			
							[New York]				

Source: 6:79,84,103,119,137,138 / 7:92 / 8:16,21,28,32,60,70,76,88 / 20:2,3,4,81,82,83,91,93,102,104 / 26:177

Group T — Record 2

1720	Tryall	Sloop		Joseph	Rhode / Rhodes	Start			>	New York	[21 Nov 1720]
M-R-025											
S-T-015							Rhode Island			[New York]	(2 Jan 1721)
						>	Barbados				
							[Lesser Antilles]				

Source: 5:133 / 6:8

Group T — Record 3

1723	Two Brothers	Sloop		Samuel	Lobdell / Londel	Start	St Christopher		>	New York	23 Apr 1723
M-L-027											[6 May 1723]
S-T-016							[Leeward Islands]			[New York]	[27 May 1723]
						>	St Christopher				
							[Leeward Islands]				

Source: 8:45,50,60

U – V	Year	Name	Type	Burden	First Name	Last Name	Length	Port	Arrival / Entered Inwards	Length	Port	Arrival / Entered Inwards	56
	MSTR ID#	Registry Location						State / Country	Custom In / Entered Out		State / Country	Custom In / Entered Out	
	SHIP ID#								Custom Out / Cleared Out			Custom Out / Cleared Out	
									Departure			Departure	
	Source							Notes					

	1720 – 1723	*Unity*	Snow		Robert	Leonard	Start	New York	[18 Jul 1720]	>	Barbados	
	M-L-028	New York, New York						[New York]	[22 Aug 1720]		[Lesser Antilles]	
	S-U-002											
							>	New York	[21 Nov 1720]	>		
									(27 Feb 1721)			
								[New York]	[7 May 1721]		Holland	
							>	Cowes		>	New York	3 Nov 1721
												(19 Dec 1721)
								[England]	About 24 Sept 1721		[New York]	[19 Mar 1722]
							>			[>]	Cowes	
								Holland			[England]	
							>	New York	[29 Oct 1722]	>	Bonaire	[25 Jan 1723]
									[12 Nov 1722]			
								[New York]	(24 Dec 1722)		[Leeward Antilles]	Taken / Pirates
							>	Curacao	Taken / In Fight of the Island			
								[Leeward Antilles]	Snow & 4 Men Taken			
	5:78,92,133 / 6:23,46,130,148 / 7:34,125,132,152 / 8:26,76											

	1721 – 1722	*Victory*	Sloop		Samuel	Saltus	Start	Barbados		>	Martinique	
	M-S-054							[Lesser Antilles]			[Lesser Antilles]	
	S-V-003											
							>	New York	26 Nov 1721	>	Barbados	
									(19 Dec 1721)			
								[New York]	(1 Jan 1722)		[Lesser Antilles]	
	6:138,148 / 7:4											

Group							Page
W							57

Record 1

Year	1721 – 1723
Name	William
Type	Sloop
Burden	
MSTR ID#	M-E-008
SHIP ID#	S-W-011
Registry Location	
Captain / Master	William Ellison

Passage Length	Port	State / Country	Arrival/Entered Inwards · Custom In/Entered Out · Custom Out/Cleared Out · Departure	Passage Length	Port	State / Country	Arrival/Entered Inwards · Custom In/Entered Out · Custom Out/Cleared Out · Departure
Start	Anguilla	[Leeward Islands]		>	Nevis	[Leeward Islands]	
>	New York	[New York]	2 Jun 1721 / [5 Jun 1721] / [19 Jun 1721]	>	London	[England]	
>	Bristol	[England]	1 Sept 1721	>	New York	[New York]	26 Oct 1721 / [13 Nov 1721] / [20 Nov 1721]
>	North Carolina			[>]	Barbados	[Lesser Antilles]	
>	New York	[New York]	8 Jul 1722 / [3 Sept 1722]	>	North Carolina		
>	New York	[New York]	17 Apr 1723 / [3 Dec 1723] / (17 Dec 1723)	>	Jamaica	[Greater Antilles]	

Source: 6:58,63,125,132,137 / 7:82,105 / 8:42,134,138

Record 2

Year	1720 – 1722
Name	William
Type	Sloop
Burden	
MSTR ID#	M-C-008
SHIP ID#	S-W-001
Registry Location	
Captain / Master	Samuel Cooper

Passage Length	Port	State / Country	Arrival/Entered Inwards · Custom In/Entered Out · Custom Out/Cleared Out · Departure	Passage Length	Port	State / Country	Arrival/Entered Inwards · Custom In/Entered Out · Custom Out/Cleared Out · Departure
Start	Bermuda			>	Philadelphia	[Pennsylvania]	23 Oct 1720 / [3 Nov 1720] / [24 Nov 1720]
>	Montserrat	[Leeward Islands]		[>]	St Christopher	[Leeward Islands]	
>	Anguilla	[Leeward Islands]		>	Philadelphia	[Pennsylvania]	[4 May 1721] / [25 May 1721]
>	Bermuda			>	Philadelphia	[Pennsylvania]	[2 Nov 1721] / [9 Nov 1721] / [7 Dec 1721]
>	Barbados	[Lesser Antilles]		[>]	Bermuda		
>	New York	[New York]	[30 Apr 1722] / [21 May 1722]	>	Curacao	[Leeward Antilles]	
[>]	Turks Island			>	New York	[New York]	[29 Oct 1722] / [11 Nov 1722] / [3 Dec 1722]
>	Barbados	[Lesser Antilles]					

Source: 5:120,123,133 / 6:42,44,53,125,130,140 / 7:51,60,126,132,144

W

MSTR ID# / SHIP ID#	Name	Type	Burden	First Name	Last Name	Length	Port / State / Country	Custom In / Entered Out / Custom Out / Cleared Out / Departure	Length	Port / State / Country	Custom In / Entered Out / Custom Out / Cleared Out / Departure
1720 M-H-041 S-W-012	William	Sloop		Benjamin	Hill	Start	Virginia		>	New York [New York]	20 Apr 1720 [2 May 1720] [2 May 1720]
						>	Virginia				
Source: 5:40,41,45											
1720 M-S-055 S-W-013	William	Sloop		John	Seymour	Start	New York [New York]	[12 Sept 1720] [19 Sept 1720]	>	Virginia	
Source: 5:99,103											
1722 M-C-040 S-W-014	William	Sloop		William	Cooper	Start	New York [New York]	[7 May 1722]	>	Curacao [Leeward Antilles]	
Source: 7:54											
1722 M-H-042 S-W-015	William	Sloop		Nicholas	Hinson	Start	Nevis [Leeward Islands]		>	New York [New York]	20 Jun 1722 [2 Jul 1722] [16 Jul 1722]
						>	Nevis [Leeward Islands]				
Source: 7:75,79,85											
1723 M-E-009 S-W-016	William	Sloop		Joseph	Evans	Start	Bermuda		>	New York [New York]	26 Oct 1723 [4 Nov 1723] [11 Nov 1723]
						>	Barbados [Lesser Antilles]				
Source: 8:118,122,126											
1723 M-V-014 S-W-017	William & John	Sloop		John	Veare	Start	New York [New York]	[20 May 1723] [20 May 1723]	>	North Carolina	
Source: 8:58											
1720 M-G-029 S-W-018	William & Mary	Sloop		Richard Stephenson	Grimston	Start	New York [New York]	[12 Sept 1720] [12 Sept 1720]	>	Rhode Island	
Source: 5:99											
1722 M-H-043 S-W-019	William & Sarah	Schooner		Alexander	Hall	Start	South Carolina		>	New York [New York]	[29 Oct 1722] [29 Oct 1722] [5 Nov 1722]
						>	Rhode Island				
Source: 7:125,126,130											

Group														Page
Y	Ship					Captain / Master		Passage	Arrival / Departure 1			Passage	Arrival / Departure 2	59
	SHIP ID#	Registry Location	Name	Type	Burden	First Name	Last Name	Length	Port	Custom In / Entered Out	State / Country	Length	Port	
	MSTR ID#								Arrival / Entered Inwards	Custom Out / Cleared Out	Departure		Arrival / Entered Inwards	
													Custom Out / Cleared Out	
													Departure	
						Source						Notes		

Year	Name	Type	Burden	First Name	Last Name	Passage	Port	Custom In/Out	State/Country	Passage	Port	State/Country	Notes
1722	Young Benjamin	Sloop		Owen	Carthy	Start	New York	[3 Sept 1722]	Barbados	>	New York	[Lesser Antilles]	
M-C-041								[10 Sept 1722]					
S-Y-001													
								23 Apr 1723					
						<	New York	[22 Jul 1723]	Barbados	>	New York	[Lesser Antilles]	
								[5 Aug 1723]					
7:105,108 / 8:45,81,86													

Year	Name	Type	Burden	First Name	Last Name	Length	Port	Custom In / Entered Out	Length	Port	Custom In / Entered Out
MSTR ID#	Registry Location						State / Country	Custom Out / Cleared Out		State / Country	Custom Out / Cleared Out
SHIP ID#								Departure			Departure
Source							Notes				

1720 – 1722	George	Sloop		Matthew	Wolf	Start	New York	[16 May 1720]	>		
M-W-039							[New York]	[16 May 1720]		Rhode Island	
S-G-016											
						>	Boston				
							[Massachusetts]				
							NO SUPPORTING DATA TO LINK TIMELINE				
						Start	New York	[24 Apr 1721]	>	Barbados	
							[New York]	[7 May 1721]		[Lesser Antilles]	
						>	New York	15 Jul 1721	>	Barbados	
								[24 Jul 1721]			
							[New York]	[31 Jul 1721]		[Lesser Antilles]	
						>	St Martin		23 Days	Perth Amboy	22 Oct 1721
							[Leeward Islands]	30 Sept 1721		[New Jersey]	
						>	New York		>	Barbados	
							[New York]	[5 Dec 1721]		[Lesser Antilles]	
						[>]	St Martin		40 Days	New York	10 Mar 1722
											[2 Apr 1722]
							[Leeward Islands]			[New York]	[9 Apr 1722]
						>	Barbados		18 Days	New York	24 Jun 1722
											[16 Jul 1722]
							[Lesser Antilles]			[New York]	[23 Jul 1722]
						>	Barbados	XXXXXXXXXXXXXX			
								XXXXXXXXXXXXXX			
							[Lesser Antilles]	XXXXXXXXXXXXXX			
				XXXXXXXXXX XXXXXXXXXX Captain / Master Changed Ships XXXXXXXXXX XXXXXXXXXX				XXXXXXXXXXXXXX			
1722 – 1723	Content	Brigantine				Start	Barbados		>	Philadelphia	
							[Lesser Antilles]			[Pennsylvania]	
S-C-027											
						>	New York	[10 Dec 1722]	>	Barbados	
								(4 Mar 1723)			
							[New York]	[8 Apr 1723]		[Lesser Antilles]	
						[>]	St Lucia		>	New York	[9 Sept 1723]
											[23 Sept 1723]
							[Lesser Antilles]			[New York]	[14 Oct 1723]
						>	Jamaica				
							[Greater Antilles]				

5:53 / 6:42,46,79,84,87,122,144 / 7:31,40,42,76,85,89,144 / 8:24,98,106,112 / 23:59 / 26:177

Multi 60

Group	Ship				Captain / Master		Passage	Arrival / Departure 1		Passage	Arrival / Departure 2		Page
	Year	Name	Type	Burden	First Name	Last Name	Length	Port	Arrival / Entered Inwards	Length	Port	Arrival / Entered Inwards	
Multi									Custom In / Entered Out			Custom In / Entered Out	61
	MSTR ID#	Registry Location						State / Country	Custom Out / Cleared Out		State / Country	Custom Out / Cleared Out	
	SHIP ID#								Departure			Departure	
		Source							Notes				

	1719 – 1721	Mary & Hannah	Sloop		Jacob	Phenix / Phoenix	Start	New York		>	Curacao		
	M-P-030								(22 Dec 1719)				
	S-M-057							[New York]			[Leeward Antilles]		

	>	New York	25 Mar 1720	>	Curacao
			[23 Apr 1720]		
		[New York]	[16 May 1720]		[Leeward Antilles]
	19 Days	New York	21 Jul 1720	>	Antigua
			[8 Aug 1720]		
		[New York]	[22 Aug 1720]		[Leeward Islands]
	>	New York	4 Nov 1720	>	
			(19 Dec 1720)		
		[New York]	(19 Dec 1720)		North Carolina
	[>]	St Eustatius		>	New York	2 Jul 1721
						[24 Jul 1721]
		[Leeward Islands]			[New York]	[31 Jul 1721]
	>	Barbados				
		[Lesser Antilles]				

XXXXXXXXX XXXXXXXXXX Captain / Master Changed Ships XXXXXXXXX XXXXXXXXXX

	1722 – 1723	Jacob	Sloop				Start	New York	[7 May 1722]	>	Jamaica	
									[14 May 1722]			
	S-J-022							[New York]			[Greater Antilles]	

	>	New York	15 Aug 1722	>	Jamaica
			[1 Oct 1722]		
		[New York]	[15 Oct 1722]		[Greater Antilles]
	>	New York	[9 Apr 1723]	>	Jamaica
			[13 May 1723]		
		[New York]	[20 May 1723]		[Greater Antilles]
	15 Days	New York	11 Aug 1723	>	Jamaica
			[19 Aug 1723]		
		[New York]	[2 Sept 1723]		[Greater Antilles]
	>	New York	24 Nov 1723	>	Jamaica
			(31 Dec 1723)		
		[New York]	(31 Dec 1723)		[Greater Antilles]

5:4,32,41,53,82,88,92,126 / 6:4,71,84,87 / 7:54,57,98,114,122 / 8:54,58,88,91,96,130,142 / 26:177

Multi	MSTR ID# / SHIP ID#	Registry Location		First Name	Last Name	Length	State / Country	Custom In / Entered Out / Custom Out / Cleared Out Departure	Length	State / Country	Custom In / Entered Out / Custom Out / Cleared Out Departure	62
		Source						Notes				
	1720	Catherine	Sloop	Peter	Simon / Simmons	Start	New York	[9 May 1720]	>	St Christopher	Never Left For Port	
	M-S-056						[New York]	XXXXXXXXXXXXXX XXXXXXXXXXXXXX		[Leeward Islands]	See Next Ship Or Captain	
	S-C-028											
					XXXXXXXXX XXXXXXXXX Captain / Master Changed Ships XXXXXXXXX XXXXXXXXX							
	1720 – 1722	Margaret	Sloop			Start	New York	XXXXXXXXXXXXXX XXXXXXXXXXXXXX	>	St Christopher		
	S-M-058						[New York]	[23 May 1720]		[Leeward Islands]		
						[>]	New York		>	Madeira Island		
							[New York]	[8 Aug 1720]		[Portugal]		
						[>]	St Thomas		21 Days	New York	26 Apr 1721 / [7 May 1721] / [22 May 1721]	
							[Virgin Islands]			[New York]		
						>	St Thomas		12 Days	New York	11 Aug 1721 / [21 Aug 1721] / [28 Aug 1721]	
							[Virgin Islands]			[New York]		
						>	Barbados		[>]	Curacao		
							[Lesser Antilles]			[Leeward Antilles]		
						>	New York	2 Nov 1721 / (19 Dec 1721) / (1 Jan 1722)	>	Barbados		
							[New York]			[Lesser Antilles]		
						[>]	St Thomas		>	New York	17 May 1722 / [4 Jun 1722] / [11 Jun 1722]	
							[Virgin Islands]			[New York]		
						>	St Thomas		>	New York	[13 Aug 1722] / [12 Nov 1722] / [3 Dec 1722]	
							[Virgin Islands]			[New York]		
						>	Barbados					
							[Lesser Antilles]					
		5:50,56,88 / 6:44,46,52,92,94,96,130,148 / 7:4,60,67,70,96,132,144										

Group	Ship				Captain / Master		Passage	Arrival / Departure 1		Passage	Arrival / Departure 2		Page
	Year	Name	Type	Burden	First Name	Last Name	Length	Port	Arrival / Entered Inwards	Length	Port	Arrival / Entered Inwards	
Multi									Custom In / Entered Out			Custom In / Entered Out	63
	MSTR ID#	Registry Location						State / Country	Custom Out / Cleared Out		State / Country	Custom Out / Cleared Out	
	SHIP ID#								Departure			Departure	
	Source							Notes					

	1720 – 1722	Anne / Ann	Sloop		Daniel	Massey / Masse / Masie	Start	Jamaica		>	Pettiguavis		
	M-M-037							[Greater Antilles]			[Location Unkn]		
	S-A-025												

							>	New York	1 Apr 1720	>	Jamaica		
									[18 Apr 1720]				
								[New York]	[2 May 1720]		[Greater Antilles]		

NO SUPPORTING DATA TO LINK TIMELINE

| | | | | | | | Start | New York | [5 Dec 1720] | > | Jamaica | | |
| | | | | | | | | [New York] | (19 Dec 1720) | | [Greater Antilles] | | |

							26 Days	New York	2 Apr 1721	>	Jamaica		
									[15 May 1721]				
								[New York]	[5 Jun 1721]		[Greater Antilles]		

							[>]	Leogand		1 Month	New York	16 Sept 1721	
												[20 Nov 1721]	
								[Location Unkn]			[New York]	[5 Dec 1721]	

| | | | | | | | > | Jamaica | | | | | |
| | | | | | | | | [Greater Antilles] | | | | | |

NO SUPPORTING DATA TO LINK TIMELINE

| | | | | | | | Start | Jamaica | | > | Hispaniola | | |
| | | | | | | | | [Greater Antilles] | | | [Greater Antilles] | | |

| | | | | | | | > | New York | [29 Oct 1722] | | | | |
| | | | | | | | | [New York] | | | | | |

XXXXXXXXX XXXXXXXXXX Captain / Master Changed Ships XXXXXXXXX XXXXXXXXXX

	1723	Good Intent	Sloop				Start	New York	[10 Jun 1723]	>	Port Royal		
									[24 Jun 1723]				
	S-G-017							[New York]			[Jamaica]		

							>	New York	24 Aug 1723	>	Suriname		
									[14 Oct 1723]				
								[New York]	[28 Oct 1723]		[South America]		

| 5:34,38,45,141 / 6:36,49,58,106,137,144 / 7:125 / 8:65,70,94,112,118 | Passage Length: Jamaica → Pettiguavis → New York / Took 8 Weeks Total |

	Year	Name	Type	Burden	First Name	Last Name	Length	Port	Arrival / Entered Inwards	Length	Port	Arrival / Entered Inwards
Multi	MSTR ID#	Registry Location						State / Country	Custom In / Entered Out		State / Country	Custom In / Entered Out
	SHIP ID#								Custom Out / Cleared Out			Custom Out / Cleared Out
		Source							Departure			Departure
									Notes			

	1720	*Anne*	Sloop		*Terret*	Lester	Start	New York		>	Jamaica	
	M-L-029							[New York]	[22 Aug 1720]		[Greater Antilles]	
	S-A-026											
	XXXXXXXXX XXXXXXXXX Captain / Master Changed Ships XXXXXXXXX XXXXXXXXX
	1721 – 1722	*Nassau*	Brigantine				Start	New York	[20 Mar 1721]	>	Jamaica	
								[New York]	[24 Apr 1721]		[Greater Antilles]	
	S-N-013											
							>	New York	25 Jul 1721	>	Jamaica	
									[7 Aug 1721]			
								[New York]	[4 Sept 1721]		[Greater Antilles]	
							[>]	Barbados		>	Barbados	25 Oct 1721
								[Lesser Antilles]	25 Oct 1721		[Lesser Antilles]	Taken / Pirates
							>	Barbados	25 Oct 1721	>	Antigua	
								[Lesser Antilles]	Released / Pirates		[Leeward Islands]	10 Nov 1721
							>		Put Into Port	>	New York	25 Dec 1721
												(29 Jan 1722)
								Rhode Island	Distress of Weather		[New York]	(26 Feb 1722)
							>	Jamaica		>	New York	2 Jul 1722
												[23 Jul 1722]
								[Greater Antilles]			[New York]	[8 Oct 1722]
												5 – 8 Oct 1722
								London				
								[England]				
	XXXXXXXXX XXXXXXXXX Captain / Master Changed Ships XXXXXXXXX XXXXXXXXX
	1723	*Brown Betty*	Brigantine				Start	New York	[28 Oct 1723]	>	Jamaica	
	S-B-033							[New York]	[18 Nov 1723]		[Greater Antilles]	
		5:92 / 6:32,42,87,90,100 / 7:4,13,26,79,89,110,114,118 / 8:118,128							Released / Pirates: 25 Oct 1721 - Sailed for Antigua w/ Captain Nicholas Webb, Captain Stuckley & 13 hands on board				
								Saved / Ships Crew: 2 Jul 1722 – Men from a London & Bristol ship, that were stranded in the Bay of Mexico					

Group	Year	Name	Type	Burden	ID / Registry / Source	First Name	Last Name	Passage Length	Port / State-Country	Arrival/Custom/Departure	Passage Length	Port / State-Country	Arrival/Custom/Departure	Page
Multi														65
	1721	Clarendon Packet	Sloop		M-B-006 / S-C-006	Elisha	Bennett	Start	New York / [New York]	[5 Jun 1721] / [19 Jun 1721]	>	Boston / [Massachusetts]		
								>	New York / [New York]	20 Jul 1721 / [4 Sept 1721] / [25 Sept 1721]	>	Boston / [Massachusetts]	[11 Nov 1721]	
								>	New York / [New York]	[20 Nov 1721]	>	Philadelphia / [Pennsylvania]	[7 Dec 1721] / [7 Dec 1721] / [19 Dec 1721]	
								>	New York / [New York]	(19 Dec 1721)	>			

XXXXXXXXXX XXXXXXXXXX Captain / Master Changed Ships XXXXXXXXXX XXXXXXXXXX

Group	Year	Name	Type	Burden	ID / Registry / Source	First Name	Last Name	Passage Length	Port / State-Country	Arrival/Custom/Departure	Passage Length	Port / State-Country	Arrival/Custom/Departure	Page
	1723	Susanna & Judith	Sloop		S-S-067			Start	New York / [New York]	(5 Feb 1723) / XXXXXXXXXXXXXX / XXXXXXXXXXXXXX	>	Barbados / [Lesser Antilles]	Never Left For Port / See Next Ship Or Captain	

XXXXXXXXXX Changed Departure Location XXXXXXXXXX

Group	Year	Name	Type	Burden	ID / Registry / Source	First Name	Last Name	Passage Length	Port / State-Country	Arrival/Custom/Departure	Passage Length	Port / State-Country	Arrival/Custom/Departure	Page
								Start	New York / [New York]	XXXXXXXXXXXXXX / XXXXXXXXXXXXXX / (5 Feb 1723)	>	Virginia		

XXXXXXXXXX XXXXXXXXXX Captain / Master Changed Ships XXXXXXXXXX XXXXXXXXXX

Group	Year	Name	Type	Burden	ID / Registry / Source	First Name	Last Name	Passage Length	Port / State-Country	Arrival/Custom/Departure	Passage Length	Port / State-Country	Arrival/Custom/Departure	Page
	1723		Sloop		S-?-077			Start	Virginia		>	New York / [New York]	5 Jun 1723	

Source: 6:58,63,84,100,108,137,140,146,148 / 8:16,65 / 23:59

Group	Year	Name	Type	Burden	ID / Registry / Source	First Name	Last Name	Passage Length	Port / State-Country	Arrival/Custom/Departure	Passage Length	Port / State-Country	Arrival/Custom/Departure	Page
	1720 – 1722	Hunter	Sloop		M-A-018 / S-H-030	John	Ablin	Start	New York / [New York]	[11 Jul 1720] / [25 Jul 1720]	>	Suriname / [South America]		
								>	New York / [New York]	30 Nov 1720 / (27 Feb 1721) / [13 Mar 1721]	>	Suriname / [South America]		
								>	New York / [New York]	[26 Jun 1721] / [17 Jul 1721] / [31 Jul 1721]	>	Suriname / [South America]		
								>	Bermuda		>	New York / [New York]	16 Mar 1722 / [2 Apr 1722] / XXXXXXXXXXXXXX / XXXXXXXXXXXXXX	
								>	Suriname / [South America]	Never Left For Port / See Next Ship Or Captain				

XXXXXXXXXX XXXXXXXXXX Captain / Master Changed Ships XXXXXXXXXX XXXXXXXXXX

Group	Year	Name	Type	Burden	ID / Registry / Source	First Name	Last Name	Passage Length	Port / State-Country	Arrival/Custom/Departure	Passage Length	Port / State-Country	Arrival/Custom/Departure	Page
	1722	Hopewell	Sloop		S-H-031			Start	New York / [New York]	XXXXXXXXXXXXXX / XXXXXXXXXXXXXX / [28 May 1722]	>	Suriname / [South America]		
								>	New York / [New York]	7 Sept 1722 / [15 Oct 1722] / [29 Oct 1722]	>	Suriname / [South America]		

Source: 5:75,82,141 / 6:23,28,67,79,87 / 7:34,40,63,108,122,126

MSTR ID# / SHIP ID#	Registry Location		First Name	Last Name	Length	Port / State / Country	Custom In / Entered Out / Custom Out / Cleared Out / Departure	Length	Port / State / Country	Custom In / Entered Out / Custom Out / Cleared Out / Departure
1720 – 1721 M-O-007 S-E-035	Elizabeth & Catherine	Brigantine	Isaiah	Overy	Start	London [England]		10 Weeks	New York [New York]	23 Jun 1720 [5 Sept 1720] [28 Nov 1720] 2 Dec 1720
					>	London [England]	[? Jan 1721] XXXXXXXXXXXXXX XXXXXXXXXXXXXX XXXXXXXXXXXXXX			

XXXXXXXXX XXXXXXXXX Captain / Master Changed Ships XXXXXXXXX XXXXXXXXX

1721 S-H-032	Hope	Brigantine			Start	London [England]	XXXXXXXXXXXXXX XXXXXXXXXXXXXX XXXXXXXXXXXXXX 26 May 1721	>	Plymouth [England]	10 Jun 1721
					>	New York [New York]	2 Aug 1721 [14 Aug 1721] [16 Oct 1721] 21 Oct 1721	>	Beachy Head England	?? ??? 1721 Drove on Shore
					&	Ships Crew & Part of Cargo Saved Ship & Part of Cargo Was Lost		>	London [England]	Never Reached Port Lost Before Arrival

XXXXXXXXX XXXXXXXXX Captain / Master Changed Ships XXXXXXXXX XXXXXXXXX

| 1722 S-M-059 | Mackworth | Brigantine | | | Start | Swansea [Wales] | | 15 Weeks | New York [New York] | 15 Aug 1722 [27 Aug 1722] [10 Sept 1722] |
| | | | | | > | Swansea [Wales] | | | | |

5:70,96,126,133,136 / 6:40,87,90,92,108,111,114,119,122,141 / 7:40,45,98,102,108 / 23:51   Source 7:98 / 15 Aug 1722 – Brought a Company of Miners

| 1720 M-G-010 S-B-013 | Bedminster | Ship | James | Gordon | Start | Bristol [England] | | 11 Weeks & 3 Days | Philadelphia [Pennsylvania] | 18 Jun 1720 [7 Jul 1720] [14 Jul 1720] |
| | | | | | > | South Carolina | | | | |

XXXXXXXXX XXXXXXXXX Captain / Master Changed Ships XXXXXXXXX XXXXXXXXX

1721 – 1722 S-P-014	Pennsylvania Merchant	Ship			Start	Bristol [England]	3 Apr 1721	>	Philadelphia [Pennsylvania]	26 Jun 1721 [17 Aug 1721] [26 Oct 1721]
					>	Bristol [England]		>	Philadelphia [Pennsylvania]	[17 May 1722] [24 May 1722] [28 Jun 1722]
					>	Port Royal Jamaica	28 Aug 1722 Drove on Shore	&		Ships Crew Saved Ship Was Lost
					>	Port Royal Jamaica	Lost In Harbor / Hurricane			

XXXXXXXXX XXXXXXXXX Captain / Master Changed Ships XXXXXXXXX XXXXXXXXX

| 1723 S-E-008 | Elizabeth | Sloop | | | Start | New York [New York] | [10 Jun 1723] [1 Jul 1723] | > | Bristol [England] | |

5:67,72,75 / 6:60,67,92,122 / 7:58,60,76,146 / 8:62,65,73

Group	Year	Ship Name	Type	Burden	First Name	Last Name	Passage Length	Arr/Dep 1 Port	Arr/Dep 1 State/Country	Arrival / Entered Inwards · Custom In / Entered Out · Custom Out / Cleared Out · Departure	Passage Length	Arr/Dep 2 Port	Arr/Dep 2 State/Country	Arrival / Entered Inwards · Custom In / Entered Out · Custom Out / Cleared Out · Departure	Page
Multi															67
	1720	*Concord*	Sloop		John	Dickenson / Dickinson	Start		Rhode Island	[9 Jan 1720]	>	Barbados	[Lesser Antilles]		
	M-D-005 / S-C-013														

XXXXXXXXXX XXXXXXXXXX Captain / Master Changed Ships XXXXXXXXXX XXXXXXXXXX

	1720 – 1721	*Deborah*	Sloop				Start	Bermuda			>	Philadelphia	[Pennsylvania]	[7 Apr 1720] / [21 Apr 1720] / [12 May 1720]	
	S-D-009						>	Bermuda			>	Turks Island			
							>	New York	[New York]	16 Oct 1720 / [31 Oct 1720] / [14 Nov 1720]	>	Barbados	[Lesser Antilles]		
							[>]	Bermuda			>	Philadelphia	[Pennsylvania]	[13 Apr 1721] / [27 Apr 1721] / [11 May 1721]	
							>	Jamaica	[Greater Antilles]		>	Philadelphia	[Pennsylvania]	20 Aug 1721 / [31 Aug 1721] / [28 Sept 1721]	
							>	Jamaica	[Greater Antilles]						

NO SUPPORTING DATA TO LINK TIMELINE

| | 1723 | *Deborah* | Sloop | | | | Start | Bermuda | | | > | New York | [New York] | 15 Sept 1723 / [23 Sept 1723] / [14 Oct 1723] | |
| | S-D-009 | | | | | | > | Jamaica | [Greater Antilles] | | | | | | |

Source: 5:18,34,38,50,115,123,129 / 6:38,42,46,94,96,108 / 8:100,106,112

| | 1720 | *Mary Hope* | Sloop | | John | Cassly / Casely | Start | Philadelphia | [Pennsylvania] | [6 Oct 1720] / [13 Oct 1720] | > | | Virginia | | |
| | M-C-011 / S-M-022 | | | | | | > | Philadelphia | [Pennsylvania] | 28 Nov 1720 / XXXXXXXXXXXXXX / XXXXXXXXXXXXXX / XXXXXXXXXXXXXX | | | | | |

NO SUPPORTING DATA TO LINK TIMELINE

| | 1723 | *Mary Hope* | Scallop | | | | Start | Philadelphia | [Pennsylvania] | [26 Sept 1723] | > | New York | [New York] | [21 Oct 1723] / [21 Oct 1723] | |
| | S-M-023 | | | | | | > | Philadelphia | [Pennsylvania] | | | | | | |

Source: 5:110,112,136 / 8:103,114

Year	Name	Type	Burden	First Name	Last Name	Length	Port	Custom In / Entered Out	Length	Port	Custom In / Entered Out
MSTR ID#							State / Country	Custom Out / Cleared Out		State / Country	Custom Out / Cleared Out
SHIP ID#	Registry Location							Departure			Departure
	Source							Notes			

Ship 1 — S-?-078

1721		Sloop		John	Stant / Stout	Start	Bay of Honduras		>	New York	25 May 1721
M-S-012										[New York]	
S-?-078											

XXXXXXXXXX XXXXXXXXXX Captain / Master Changed Ships XXXXXXXXXX XXXXXXXXXX

1721	William & Sarah	Sloop				Start	New York	[16 Oct 1721]	>	Barbados	
								[13 Nov 1721]			
S-W-020							[New York]			[Lesser Antilles]	

XXXXXXXXXX XXXXXXXXXX Captain / Master Changed Ships XXXXXXXXXX XXXXXXXXXX

1722	Mary	Sloop				Start	Barbados		>	Philadelphia	[26 Apr 1722]
											[17 May 1722]
S-M-005							[Lesser Antilles]			[Pennsylvania]	[31 May 1722]
						>	Barbados			Martinique	
							[Lesser Antilles]			[Lesser Antilles]	
						>	Perth Amboy	16 Oct 1722			
							[New Jersey]				

NO SUPPORTING DATA TO LINK TIMELINE

						Start	St Thomas		>	New York	7 Jun 1723
							[Virgin Islands]			[New York]	[19 Aug 1723]
						>	Barbados				
							[Lesser Antilles]				

6:56,119,132 / 7:48,58,64 / 8:65,91 / 23:66

Ship — S-W-021

1722	William & John	Sloop		John	Greenock	Start	New York	[16 Jul 1722]	>		
M-G-030								[30 Jul 1722]			
S-W-021							[New York]			Virginia	

XXXXXXXXXX XXXXXXXXXX Captain / Master Changed Ships XXXXXXXXXX XXXXXXXXXX

| 1722 | | Schooner | | | | Start | | | > | New York | 27 Sept 1722 |
| S-?-079 | | | | | | | Virginia | | | [New York] | |

7:85,92,114

Ship — S-?-080

1722		Sloop		Peter	Sergent	Start	Boston		>	New York	[15 Oct 1722]
M-S-057								[6 Oct 1722]			
S-?-080							[Massachusetts]			[New York]	

XXXXXXXXXX XXXXXXXXXX Captain / Master Changed Ships XXXXXXXXXX XXXXXXXXXX

1722	Mary	Schooner				Start	New York		>		
								[21 Oct 1722]			
S-M-060							[New York]			Connecticut	

7:122 / 20:62

Ship — S-?-081

1722		Sloop		Benjamin	Moyon	Start	Boston		>	New York	[26 Nov 1722]
M-M-038											
S-?-081							[Massachusetts]			[New York]	

XXXXXXXXXX XXXXXXXXXX Captain / Master Changed Ships XXXXXXXXXX XXXXXXXXXX

1723	Joanna & Judith	Sloop				Start	New York	[1 Jul 1723]	>		
								[1 Jul 1723]			
S-J-023							[New York]			Virginia	

7:138 / 8:73

Interact	Ship				Captain / Master		Passage	Arrival / Departure 1		Passage	Arrival / Departure 2		Page
	Year	Name	Type	Burden	First Name	Last Name	Length	Port / State/Country	Arrival/Entered Inwards / Custom In/Entered Out / Custom Out/Cleared Out / Departure	Length	Port / State/Country	Arrival/Entered Inwards / Custom In/Entered Out / Custom Out/Cleared Out / Departure	
	MSTR ID# / SHIP ID#	Registry Location											
	Source								Notes				

Entry 1

- Year: 1720 – 1723
- Name: *Eagle*
- Type: Brigantine
- MSTR ID#: M-E-010
- SHIP ID#: S-E-036
- Captain/Master: James Eustace
- Page: 69

Passage Length	Port 1	State/Country 1	Arr/Dep 1 dates	Passage Length	Port 2	State/Country 2	Arr/Dep 2 dates
Start	New York	[New York]	(14 Mar 1720) / 26 – 28 Apr 1720 / 28 Apr 1720	>	Bristol	[England]	20 Aug 1720
>	New York	[New York]	30 Oct 1720 / [14 Nov 1720] / (19 Dec 1720)	>	Barbados	[Lesser Antilles]	
[>]	St Christopher	[Leeward Islands]		2 Days	St Eustatius	[Leeward Islands]	
18 Days	New York	[New York]	8 Apr 1721 / [17 Apr 1721] / [22 May 1721]	>	Bristol	[England]	
>	Milford Haven	[Wales]		6 Weeks	New York	[New York]	2 Nov 1721 / [20 Nov 1721] / [2 Apr 1722] / 12 Apr 1722
>	Bristol	[England]		>	New York	[New York]	[15 Oct 1722] / [12 Nov 1722] / (24 Dec 1722)
>	Madeira Island	[Portugal]		29 Days	New York	[New York]	21 Mar 1723 / XX [1 Apr 1723] XX / XXXXXXXXXXXXXX / XXXXXXXXXXXXXX

Source: 5:27,32,36,38,40,45,123,129 / 6:4,38,40,52,130,137 / 7:20,26,32,40,122,132,151 / 8:32

(Cross-reference: > M-B-068 / S-E-036 / Page # 69)

Entry 2

(Cross-reference: M-E-010 / S-E-036 / Page # 69 <)

- Year: 1723
- Name: *Eagle*
- Type: Brigantine
- MSTR ID#: M-B-068
- SHIP ID#: S-E-036
- Captain/Master: Daniel Bloom

Passage Length	Port 1	State/Country 1	Arr/Dep 1 dates	Passage Length	Port 2	State/Country 2	Arr/Dep 2 dates
Start	New York	[New York]	XX 21 Mar 1723 XX / [1 Apr 1723] / [22 Apr 1723]	>	Jamaica	[Greater Antilles]	
>	Bay of Honduras			6 Weeks	New York	[New York]	12 Oct 1723 / [18 Nov 1723] / (17 Dec 1723)
>	Madeira Island	[Portugal]					

Source: 8:34,42,112,128,138

MSTR ID#		First Name	Last Name	Length	State / Country	Custom In / Entered Out	Length	State / Country	Custom In / Entered Out
SHIP ID#	Registry Location					Custom Out / Cleared Out			Custom Out / Cleared Out
	Source					Departure		Notes	Departure

2 — **70**

1719 – 1722	Port Royal	Sloop		John	Fred	Start	New York	[9 Dec 1719]	>	Curacao
M-F-014							[New York]			[Leeward Antilles]
S-P-030										
						26 Days	New York	5 Mar 1720	>	Curacao
								[11 Apr 1720]		
							[New York]	[23 Apr 1720]		[Leeward Antilles]
						17 Days	New York	22 Jun 1720	>	Curacao
								[4 Jul 1720]		
							[New York]	[18 Jul 1720]		[Leeward Antilles]
						>	New York	28 Sept 1720	>	Curacao
								[31 Oct 1720]		
							[New York]	[28 Nov 1720]		[Leeward Antilles]
						>	New York	10 Apr 1721	>	Curacao
								[24 Apr 1721]		
							[New York]	[7 May 1721]		[Leeward Antilles]
						>	New York	13 Jul 1721	>	Curacao
								[24 Jul 1721]		
							[New York]	[24 Jul 1721]		[Leeward Antilles]
						>	New York	20 Oct 1721	>	St Thomas
								[13 Nov 1721]		
							[New York]	[28 Nov 1721]		[Virgin Islands]
						19 Days	New York	30 Apr 1722	>	Curacao
								[14 May 1722]		
							[New York]	[28 May 1722]		[Leeward Antilles]
						[>]	St Thomas	8 Sept 1722	>	New York
								XX [17 Sept 1722] XX		
							[Virgin Islands]	XXXXXXXXXXXXXXX XXXXXXXXXXXXXXX		[New York]

> M-L-030 / S-P-030 / Page # 70

5:2,26,36,41,70,72,78,110,123,136 / 6:38,42,46,79,84,122,132,138 / 7:51,57,63,108

1722	Port Royal	Sloop		Ichabod	Lontit	Start	New York	XX 8 Sept 1722 XX	>	Curacao
M-L-030								[17 Sept 1722]		
S-P-030							[New York]	[24 Sept 1722]		[Leeward Antilles]
	7:110,112									

M-F-014 / S-P-030 / Page # 70 <

Interact		Ship				Captain / Master		Passage	Arrival / Departure 1		Passage	Arrival / Departure 2		Page
	Year	Name	Type	Burden		First Name	Last Name	Length	Port	Arrival / Entered Inwards	Length	Port	Arrival / Entered Inwards	
3										Custom In / Entered Out			Custom In / Entered Out	71
	MSTR ID#									Custom Out / Cleared Out			Custom Out / Cleared Out	
	SHIP ID#	Registry Location							State / Country	Departure		State / Country	Departure	
		Source							Notes					

M-S-058	1720	Hope	Sloop		Thomas	Jacobs Jr.	Start	New York	XX 5 Apr 1720 XX	>	Suriname		M-S-058
S-H-033 <	M-J-018								[23 May 1720]				S-H-033
Page # 71	S-H-033							[New York]	[6 Jun 1720]		[South America]		Page # 71
							>	New York	4 Nov 1720				
									XX (13 Feb 1721) XX				
								[New York]	XXXXXXXXXXXXXX				
									XXXXXXXXXXXXXX				
		5:56,60,125											

	1720	Hope	Sloop		Abraham	Santford	Start	Suriname		>	New York	5 Apr 1720	M-J-018
	M-S-058											XX [23 May 1720] XX	S-H-033
	S-H-033							[South America]			[New York]	XXXXXXXXXXXXXX	Page # 71
												XXXXXXXXXXXXXX	
	XXXXXXXXXX XXXXXXXXXX Captain / Master Relieved And Then Retook Command XXXXXXXXXX XXXXXXXXXX												
							Start	New York	XX 4 Nov 1720 XX	>	St Christopher		
									(13 Feb 1721)				
								[New York]	[20 Mar 1721]		[Leeward Islands]		
							>	New York	10 Jul 1721	>	Jamaica		
									[31 Jul 1721]				
								[New York]	[14 Aug 1721]		[Greater Antilles]		
							[>]	Barbados		>	New York	17 Oct 1721	
												[5 Dec 1721]	
M-J-018								[Lesser Antilles]			[New York]	(19 Dec 1721)	
S-H-033 <							>	Barbados		[>]	Jamaica		
Page # 71								[Lesser Antilles]			[Greater Antilles]		
							28 Days	New York	1 Apr 1722	>	Barbados		
									[16 Apr 1722]				
								[New York]			[Lesser Antilles]		
							>	New York	20 Jul 1722	>	Barbados		
									[30 Jul 1722]				
								[New York]	[20 Aug 1722]		[Lesser Antilles]		
							>	New York	3 Nov 1722	>	Barbados		
									(5 Feb 1723)				
								[New York]	(18 Feb 1723)		[Lesser Antilles]		
							>	New York	23 Apr 1723	>	Jamaica		
									[6 May 1723]				
								[New York]	[27 May 1723]		[Greater Antilles]		
		5:36 / 6:20,32,79,87,92,122,144,148 / 7:40,45,89,92,96,98,130 / 8:16,21,45,50,60											

4	Year	Name	Type	Burden	First Name	Last Name	Length	Port	Custom In / Entered Out	Length	Port	Custom In / Entered Out	72
	MSTR ID#	Registry Location						State / Country	Custom Out / Cleared Out		State / Country	Custom Out / Cleared Out	
	SHIP ID#								Departure			Departure	
		Source							Notes				

	1720 – 1722	Huntington	Sloop		John	Vanbrugh / Van Brugh / Vanbrugn / Vanbrough	Start	Saltertuda		20 Days	New York	20 Apr 1720 [2 May 1720]
	M-V-015							[Location Unkn]			[New York]	[9 May 1720]
	S-H-034											
							>	Barbados		20 Days	New York	31 Jul 1720 [15 Aug 1720]
								[Lesser Antilles]			[New York]	[29 Aug 1720]
							>	Barbados		>	New York	2 Nov 1720 [21 Nov 1720]
								[Lesser Antilles]			[New York]	(19 Dec 1720)
							>	Madeira Island		9 Weeks	New York	29 Apr 1721 [7 May 1721]
								[Portugal]			[New York]	[22 May 1721]
							>	Barbados		23 Days	New York	4 Aug 1721 [14 Aug 1721]
								[Lesser Antilles]			[New York]	
							>	Barbados		17 Days	New York	3 Nov 1721 (26 Feb 1722)
								[Lesser Antilles]			[New York]	[19 Mar 1722]
							>	Barbados		>	New York	30 May 1722 [11 Jun 1722]
								[Lesser Antilles]			[New York]	[18 Jun 1722]
							>	Barbados		>	New York	7 Sept 1722 XX [26 Nov 1722] XX
								[Lesser Antilles]			[New York]	XXXXXXXXXXXXXX XXXXXXXXXXXXXX

XXXXXXXXX XXXXXXXXX Captain / Master Changed Ships XXXXXXXXX XXXXXXXXX

	1722 – 1723	Barbados Packet	Sloop				Start	New York	[10 Dec 1722]	>	Barbados	
								[New York]	(24 Dec 1722)		[Lesser Antilles]	
	S-B-034											
							20 Days	New York	23 Mar 1723 [1 Apr 1723]	>	Barbados	
								[New York]	[8 Apr 1723]		[Lesser Antilles]	
							23 Days	New York	14 Jul 1723 [29 Jul 1723]	>	Barbados	
								[New York]	[12 Aug 1723]		[Lesser Antilles]	

5:40,41,45,50,85,90,94,125,133 / 6:4,44,46,90,92,130 / 7:26,34,67,70,74,108,144,151 / 8:32,34,78,88 / 26:177,193

	1722	Huntington	Sloop		Matthew	Gleaves	Start	New York	XX 7 Sept 1722 XX [26 Nov 1722]	>	Barbados	
	M-G-031							[New York]	[10 Dec 1722]		[Lesser Antilles]	
	S-H-034											
							>	New York				
								[New York]				

7:138,144 / 8:32

Source 8:32 – Has not arrived by 23 Mar 1723

Interact	Year	Name	Type	Burden	First Name	Last Name	Passage Length	Port / State·Country	Arrival / Entered Inwards · Custom In/Entered Out · Custom Out/Cleared Out · Departure	Passage Length	Port / State·Country	Arrival / Entered Inwards · Custom In/Entered Out · Custom Out/Cleared Out · Departure	Page
5													73

Ship: Thomas & Mary — Schooner — MSTR ID# M-B-069 — SHIP ID# S-T-017

Year	First Name	Last Name	Passage Length	Port 1	Dates 1	Passage Length 2	Port 2	Dates 2	Link
1721 – 1723	John	Brown	Start	South Carolina		7 Days	New York / [New York]	7 May 1721 / [23 Oct 1721] / [6 Nov 1721]	
			>	Barbados / [Lesser Antilles]		[>]	Anguilla / [Leeward Islands]		
			>	New York / [New York]	21 Feb 1722 (12 Mar 1722)	>	St Thomas / [Virgin Islands]		> M-L-031 / S-T-017 / Page # 73
			>	New York / [New York]	20 Jun 1722 [2 Jul 1722] [16 Jul 1722]	>	St Thomas / [Virgin Islands]		
			>	New York / [New York]	[15 Oct 1722] [21 Oct 1722] [19 Nov 1722]	>	St Thomas / [Virgin Islands]		
			29 Days	New York / [New York]	30 Jan 1723 XX (4 Mar 1723) XX XXXXXXXXXXXXX XXXXXXXXXXXXX				

XXXXXXXXXX XXXXXXXXXX Captain / Master Relieved And Then Retook Command XXXXXXXXXX XXXXXXXXXX

SHIP ID# S-T-017 (link: M-L-031 / S-T-017 / Page # 73)

Year	Passage Length	Port 1	Dates 1	Passage Length 2	Port 2	Dates 2
1723	Start	New York / [New York]	XX 7 Jun 1723 XX [17 Jun 1723] [1 Jul 1723]	>	St Thomas / [Virgin Islands]	
	>	New York / [New York]	15 Sept 1723 [28 Oct 1723] [25 Nov 1723]	>	St Thomas / [Virgin Islands]	

Source: 6:46,122,130 / 7:26,32,75,79,85,122,136 / 8:15,68,73,100,118,130 / 20:82

Ship: Thomas & Mary — Schooner — MSTR ID# M-L-031 — SHIP ID# S-T-017 (link: M-B-069 / S-T-017 / Page # 73)

Year	First Name	Last Name	Passage Length	Port 1	Dates 1	Passage Length 2	Port 2	Dates 2	Link
1723	Henry	Lawrence	Start	New York / [New York]	XX 30 Jan 1723 XX (4 Mar 1723) [25 Mar 1723]	>	St Thomas / [Virgin Islands]		> M-B-069 / S-T-017 / Page # 73
			>	New York / [New York]	7 Jun 1723 XX [17 Jun 1723] XX XXXXXXXXXXXXX XXXXXXXXXXXXX				

XXXXXXXXXX XXXXXXXXXX Captain / Master Changed Ships XXXXXXXXXX XXXXXXXXXX

Ship: Judith — Sloop — SHIP ID# S-J-024

Year	Passage Length	Port 1	Dates 1	Passage Length 2	Port 2	Dates 2
1723	Start	New York / [New York]	[25 Nov 1723] (31 Dec 1723)	>	Jamaica / [Greater Antilles]	

Source: 8:24,32,65,130,142

MSTR ID# / SHIP ID#	Registry Location		First Name	Last Name	Length	State / Country	Custom In / Entered Out / Custom Out / Cleared Out / Departure	Length	State / Country	Custom In / Entered Out / Custom Out / Cleared Out / Departure	
	Source						Notes				
1721 – 1722 M-H-044 S-S-068	Sunderland	Ship	Thomas	Hopkins	Start	New York [New York]	(13 Feb 1721) [17 Apr 1721]	>	Jamaica [Greater Antilles]		
					[>]	London [England]	[? Jan 1722]	>	Downs [England]	25 Feb 1722	> M-W-040 S-S-068 Page # 74
					>	New York [New York]	20 Apr 1722 XX [7 May 1722] XX XXXXXXXXXXXXXX XXXXXXXXXXXXXX				
	6:20,40 / 7:8,47					(Known Passengers / Passengers) New York / Inward – 20 Apr 1722 – Count 25+					
1722 – 1723 M-W-040 S-S-068	Sunderland	Ship	Joseph	Wilson	Start	New York [New York]	XX 20 Apr 1722 XX [7 May 1722] [18 Jun 1722] 19 Jun 1722	>	Sandy Hook [New Jersey]	20 Jun 1722	
					>	London [England]		>	New York [New York]	[12 Nov 1722] [24 Dec 1722] [24 Dec 1722]	
					>	London [England]		>	Lymington [England]	17 Mar 1723	M-H-044 S-S-068 Page # 74 <
					>	New York [New York]	17 May 1723 [27 May 1723] [24 Jun 1723]	>	London [England]	4 Aug 1723 20 Sept 1723	
					>	New York [New York]	11 Nov 1723				
	7:54,60,63,74,122,132,151,152 / 8:58,60,65,70,109,128										

Interact	Ship				Captain / Master		Passage	Arrival / Departure 1		Passage	Arrival / Departure 2		Page
	Year	Name	Type	Burden	First Name	Last Name	Length	Port	Arrival / Entered Inwards	Length	Port	Arrival / Entered Inwards	
									Custom In / Entered Out			Custom In / Entered Out	
7	MSTR ID#	Registry Location							Custom Out / Cleared Out			Custom Out / Cleared Out	75
	SHIP ID#							State / Country	Departure		State / Country	Departure	
	Source							Notes					

Record 1

	Year	Name	Type	MSTR/SHIP ID#	First Name	Last Name	Passage	Port (Arr/Dep 1)	State/Country	Dates 1	Passage 2	Port (Arr/Dep 2)	State/Country	Dates 2
■	1722	Hannah	Sloop	M-S-059 / S-H-035	William	Smith	Start	New Providence	[Bahamas]		14 Days	New York	[New York]	10 Feb 1722
							[>]		Bahamas		>	New York	[New York]	20 Apr 1722 / [30 Apr 1722]
							>	New Providence	[Bahamas]		12 Days	New York	[New York]	16 Jun 1722 / XX [25 Jun 1722] XX / XXXXXXXXXXXXXX / XXXXXXXXXXXXXX

> M-S-060 / S-H-035 / Page # 75

Source: 7:20,47,52,73

Notes: (Known Passengers / Passengers) New York / Inward – 16 Jun 1722 – Count 1+

Record 2

	Year	Name	Type	MSTR/SHIP ID#	First Name	Last Name	Passage	Port (Arr/Dep 1)	State/Country	Dates 1	Passage 2	Port (Arr/Dep 2)	State/Country	Dates 2
■	1720 – 1721	Mermaid / Maremaid	Sloop	M-S-060 / S-M-062	Burger	Sipkins	Start	Curacao	[Leeward Antilles]		>	St Thomas	[Virgin Island]	
							>	New York	[New York]	16 Apr 1720 / [23 May 1720] / [13 Jun 1720]	>	Jamaica	[Greater Antilles]	
							[>]	Charles Town	[South Carolina]	[? Aug 1720]	>	New York	[New York]	[5 Sept 1720] / [12 Sept 1720] / [3 Oct 1720]
							>		South Carolina		[>]	Barbados	[Lesser Antilles]	
							>	New York	[New York]	11 Apr 1721 / [24 Apr 1721] / XXXXXXXXXXXXXX / XXXXXXXXXXXXXX	>	Barbados (Never Left For Port)	[Lesser Antilles] (See Next Ship Or Captain)	

XXXXXXXXXX XXXXXXXXXX Captain / Master Changed Ships XXXXXXXXXX XXXXXXXXXX

Record 3

	Year	Name	Type	SHIP ID#	First Name	Last Name	Passage	Port (Arr/Dep 1)	State/Country	Dates 1	Passage 2	Port (Arr/Dep 2)	State/Country	Dates 2
	1721	Mary	Sloop	S-M-061			Start	New York	[New York]	XXXXXXXXXXXXXX / XXXXXXXXXXXXXX / [7 May 1721]	>	Barbados	[Lesser Antilles]	

XXXXXXXXXX XXXXXXXXXX Captain / Master Changed Ships XXXXXXXXXX XXXXXXXXXX

Record 4

	Year	Name	Type	SHIP ID#	First Name	Last Name	Passage	Port (Arr/Dep 1)	State/Country	Dates 1	Passage 2	Port (Arr/Dep 2)	State/Country	Dates 2
	1722 – 1723	Hannah	Sloop	S-H-035			Start	New York	[New York]	XX 16 Jun 1722 XX / [25 Jun 1722] / [2 Jul 1722]	>	Antigua	[Leeward Islands]	
							>	New York	[New York]	26 Sept 1722 / [3 Dec 1722] / [10 Dec 1722]	>	Bermuda		
							[>]	Curacao	[Leeward Antilles]	[? Feb 1723] / Taken / Pirates	>	Curacao	[Leeward Antilles]	Taken / In Fight of the Island
							>	Curacao	[Leeward Antilles]	[? Feb 1723] / Retaken / Pirates				

M-S-059 / S-H-035 / Page # 75 <

Source: 5:38,56,63,88,96,99,110 / 6:40,42,46 / 7:76,79,114,144 / 8:26

Interact	Ship				Captain / Master		Passage	Arrival / Departure 1		Passage	Arrival / Departure 2		Page
	Year	Name	Type	Burden	First Name	Last Name	Length	Port	Arrival / Entered Inwards	Length	Port	Arrival / Entered Inwards	
8	MSTR ID#	Registry Location							Custom In / Entered Out			Custom In / Entered Out	76
	SHIP ID#							State / Country	Custom Out / Cleared Out		State / Country	Custom Out / Cleared Out	
		Source							Departure			Departure	
									Notes				

	1720	Sweet Fancy	Sloop		James	Davis	Start	St Christopher		>	New York	27 Aug 1720	
	M-D-028											[19 Sept 1720]	
	S-S-069							[Leeward Islands]			[New York]	XX [26 Sept 1720] XX	> M-D-029 / S-S-069 / Page # 76
												XXXXXXXXXXXXXX	
							>	St Christopher	Never Left For Port				
								[Leeward Islands]	See Next Ship Or Captain				
		5:94,103											

M-D-028 / S-S-069 / Page # 76	<	1720	Sweet Fancy	Sloop		Isa.	Davis	Start	New York	XXXXXXXXXXXXXX	>	St Christopher	
		M-D-029								XX [19 Sept 1720] XX			
		S-S-069							[New York]	[26 Sept 1720]		[Leeward Islands]	
			5:107										

Interact	Ship				Captain / Master		Passage	Arrival / Departure 1		Passage	Arrival / Departure 2		Page
	Year	Name	Type	Burden	First Name	Last Name	Length	Port	Arrival / Entered Inwards	Length	Port	Arrival / Entered Inwards	
9	MSTR ID#	Registry Location							Custom In / Entered Out			Custom In / Entered Out	76
	SHIP ID#							State / Country	Custom Out / Cleared Out		State / Country	Custom Out / Cleared Out	
		Source							Departure			Departure	
									Notes				

	1722	Bermuda	Sloop		William	Burrows	Start	Bay of Honduras		>	New York	[14 May 1722]	
	M-B-070											[28 May 1722]	
	S-B-035										[New York]	[25 Jun 1722]	
							>	Jamaica		[>]	Honduras		> M-T-030 / S-B-035 / Page # 76
								[Greater Antilles]					
							>	New York	[12 Nov 1722]				
									XX (24 Dec 1722) XX				
								[New York]	XXXXXXXXXXXXXX				
									XXXXXXXXXXXXXX				
		7:57,63,76,132											

M-B-070 / S-B-035 / Page # 76	<	1722 – 1723	Bermuda	Sloop		Barnabas	Turhill / Tithill		New York	XX [12 Nov 1722] XX	>	Curacao	
		M-T-030								(24 Dec 1722)			
		S-B-035							[New York]	(8 Jan 1723)		[Leeward Antilles]	
			7:151 / 8:5										

Interact	Ship				Captain / Master		Passage	Arrival / Departure 1		Passage	Arrival / Departure 2		Page
	Year	Name	Type	Burden	First Name	Last Name	Length	Port	Arrival / Entered Inwards	Length	Port	Arrival / Entered Inwards	
10									Custom In / Entered Out			Custom In / Entered Out	77
	MSTR ID#								Custom Out / Cleared Out			Custom Out / Cleared Out	
	SHIP ID#	Registry Location						State / Country	Departure		State / Country	Departure	
		Source							Notes				

	1719 – 1721	Cornelia	Sloop		Thomas	Hook / Hooke	Start	New York	(22 Dec 1719)	>	Curacao		
	M-H-045								(5 Jan 1720)				
	S-C-029							[New York]			[Leeward Antilles]		
							[>]	Jamaica		>	New York	9 May 1720	
												[23 May 1720]	
								[Greater Antilles]			[New York]	[6 Jun 1720]	
							>	Jamaica		>	New York	1 Oct 1720	> M-B-071
												(27 Feb 1721)	S-C-029
								[Greater Antilles]			[New York]	[3 Apr 1721]	Page # 77
							>	Jamaica		>	New York	17 Aug 1721	
												[23 Oct 1721]	
								[Greater Antilles]			[New York]	XX [20 Nov 1721] XX	
												XXXXXXXXXXXXXX	
							>	Jamaica	Never Left For Port				
								[Greater Antilles]	See Next Ship Or Captain				

XXXXXXXXX XXXXXXXXXX Captain / Master Changed Ships XXXXXXXXXX XXXXXXXXXX

	1722	Mary	Sloop				Start	New York	[28 May 1722]	>	Jamaica		
									[18 Jun 1722]				
	S-M-063							[New York]			[Greater Antilles]		

5:4,8,53,56,60,110 / 6:23,34,36,94,122 / 7:63,74

M-H-045	1721 – 1722	Cornelia	Sloop		Phillip / Philip	Boiles	Start	New York	XXXXXXXXXXXXXX	>	Jamaica		
S-C-029	M-B-071								XX [23 Oct 1721] XX				
Page # 77	S-C-029							[New York]	[20 Nov 1721]		[Greater Antilles]		
							>	New York	3 Apr 1722				
								[New York]					

6:137 / 7:42

Interact	Ship				Captain / Master		Passage	Arrival / Departure 1		Passage	Arrival / Departure 2		Page
	Year	Name	Type	Burden	First Name	Last Name	Length	Port	Arrival / Entered Inwards	Length	Port	Arrival / Entered Inwards	
11									Custom In / Entered Out			Custom In / Entered Out	77
	MSTR ID#								Custom Out / Cleared Out			Custom Out / Cleared Out	
	SHIP ID#	Registry Location						State / Country	Departure		State / Country	Departure	
		Source							Notes				

	1720 – 1721	Elizabeth	Sloop		Edward	Evans	Start	St Thomas		20 Days	New York	24 Jul 1720	
	M-E-011											[8 Aug 1720]	
	S-E-037							[Virgin Islands]			[New York]	[22 Aug 1720]	
							>	Nevis					> M-E-012
													S-E-037
								[Leeward Islands]					Page # 77
								NO SUPPORTING DATA TO LINK TIMELINE					
							Start	New York	[25 Sept 1721]	>	Barbados	Never Left For Port	
									XX [2 Oct 1721] XX			See Next Ship Or Captain	
								[New York]	XXXXXXXXXXXXXX		[Lesser Antilles]		

5:82,88,92 / 6:108

M-E-011	1721	Elizabeth	Sloop		David	Evans	Start	New York	XXXXXXXXXXXXXX	>	Barbados		
S-E-037	M-E-012								XX [25 Sept 1721] XX				
Page # 77	S-E-037							[New York]	[2 Oct 1721]		[Lesser Antilles]		

6:111

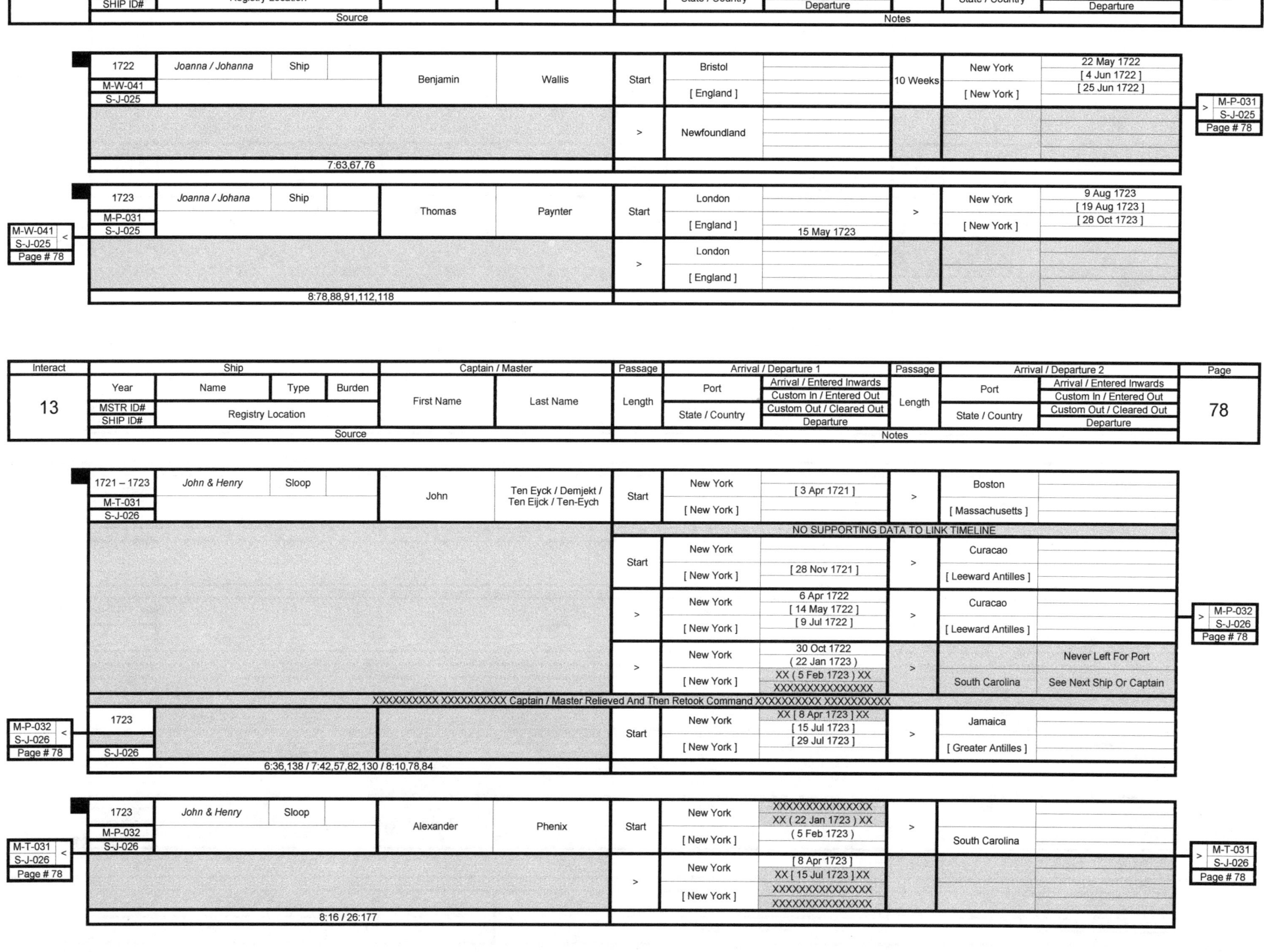

Interact	Ship				Captain / Master		Passage	Arrival / Departure 1		Passage	Arrival / Departure 2		Page
	Year	Name	Type	Burden	First Name	Last Name	Length	Port	Arrival / Entered Inwards / Custom In / Entered Out	Length	Port	Arrival / Entered Inwards / Custom In / Entered Out	
14	MSTR ID#	Registry Location						State / Country	Custom Out / Cleared Out / Departure		State / Country	Custom Out / Cleared Out / Departure	**79**
	SHIP ID#												
	Source							Notes					

	1723	James & Mary	Ship		Robert	Law	Start	Liverpool		1 Week			
M-L-032								[England]			Ireland		> M-P-032 / S-J-028 / Page # 79
S-J-028							10 Weeks	New York	[8 Jul 1723] / XX [22 Jul 1723] XX / XXXXXXXXXXXXXX / XXXXXXXXXXXXXX				
								[New York]					

XXXXXXXXX XXXXXXXXX Captain / Master Changed Ships XXXXXXXXX XXXXXXXXX

	1723	James & Joseph	Snow				Start	New York	(17 Dec 1723)	>	Barbados		
S-J-027								[New York]			[Lesser Antilles]		
8:76,138													

M-T-031 / S-J-028 / Page # 79 <	1723	James & Mary	Ship		David	Agnew	Start	New York	XX [8 Jul 1723] XX / [22 Jul 1723] / [26 Aug 1723]	>	Liverpool		
	M-A-019							[New York]			[England]		
	S-J-028												
8:81,94													

Interact	Ship				Captain / Master		Passage	Arrival / Departure 1		Passage	Arrival / Departure 2		Page
	Year	Name	Type	Burden	First Name	Last Name	Length	Port	Arrival / Entered Inwards / Custom In / Entered Out	Length	Port	Arrival / Entered Inwards / Custom In / Entered Out	
15	MSTR ID#	Registry Location						State / Country	Custom Out / Cleared Out / Departure		State / Country	Custom Out / Cleared Out / Departure	**79**
	SHIP ID#												
	Source							Notes					

	1720 – 1721	Mary	Sloop		Joseph	Wilson	Start	New York	(2 Feb 1720) / (16 Feb 1720) / 9 Feb 1720	>	Jamaica		
M-W-042								[New York]			[Greater Antilles]		
S-M-064							>	New York	9 May 1720 / [20 Jun 1720] / [27 Jun 1720]	>	Jamaica		
								[New York]			[Greater Antilles]		> M-M-039 / S-M-064 / Page # 79
							28 Days	New York	28 Sept 1720 / [24 Oct 1720] / [31 Oct 1720]	>	Jamaica		
								[New York]			[Greater Antilles]		
							22 Days	New York	27 Apr 1721 / XX [29 May 1721] XX / XXXXXXXXXXXXXX / XXXXXXXXXXXXXX				
								[New York]					
5:16,20,50,67,70,110,120,123 / 6:44													

M-W-042 / S-M-064 / Page # 79 <	1721 – 1722	Mary	Sloop		Andrew	Mansfield	Start	New York	XX 27 Apr 1721 XX / [29 May 1721] / [5 Jun 1721]	>	Madeira Island		
	M-M-039							[New York]			[Portugal]		
	S-M-064						>	New York	20 Sept 1721 / [6 Nov 1721] / [20 Nov 1721]	>	Jamaica		
								[New York]			[Greater Antilles]		
							7 Weeks	New York	24 Feb 1722 / (12 Mar 1722) / [19 Mar 1722]	>	Madeira Island		
								[New York]			[Portugal]		
							6 Weeks	New York	15 Jun 1722 / [25 Jun 1722] / [2 Jul 1722]	>	Jamaica		
								[New York]			[Greater Antilles]		
6:56,58,108,130,137 / 7:26,32,34,73,76,79													

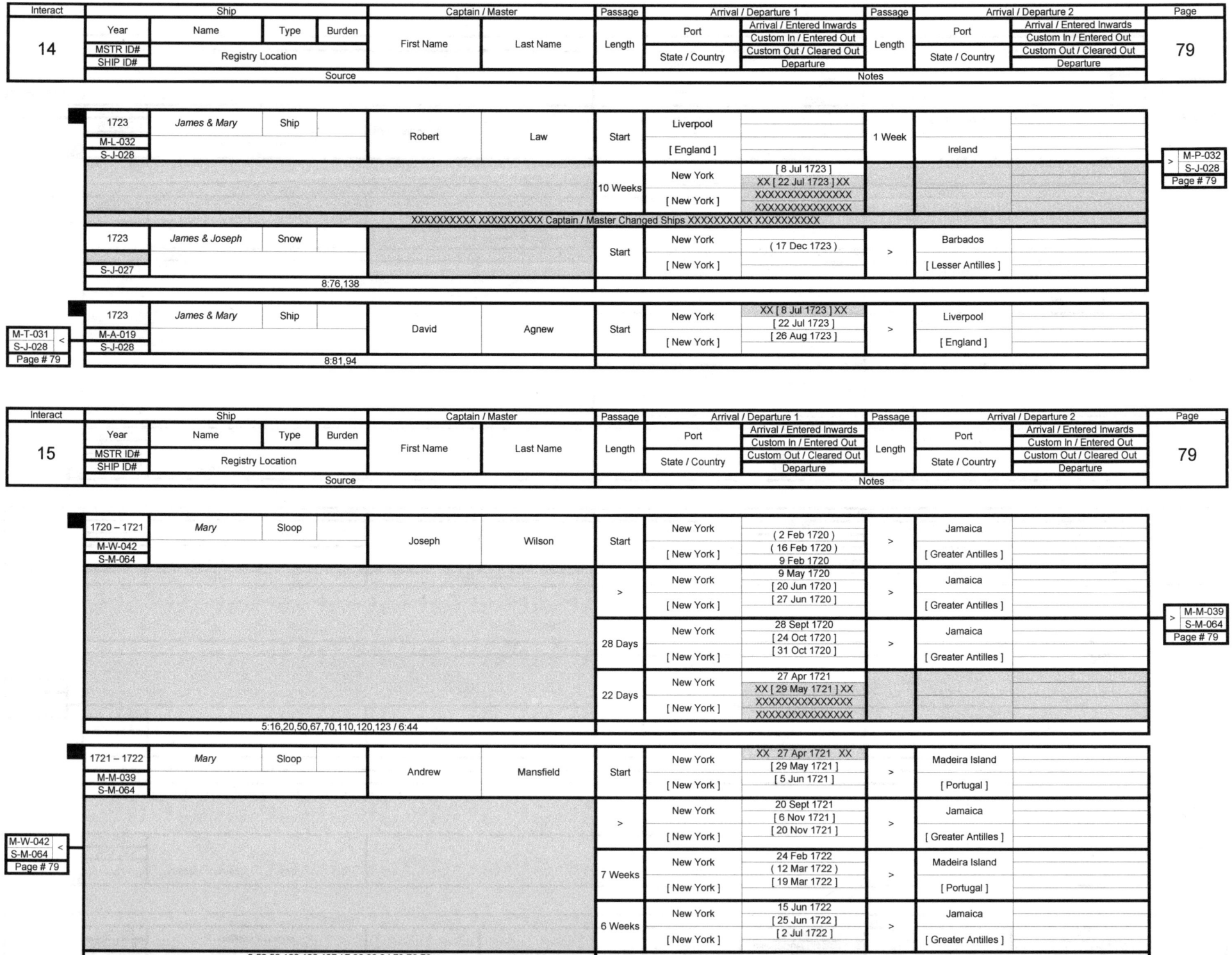

Interact 16 — Page 80

Year	Ship Name	Type	Burden	Captain First	Captain Last	Passage	Arrival/Departure 1 Port	A/D 1 Dates	Passage	Arrival/Departure 2 Port	A/D 2 Dates	Link
1719 / M-M-040 / S-M-065	Mary / Mary Galley	Ship	200 Tons	John	Moulton / Molton	Start	St Christopher [Leeward Islands]		>	St Christopher [Leeward Islands]	23 Dec 1719 / Taken / Spanish Privateer	> M-?-??? / S-M-065 / Page # 80
						>	London [England]	Never Reached Port / Taken / Spanish Privateer				
XXXXXXXXXX XXXXXXXXXX Ship Taken And Then Retook Command XXXXXXXXXX XXXXXXXXXX												
1720 / S-M-065						Start	New York [New York]	XX 19 Jan 1720 XX / [27 Jun 1720] / [22 Aug 1720] / 28 Aug 1720	>	London [England]		
Source: 5:16,38,70,75,78,85,90,92,94							Arrived In New York: 15 Apr 1720 on the Sloop Sarah (S-S-048) / To Retake Command of the Ship Mary Galley				

| 1719 – 1720 / M-M-040 / S-M-065 | Mary / Mary Galley | Ship | 200 Tons | NO CAPTAIN | | Start | St Christopher [Leeward Islands] | 25 Dec 1719 / Retaken / Spanish Privateer | > | New York [New York] | 19 Jan 1720 / XX [27 Jun 1720] XX / XXXXXXXXXXXXXXX / XXXXXXXXXXXXXXX | > M-M-040 / S-M-065 / Page # 80 |

< M-M-040 / S-M-065 / Page # 80 — M-?-??? / S-M-065

Source: 5:16
Ship Retaken By: Captain Hickford (M-H-037) at St Christopher's – Taken to New York for salvage

Interact 17 — Page 80

Year	Ship Name	Type	Burden	Captain First	Captain Last	Passage	A/D 1 Port	A/D 1 Dates	Passage	A/D 2 Port	A/D 2 Dates	Link
1720 / M-H-046 / S-H-036	Hamilton	Sloop		James	Hester	Start	Nevis [Leeward Islands]	17 Jul 1720 / [25 Jul 1720] / [8 Aug 1720]	14 Days	New York [New York]		> M-S-061 / S-H-036 / Page # 80
						>	Nevis [Leeward Islands]					
Source: 5:78,82,88												

1721 – 1723 / M-S-061 / S-H-036	Hamilton	Sloop		George	Sharp / Sharpe	Start	Nevis [Leeward Islands]		>	New York [New York]	[19 Jun 1721] / [26 Jun 1721] / [10 Jul 1721]	
						>	Nevis [Leeward Islands]		>	New York [New York]	[6 Aug 1722] / [13 Aug 1722] / [10 Sept 1722]	
						>	Nevis [Leeward Islands]		>	Boston [Massachusetts]	[8 Jun 1723] / [22 Jun 1723]	
						>	New York [New York]	[8 Jul 1723] / [15 Jul 1723] / [29 Jul 1723]	>	Nevis [Leeward Islands]		

< M-H-046 / S-H-036 / Page # 80

Source: 6:63,67,76 / 7:94,96,108 / 8:76,78 / 20:97,99 / 26:193

Interact	Ship				Captain / Master		Passage	Arrival / Departure 1		Passage	Arrival / Departure 2		Page
	Year	Name	Type	Burden	First Name	Last Name	Length	Port	Arrival / Entered Inwards / Custom In / Entered Out	Length	Port	Arrival / Entered Inwards / Custom In / Entered Out	
18	MSTR ID#								Custom Out / Cleared Out			Custom Out / Cleared Out	81
	SHIP ID#	Registry Location						State / Country	Departure		State / Country	Departure	
	Source							Notes					
	1720	John Galley	Ship		Isaac	Butler	Start	Perth Amboy	[21 Jan 1720]	>	Madeira Island		
	M-B-071								[29 Jan 1720]				
	S-J-029							[New Jersey]			[Portugal]		
							>	New York	29 Jul 1720				
									XX [29 Aug 1720] XX				
								[New York]	XXXXXXXXXXXXXXX				
									XXXXXXXXXXXXXXX				
	XXXXXXXXXX XXXXXXXXXX Captain / Master Changed Ships XXXXXXXXXX XXXXXXXXXX												
	1721	Prophet Elias	Ship				Start	New York	[12 Jun 1721]	>	Antigua		
	S-P-031							[New York]			[Leeward Islands]		
	5:12,16,85 / 6:60 / 23:46,47												
	1720 – 1721	John Galley	Ship		Samuel	Lancolet / Lancelott	Start	New York	XX 29 Jul 1720 XX	>	Jamaica		
	M-L-033								[29 Aug 1720]				
	S-J-029							[New York]	[3 Oct 1720]		[Greater Antilles]	19 Dec 1720	
							>	New York	19 Jan 1721	>	Jamaica	XXXXXXXXXXXXXXX	
									(27 Feb 1721)			XXXXXXXXXXXXXXX	
								[New York]	[3 Apr 1721]		[Greater Antilles]	XXXXXXXXXXXXXXX	
	XXXXXXXXXX XXXXXXXXXX Captain / Master Changed Ships XXXXXXXXXX XXXXXXXXXX												
	1721	Haywood Galley	Ship				Start	Jamaica	XXXXXXXXXXXXXXX	>	New York	11 Aug 1721	
	S-H-037							[Greater Antilles]			[New York]	[28 Aug 1721]	
							>	London					
								[England]					
	5:94,110 / 6:16,23,36,92,96							Only came into New York on 11 Aug 1721 to repair leak					

Side reference boxes:
- (top right) > M-L-033 / S-J-029 / Page # 81
- (left, second entry) M-B-071 / S-J-029 / Page # 81 <

	MSTR ID#		Registry Location		First Name	Last Name	Length	State / Country	Custom In / Entered Out	Length	State / Country	Custom In / Entered Out	
19	SHIP ID#								Custom Out / Cleared Out Departure			Custom Out / Cleared Out Departure	82
			Source						Notes				

	1722 – 1723	*Jolly*	Sloop		John	Theobald / Theobalds / Theohalds	Start	Boston	[31 Mar 1722]	>	New York	[23 Apr 1722]	
	M-T-032							[Massachusetts]	[14 Apr 1722]		[New York]	[14 May 1722]	
	S-J-030												
							>	Boston	[26 May 1722]	>	New York	[18 Jun 1722]	
									[9 Jun 1722]			[16 Jul 1722]	
								[Massachusetts]			[New York]	[23 Jul 1722]	
							>	Boston					
								[Massachusetts]					
									NO SUPPORTING DATA TO LINK TIMELINE				
							Start	Boston	[4 May 1723]	>	New York	6 Aug 1723	> M-C-042
								[Massachusetts]	[27 Jul 1723]		[New York]	XX [19 Aug 1723] XX	S-J-030
												XXXXXXXXXXXXXX	Page # 82
			7:48,57,74,85,89 / 8:88 / 20:35,37,43,45,92,104									XXXXXXXXXXXXXX	

	1722	*Joseph*	Sloop		Elisha	Risden	Start	New York	(15 Jan 1722)	>	North Carolina		
	M-R-026							[New York]	(29 Jan 1722)				
	S-J-031												
							>	New York	11 Apr 1722	>	North Carolina		
								[New York]	[23 Apr 1722]				
							>	New York	20 Jul 1722	>	Boston		> M-C-042
									[17 Sept 1722]				S-J-031
								[New York]	[17 Sept 1722]		[Massachusetts]	[6 Oct 1722]	Page # 82
							>	New York	[15 Oct 1722]				
									XX [11 Mar 1723] XXX				
								[New York]	XXXXXXXXXXXXXX				
									XXXXXXXXXXXXXX				
			7:8,13,45,48,89,110,122 / 20:62										

	1723	*Joseph*	Sloop		Samuel	Crony / Croney	Start	New York	XX [15 Oct 1722] XX	>	Antigua		
M-R-026	M-C-042								[11 Mar 1723]				> M-V-016
S-J-031 <	S-J-031							[New York]	[18 Mar 1723]		[Leeward Islands]		S-J-031
Page # 82													Page # 82
							[>]	Bermuda		>	New York	22 Apr 1723	
												XX [8 Jul 1723] XX	
											[New York]	XXXXXXXXXXXXXX	
												XXXXXXXXXXXXXX	
					XXXXXXXXXX XXXXXXXXX Captain / Master Changed Ships XXXXXXXXX XXXXXXXXX								

	1723	*Jolly*	Sloop				Start	New York	XX 6 Aug 1723 XX	>	Barbados		
M-T-032	S-J-030								[19 Aug 1723]				
S-J-030 <								[New York]	[2 Sept 1723]		[Lesser Antilles]		
Page # 82													
			8:26,28,45,91,96										

	1723	*Joseph*	Sloop		Tunis / Tunes	Vangeider / Vangelder	Start	New York	XX 22 Apr 1723 XX	>	Jamaica		
M-C-042	M-V-016								[8 Jul 1723]				
S-J-031 <	S-J-031							[New York]	[15 Jul 1723]		[Greater Antilles]		
Page # 82													
					XXXXXXXXXX XXXXXXXXX Captain / Master Changed Ships XXXXXXXXX XXXXXXXXX								

	1723	*Adventure*	Sloop				Start	New York	(31 Dec 1723)	>			
	S-A-027							[New York]	(31 Dec 1723)		North Carolina		
			8:76,78,142										

Interact		Year	Name	Type	Burden	First Name	Last Name	Length	Port	Arrival / Entered Inwards / Custom In / Entered Out / Custom Out / Cleared Out	Length	Port	Arrival / Entered Inwards / Custom In / Entered Out / Custom Out / Cleared Out	Page
		MSTR ID#	Registry Location						State / Country	Departure		State / Country	Departure	
20														83

Record 1

	Year	Name	Type	Burden	First Name	Last Name	Length	Port / State	A/D 1 dates	Length	Port / State	A/D 2 dates
	1722	*Unity*	Sloop		David	Carmer	Start	Boston [Massachusetts]		>	New York [New York]	(19 Dec 1721) (12 Feb 1722)
M-C-043 / S-U-003							>	Boston [Massachusetts]	[31 Mar 1722]	>	Rhode Island	> M-B-072 / S-U-003 / Page # 83
							>	New York [New York]	[23 Apr 1722] [30 Apr 1722] XXXXXXXXXXXXXX XXXXXXXXXXXXXX	>	Boston [Massachusetts]	Never Left For Port / See Next Ship Or Captain

XXXXXXXXXX XXXXXXXXXX Captain / Master Relieved And Then Retook Command XXXXXXXXXX XXXXXXXXXX

	Year						Length	Port / State	A/D 1	Length	Port / State	A/D 2
M-B-072 / S-U-003 / Page # 83	1722 – 1723	S-U-003					Start	Boston [Massachusetts]	XXXXXXXXXXXXXX	>	New York [New York]	4 Nov 1722 (4 Mar 1723) XX [11 Mar 1723] XX XXXXXXXXXXXXXX > M-S-062 / S-U-003 / Page # 84
							>	Boston [Massachusetts]	Never Left For Port / See Next Ship Or Captain			

XXXXXXXXXX XXXXXXXXXX Captain / Master Relieved And Then Retook Command XXXXXXXXXX XXXXXXXXXX

	Year						Length	Port / State	A/D 1	Length	Port / State	A/D 2
M-E-013 / S-U-003 / Page # 84	1723	S-U-003					Start	Boston [Massachusetts]	XXXXXXXXXXXXXX XXXXXXXXXXXXXX	>	New York [New York]	[3 Dec 1723]

Source: 6:148 / 7:20,48,52,130 / 8:24,134 / 20:35

Record 2

	Year	Name	Type	Burden	First Name	Last Name	Length	Port / State	A/D 1	Length	Port / State	A/D 2
	1722	*Unity*	Sloop		Samuel	Broadhurst / Brodhurst	Start	New York [New York]	XXXXXXXXXXXXXX XXXXXXXXXXXXXX	>	Boston [Massachusetts]	[12 May 1722] [12 May 1722]
M-B-072 / S-U-003												
M-C-043 / S-U-003 / Page # 83							>	New York [New York]	[4 Jun 1722] [11 Jun 1722] [25 Jun 1722]	>	Boston [Massachusetts]	[7 Jul 1722]
							>	New York [New York]	[30 Jul 1722] [3 Sept 1722]	>	Boston [Massachusetts]	[8 Sept 1722] > M-C-043 / S-U-003 / Page # 83
							>	New York [New York]	14 Sept 1722 [1 Oct 1722] [1 Oct 1722]	>	Boston [Massachusetts]	XXXXXXXXXXXXXX XXXXXXXXXXXXXX XXXXXXXXXXXXXX

XXXXXXXXXX XXXXXXXXXX Captain / Master Relieved And Then Retook Command XXXXXXXXXX XXXXXXXXXX

	Year						Length	Port / State	A/D 1	Length	Port / State	A/D 2
M-S-062 / S-U-003 / Page # 84	1723	S-U-003					Start	New York [New York]	XX [1 Jul 1723] XX [8 Jul 1723] [15 Jul 1723]	>	Boston [Massachusetts]	[27 Jul 1723] [3 Aug 1723]
							>	New York [New York]	6 Aug 1723 XX [16 Sept 1723] XX XXXXXXXXXXXXXX XXXXXXXXXXXXXX			> M-E-013 / S-U-003 / Page # 84

Source: 7:67,70,76,92,105,110,114 / 8:76,78,88 / 20:41,49,58,104,105

Year / MSTR ID# / SHIP ID#	Name	Type	Burden	First Name	Last Name	Length	Port / State-Country	Arrival / Custom In / Custom Out / Departure	Length	Port / State-Country	Arrival / Custom In / Custom Out / Departure
1723 / M-S-062 / S-U-003	Unity	Sloop		Bartholemew	Skaats / Skaars	Start	New York / [New York]	XXXXXXXXXXXXXX / XX (4 Mar 1723) XX / [11 Mar 1723]	>	Boston / [Massachusetts]	[23 Mar 1723] / [23 Mar 1723] / [6 Apr 1723]
						>	New York / [New York]	[15 Apr 1723] / [6 May 1723] / [13 May 1723]	>	Boston / [Massachusetts]	[1 Jun 1723] / [1 Jun 1723] / [8 Jun 1723]
						>	New York / [New York]	[1 Jul 1723] / XX [8 Jul 1723] XX / XXXXXXXXXXXXXX / XXXXXXXXXXXXXX			

Source: 8:26,39,45,50,54,73 / 20:86,88,96,97

Year / MSTR ID# / SHIP ID#	Name	Type	Burden	First Name	Last Name	Length	Port / State-Country	Arrival / Custom In / Custom Out / Departure	Length	Port / State-Country	Arrival / Custom In / Custom Out / Departure
1723 / M-E-013 / S-U-003	Unity	Sloop		John	English / Inglish	Start	New York / [New York]	XX 6 Aug 1723 XX / [16 Sept 1723] / [30 Sept 1723]	>	Boston / [Massachusetts]	[19 Oct 1723] / XXXXXXXXXXXXXX / XXXXXXXXXXXXXX
						>	New York / [New York]	Never Left For Port / See Next Ship Or Captain			

Source: 8:100,106 / 20:116

Interact	Year	Name	Type	Burden	First Name	Last Name	Passage Length	Port	Arrival / Departure 1	Passage Length	Port	Arrival / Departure 2	Page
	MSTR ID#												
	SHIP ID#	Registry Location						State / Country			State / Country		
	Source								Notes				
21													85

Friendship (Sloop) — M-O-008 / S-F-015 — 1720–1722

Captain: Richard Oivian / Tivian / Vivian			
Passage Length	Port 1	Arrival/Departure 1	Port 2 / Arrival/Departure 2
Start	New York / [New York]	[16 May 1720] / XXXXXXXXXXXXXX / XXXXXXXXXXXXXX	> St Thomas / [Virgin Islands] — Never Left For Port / See Next Ship Or Captain

XXXXXXXXXX Changed Departure Location XXXXXXXXXX

Passage Length	Port 1	Arrival/Departure 1	Passage Length	Port 2	Arrival/Departure 2
Start	New York / [New York]	XXXXXXXXXXXXXX / XXXXXXXXXXXXXX / [13 Jun 1720]	>	Curacao / [Leeward Antilles]	
>	New York / [New York]	15 Aug 1720 / [22 Aug 1720] / [29 Aug 1720]	>	Curacao / [Leeward Antilles]	
[>]	New York / [New York]	[28 Nov 1720] / (2 Jan 1721)	>	Barbados / [Lesser Antilles]	
[>]	Curacao / [Leeward Antilles]		>	New York / [New York]	24 Mar 1721 / [1 May 1721] / [7 May 1721]
>	Barbados / [Lesser Antilles]		[>]	New York / [New York]	[24 Jul 1721] / [7 Aug 1721]
>	Curacao / [Leeward Antilles]		[>]	Jamaica / [Greater Antilles]	
>	New York / [New York]	26 Nov 1721 / (26 Feb 1722) / (12 Mar 1722)	>	Curacao / [Leeward Antilles]	
25 Days	New York / [New York]	16 Jun 1722 / XX [20 Aug 1722] XX / XXXXXXXXXXXXXX / XXXXXXXXXXXXXX			

> M-M-041 / S-F-015 / Page # 86

Source: 5:53,63,92,94,136 / 6:8,34,44,46,84,90,138 / 7:26,32,73

Charlotte (Pink) — M-L-034 / S-C-030 — 1720

Captain: Andrew Law			
Passage Length	Port 1	Arrival/Departure 1	Passage Length	Port 2	Arrival/Departure 2
---	---	---	---	---	---
Start	New York / [New York]	(14 Mar 1720) / [28 Mar 1720]	>	Barbados / [Lesser Antilles]	
[>]	St Thomas / [Virgin Islands]		17 Days	New York / [New York]	23 Jun 1720 / XX [11 Jul 1720] XX / XXXXXXXXXXXXXX / XXXXXXXXXXXXXX

> M-M-041 / S-C-030 / Page # 86

XXXXXXXXXX XXXXXXXXXX Captain / Master Changed Ships XXXXXXXXXX XXXXXXXXXX

Rachael / Rachel (Brigantine) — S-R-018 — 1720

Passage Length	Port 1	Arrival/Departure 1	Passage Length	Port 2	Arrival/Departure 2
Start	New York / [New York]	[17 Oct 1720] / [28 Nov 1720]	>	Jamaica / [Greater Antilles]	

Source: 5:27,32,70,115,136

	MSTR ID#		Registry Location		First Name	Last Name	Length	State / Country	Custom In / Entered Out	Length	State / Country	Custom Out / Cleared Out	
	SHIP ID#								Custom Out / Cleared Out			Departure	
			Source						Departure		Notes		
M-L-034 S-C-030 Page # 85	<	1720 M-M-041 S-C-030	*Charlotte*	Pink	John	Mutlow / Mutlaw	Start	New York	XX 23 Jun 1720 XX [11 Jul 1720]	>		
								[New York]	[26 Sept 1720]		Holland	
					XXXXXXXXXX XXXXXXXXXX Captain / Master Changed Ships XXXXXXXXXX XXXXXXXXXX							
M-O-008 S-F-015 Page # 85	<	1722 – 1723 S-F-015	*Friendship*	Sloop			Start	New York	XX 16 Jun 1722 XX [20 Aug 1722]	>	Curacao	
								[New York]	[3 Sept 1722]		[Leeward Antilles]	
							>	New York	[12 Nov 1722] (4 Mar 1723)	>	Curacao	
								[New York]	[11 Mar 1723]		[Leeward Antilles]	
					XXXXXXXXXX XXXXXXXXXX Captain / Master Changed Ships XXXXXXXXXX XXXXXXXXXX							
		1723 S-B-036	*Burnet*	Sloop			Start	New York	[18 Nov 1723]	>	St Thomas	
								[New York]	[25 Nov 1723]		[Virgin Islands]	
			5:75,107 / 7:98,105,132 / 8:24,26,128,130									

Interact	Ship				Captain / Master		Passage	Arrival / Departure 1		Passage	Arrival / Departure 2		Page
	Year	Name	Type	Burden	First Name	Last Name	Length	Port	Arrival / Entered Inwards	Length	Port	Arrival / Entered Inwards	
22									Custom In / Entered Out			Custom In / Entered Out	87
	MSTR ID#	Registry Location						State / Country	Custom Out / Cleared Out		State / Country	Custom Out / Cleared Out	
	SHIP ID#								Departure			Departure	
	Source							Notes					

1720 – 1721	*Speedwell*	Sloop		Alexander	Phenix / Phoenix	Start	New York		>	St Christopher		
M-P-033							[New York]	[22 Aug 1720]		[Leeward Islands]		> M-V-004
S-S-009												S-S-009
												Page # 87
				>	New York	22 Nov 1720 (2 Jan 1721)	>	Curacao		
					[New York]	(16 Jan 1721)		[Leeward Antilles]		
5:92,136 / 6:8,12											

1720	*Warwick*	Sloop		John	Vesey / Vezey	Start	Bermuda		>	New York	12 Jun 1720 (27 Jun 1720)	
M-V-004										[New York]	[4 Jul 1720]	
S-W-022												
						>	Jamaica					
							[Greater Antilles]					
XXXXXXXXXX XXXXXXXXXX Captain / Master Changed Ships XXXXXXXXXX XXXXXXXXXX												
1721 – 1722	*Speedwell*	Sloop				Start	Turks Island		>	Philadelphia	[7 Sept 1721] [14 Sept 1721]	
S-S-009										[Pennsylvania]	[28 Sept 1721]	
M-P-033 <						>	Jamaica		[>]	Anguilla		> M-G-032
S-S-009							[Greater Antilles]			[Leeward Islands]		S-S-009
Page # 87												Page # 88
						>	New York	[16 Apr 1722] [23 Apr 1722]	>	Curacao		
							[New York]	[7 May 1722]		[Leeward Antilles]		
						[>]	Turks Island		>	New York	28 Jun 1722 XX [13 Aug 1722] XX	
										[New York]	XXXXXXXXXXXXXX XXXXXXXXXXXXXX	
XXXXXXXXXX XXXXXXXXXX Captain / Master Changed Ships XXXXXXXXXX XXXXXXXXXX												
1722	*Warwick*	Sloop				Start	New York	XXXXXXXXXXXXXX [16 Jul 1722]	>	Curacao		
S-W-022							[New York]	[30 Jul 1722]		[Leeward Antilles]		
							NO SUPPORTING DATA TO LINK TIMELINE					
						Start	New York	[3 Dec 1722]	>	Jamaica		
							[New York]	(24 Dec 1722)		[Greater Antilles]		
5:63,70,72 / 6:100,104,108 / 7:45,48,54,79,85,92,144,151											

Year	Name	Type	Burden	First Name	Last Name	Length	Port	Custom In / Entered Out	Length	Port	Custom In / Entered Out
MSTR ID#							State / Country	Custom Out / Cleared Out		State / Country	Custom Out / Cleared Out
SHIP ID#	Registry Location							Departure			Departure
	Source							Notes			
1722	*Endeavor*	Sloop		Francis	Gottier	Start	New York	(15 Jan 1722)	>	Jamaica	
M-G-032							[New York]	(29 Jan 1722)		[Greater Antilles]	
S-E-038											
XXXXXXXXXX XXXXXXXXXX Captain / Master Changed Ships XXXXXXXXXX XXXXXXXXXX											
1722 – 1723	*Speedwell*	Sloop				Start	New York	XX 28 Jun 1722 XX	>	St Thomas	
								[13 Aug 1722]			
S-S-009							[New York]	[20 Aug 1722]		[Virgin Islands]	
						>	New York	[3 Dec 1722]	>	St Thomas	
								(22 Jan 1723)			
M-V-004 <							[New York]	(22 Jan 1723)		[Virgin Islands]	
S-S-009						>	New York	4 Jun 1723	>	Barbados	
Page # 87								[1 Jul 1723]			
							[New York]	[15 Jul 1723]		[Lesser Antilles]	
						[>]	New York	[2 Sept 1723]	>	Bermuda	
								[9 Sept 1723]			
							[New York]				
						>	New York	[3 Dec 1723]			
							[New York]				
	7:8,13,96,98,144 / 8:10,65,73,78,96,98,134										

Interact	Ship				Captain / Master		Passage	Arrival / Departure 1		Passage	Arrival / Departure 2		Page
	Year	Name	Type	Burden	First Name	Last Name	Length	Port	Arrival / Entered Inwards / Custom In / Entered Out	Length	Port	Arrival / Entered Inwards / Custom In / Entered Out	
23	MSTR ID#							State / Country	Custom Out / Cleared Out / Departure		State / Country	Custom Out / Cleared Out / Departure	89
	SHIP ID#	Registry Location											
	Source							Notes					

	1720 – 1721	*Overplus*	Sloop		Benjamin	Conyars / Conyers / Conyards	Start	Anguilla		>	St Thomas		
	M-C-044							[Leeward Islands]			[Virgin Islands]		
	S-O-001												
							>	New York	11 Nov 1720 / [21 Nov 1720] / [28 Nov 1720]	>	St Eustatius		
								[New York]			[Leeward Islands]		> M-T-033 / S-O-001 / Page # 90
							[>]	New York	[1 May 1721] / [15 May 1721]	>	St Eustatius		
								[New York]			[Leeward Islands]		
							[>]	Bermuda					

XXXXXXXXXX XXXXXXXXXX Captain / Master Changed Ships XXXXXXXXXX XXXXXXXXXX

	1721	*Benjamin*	Sloop				Start	Bermuda		>	New York	[6 Nov 1721] / [20 Nov 1721] / (19 Dec 1721)	
											[New York]		
	S-B-037						>	Jamaica		[>]	Tortuga		
								[Greater Antilles]			[Haiti]		
							>	New York	[2 Apr 1722] / [16 Apr 1722]	>	Jamaica		
								[New York]			[Greater Antilles]		
							[>]	Bermuda		>	New York	[6 Aug 1722] / [20 Aug 1722] / [3 Sept 1722]	
											[New York]		
							>	Jamaica		[>]	Tortuga		
								[Greater Antilles]			[Haiti]		
							>	New York	[18 Mar 1723] / [1 Apr 1723] / [8 Apr 1723]	>	Jamaica		
								[New York]			[Greater Antilles]		

5:129,133,136 / 6:44,49,130,137,148 / 7:40,45,94,98,105 / 8:28,34 / 26:177

IDs	Dates	Name	Type		Master Last	Master First	Dir	Port	State/Country	Custom Out / Cleared Out / Departure		Port	State/Country	Custom Out / Cleared Out / Departure
M-T-033 / S-?-082	1721		Sloop		Mansfield	Tucker / Tucke	Start	Saltertuda	[Location Unkn]		>	New York	[New York]	21 Apr 1721
	XXXXXXXXX XXXXXXXXX Captain / Master Changed Ships XXXXXXXXX XXXXXXXXX													
S-O-001	1721 – 1723	Overplus	Sloop				Start	Bermuda			>	New York	[New York]	17 Sept 1721 [9 Oct 1721] [30 Oct 1721]
							>	St Eustatius	[Leeward Islands]		[>]	Bermuda		
							>	New York	[New York]	17 May 1722 [28 May 1722] [11 Jun 1722]	>	Barbados	[Lesser Antilles]	
M-C-044 / S-O-001 / Page # 89								NO SUPPORTING DATA TO LINK TIMELINE						
							Start	Bermuda			>	New York	[New York]	21 May 1723 [3 Jun 1723] [10 Jun 1723]
							>	Jamaica	[Greater Antilles]		[>]	Bermuda		
							>	New York	[New York]	31 Aug 1723 [9 Sept 1723] [16 Sept 1723]	>	Jamaica	[Greater Antilles]	

Source: 6:42,106,114,125 / 7:60,63,70 / 8:60,62,65,96,98,100

Interact	Ship				Captain / Master		Passage	Arrival / Departure 1		Passage	Arrival / Departure 2		Page
	Year	Name	Type	Burden	First Name	Last Name	Length	Port	Arrival / Entered Inwards / Custom In / Entered Out	Length	Port	Arrival / Entered Inwards / Custom In / Entered Out	
24	MSTR ID#							State / Country	Custom Out / Cleared Out / Departure		State / Country	Custom Out / Cleared Out / Departure	91
	SHIP ID#	Registry Location											
	Source							Notes					

	1720	Three Brothers	Sloop		Jacob / Jacobus	Kierstead / Kierfred / Keirftede / Kierstend / Kearstede	Start	New York	[15 Aug 1720] / [5 Sept 1720]	>	Antigua		
	M-K-005							[New York]			[Leeward Islands]		> M-B-073 / S-T-018 / Page # 92
	S-T-018												
							[>]	Anguilla		>	New York	24 Nov 1720 / XX [7 May 1721] XX / XXXXXXXXXXXXXX	
								[Leeward Islands]			[New York]	XXXXXXXXXXXXXX	

XXXXXXXXXX XXXXXXXXXX Captain / Master Changed Ships XXXXXXXXXX XXXXXXXXXX

	1721 – 1723	Two Brothers	Sloop				Start	New York	XXXXXXXXXXXXXX / [24 Jul 1721] / [31 Jul 1721]	>			
	S-T-019							[New York]			South Carolina		
							>	New York	23 Sept 1721 / [2 Oct 1721] / [16 Oct 1721]	>			
								[New York]			South Carolina		

NO SUPPORTING DATA TO LINK TIMELINE

							Start	Boston	[28 Apr 1722]	>	New York	[30 Apr 1722] / [21 May 1722] / [4 Jun 1722]	
								[Massachusetts]			[New York]		
							>	Barbados					
								[Lesser Antilles]					

NO SUPPORTING DATA TO LINK TIMELINE

							Start			>	New York	22 May 1723 / [27 May 1723] / [3 Jun 1723]	
								South Carolina			[New York]		
							>	Curacao		>	New York	1 Aug 1723 / [26 Aug 1723] / [2 Sept 1723]	
								[Leeward Antilles]			[New York]		> M-K-006 / S-T-019 / Page # 91
							>	Jamaica		>	New York	11 Nov 1723 / [3 Dec 1723] / XX (17 Dec 1723) XX / XXXXXXXXXXXXXX	
								[Greater Antilles]			[New York]		
							>	Barbados	Never Left For Port				
								[Lesser Antilles]	See Next Ship Or Captain				

5:90,96,136 / 6:79,84,87,108,111,119 / 7:51,60,67 / 8:60,62,86,94,96,128,134 / 20:39

M-K-005 / S-T-019 / Page # 91 <	1723	Two Brothers	Sloop		Jesse	Kiersteade	Start	New York	XXXXXXXXXXXXXX / XX [3 Dec 1723] XX / (17 Dec 1723)	>	Barbados		
	M-K-006							[New York]			[Lesser Antilles]		
	S-T-019												
	8:138												

Year	Name	Type	Burden	First Name	Last Name	Length	Port	Custom In / Entered Out / Custom Out / Cleared Out / Departure	Length	Port	Custom In / Entered Out / Custom Out / Cleared Out / Departure
MSTR ID#							State / Country			State / Country	
SHIP ID#	Registry Location										
	Source							Notes			
1721 – 1723	Three Brothers	Sloop		Vincent	Bodin / Bodine	Start	New York	XX 24 Nov 1720 XX [7 May 1721]	>	Barbados	
M-B-073							[New York]	[29 May 1721]		[Lesser Antilles]	
S-T-018											
						[>]	St Eustatius		>	New York	[25 Sept 1721] [13 Nov 1721] [28 Nov 1721]
							[Leeward Islands]			[New York]	
						>	Suriname		[>]	Grenada	
							[South America]				
						>	New York	4 Apr 1722 [14 May 1722] [4 Jun 1722]	>	Suriname	
							[New York]			[South America]	
						[>]	St Eustatius		>	New York	[8 Oct 1722] [26 Nov 1722] [10 Dec 1722]
							[Leeward Islands]			[New York]	
						>	Suriname		[>]	St Eustatius	
							[South America]			[Leeward Islands]	
						>	Spanish Town		>	New York	19 Apr 1723 [20 May 1723] [3 Jun 1723]
							[Virgin Islands]			[New York]	
						>	Suriname		[>]	St Eustatius	
							[South America]			[Leeward Islands]	
						>	New York	9 Nov 1723 [3 Dec 1723] (17 Dec 1723)	>	Suriname	
							[New York]			[South America]	

M-K-005
S-T-018
Page # 91

6:46,56,108,132,138 / 7:42,57,67,118,138,144 / 8:42,58,62,126,138

Interact	Ship				Captain / Master		Passage	Arrival / Departure 1		Passage	Arrival / Departure 2		Page
	Year	Name	Type	Burden	First Name	Last Name	Length	Port	Arrival / Entered Inwards / Custom In / Entered Out	Length	Port	Arrival / Entered Inwards / Custom In / Entered Out	
25	MSTR ID#	Registry Location						State / Country	Custom Out / Cleared Out / Departure		State / Country	Custom Out / Cleared Out / Departure	**93**
	SHIP ID#												
	Source							Notes					

	1719	*Elizabeth*	Sloop		James	Coden / Codden	Start			>	New York	13 Dec 1719 (22 Dec 1719)	
	M-C-045							Rhode Island			[New York]		
	S-E-039												
							>	25 Dec 1719 – Cast Upon a Rock		&	Ship & Cargo Saved		
								Passing Through Hell Gate Toward The Sound			Ship & Cargo Was Damaged		
							>						
								Rhode Island					

XXXXXXXXXX XXXXXXXXXX Captain / Master Changed Ships XXXXXXXXXX XXXXXXXXXX

	1720 – 1723	*Mary*	Sloop				Start			>	New York	3 Mar 1720 (14 Mar 1720)	
								Rhode Island			[New York]	[21 Mar 1720]	
	S-M-066												
							>			>	New York		
								Rhode Island	[8 Apr 1720]		[New York]	[23 Apr 1720]	
							>			>	New York	[16 May 1720] [16 May 1720]	
								Rhode Island			[New York]	[23 May 1720]	
							>			>	New York	7 Jun 1720 [20 Jun 1720]	
								Rhode Island			[New York]	[18 Jul 1720]	
							>			>	New York	9-11 Aug 1720 [15 Aug 1720]	
								Rhode Island			[New York]	[22 Aug 1720]	
							>			>	New York	[12 Sept 1720] [12 Sept 1720]	
								Rhode Island			[New York]	[19 Sept 1720]	
							>			>	New York	16 Oct 1720 [24 Oct 1720]	
								Rhode Island			[New York]	[31 Oct 1720]	
							>			>	New York	[21 Nov 1720] [28 Nov 1720]	
								Rhode Island			[New York]	[5 Dec 1720]	
							>			>	New York	(2 Jan 1721) (2 Jan 1721)	
								Rhode Island			[New York]	(2 Jan 1721)	
							>			[>]	New York	(31 Jan 1721)	
								Rhode Island			[New York]	(13 Feb 1721)	
							>			4 Days	New York	27 Feb 1721 [6 Mar 1721]	
								Rhode Island			[New York]	[20 Mar 1721]	

>			>	New York	[10 Apr 1721]
					[17 Apr 1721]
	Rhode Island			[New York]	[17 Apr 1721]
>			[>]	New York	[22 May 1721]
	Rhode Island			[New York]	[29 May 1721]
>			>	New York	12 Jun 1721
					[19 Jun 1721]
	Rhode Island			[New York]	[26 Jun 1721]
>			>	Boston	
	Rhode Island			[Massachusetts]	[15 Jul 1721]
>			>	New York	[7 Aug 1721]
					[7 Aug 1721]
	Rhode Island			[New York]	[14 Aug 1721]
>			>	New York	[4 Sept 1721]
					[11 Sept 1721]
	Rhode Island	[1 Sept 1721]		[New York]	[11 Sept 1721]
>			>	New York	[9 Oct 1721]
					[9 Oct 1721]
	Rhode Island	[29 Sept 1721]		[New York]	[16 Oct 1721]
>			>	New York	[6 Nov 1721]
					[6 Nov 1721]
	Rhode Island			[New York]	[13 Nov 1721]
>			>	New York	[5 Dec 1721]
					(19 Dec 1721)
	Rhode Island			[New York]	(19 Dec 1721)
>			>	New York	(29 Jan 1722)
					(29 Jan 1722)
	Rhode Island			[New York]	(12 Feb 1722)
>			[>]	New York	(12 Mar 1722)
	Rhode Island			[New York]	[19 Mar 1722]
>			[>]	Boston	
	Rhode Island			[Massachusetts]	[14 Apr 1722]
>			>	New York	[30 Apr 1722]
	Rhode Island			[New York]	[14 May 1722]
>			>	New York	6 Jun 1722
					[11 Jun 1722]
	Rhode Island			[New York]	[18 Jun 1722]
>			>	New York	28 Jun 1722
					[2 Jul 1722]
	Rhode Island			[New York]	[9 Jul 1722]
>			>	New York	[30 Jul 1722]
					[30 Jul 1722]
	Rhode Island			[New York]	[6 Aug 1722]

Year	Ship	Type	Captain (First)	Captain (Last)	Status	From / State	Duration	To / State	Dates
					>	/ Rhode Island	>	New York / [New York]	[27 Aug 1722] / [27 Aug 1722] / [3 Sept 1722]
					>	[7 Sept 1722] / Rhode Island	>	New York / [New York]	14 Sept 1722 / [24 Sept 1722] / [1 Oct 1722]
					>	/ Rhode Island	[>]	New York / [New York]	[11 Mar 1723] / [8 Apr 1723]
					>	/ Rhode Island	>	New York / [New York]	23 Apr 1723 / [6 May 1723] / [13 May 1723]
					>	XXXXXXXXXXXXXX XXXXXXXXXXXXXX XXXXXXXXXXXXXX / Rhode Island			

XXXXXXXXXX XXXXXXXXXX Captain / Master Changed Ships XXXXXXXXXX XXXXXXXXXX

Year	Ship	Type	Captain (First)	Captain (Last)	Status	From / State	Duration	To / State	Dates
1723	*Hester*	Sloop			Start	XXXXXXXXXXXXXX / Rhode Island	>	New York / [New York]	[17 Jun 1723] / [17 Jun 1723] / [24 Jun 1723]
					>	/ Rhode Island	>	New York / [New York]	[22 Jul 1723] / [22 Jul 1723] / [29 Jul 1723]
					>	/ Rhode Island	>	New York / [New York]	11 Aug 1723 / [19 Aug 1723] / [19 Aug 1723]
					>	Newport / Rhode Island	>	Boston / [Massachusetts]	[7 Sept 1723] / [7 Sept 1723]
					>	Newport / Rhode Island	13 Hours	New York / [New York]	[30 Sept 1723] / [30 Sept 1723] / [7 Oct 1723]
					>	/ Rhode Island	>	New York / [New York]	26 Oct 1723 / [4 Nov 1723] / [4 Nov 1723]
					>	/ Rhode Island	>	New York / [New York]	[3 Dec 1723] / (17 Dec 1723) / (17 Dec 1723)
					>	/ Rhode Island			

5:4,8,26,27,30,38,41,53,56,62,67,78,90,92,99,103,115,120,123,133,136,141 /
6:8,16,20,23,28,32,38,40,52,56,60,63,67,87,90,92,100,103,114,119,130,132,144,148 /
7:13,20,32,34,51,57,67,70,74,79,82,92,94,102,105,110,112,114 /
8:26,45,50,54,68,70,81,84,88,91,106,109,118,122,134,138 / 20:4,10,37,58,110 / 26:177,193

Year	Ship	Type	Captain (First)	Captain (Last)	Status	From / State	Duration	To / State	Dates
1723	*Mary*	Sloop	Joseph	Gray	Start	XXXXXXXXXXXXXX / Rhode Island	>	Perth Amboy / [New Jersey]	[24 Jun 1723]

8:70

M-G-033 / S-M-066 / Page # 95

M-C-045 / S-M-066 / Page # 95 — M-G-033 / S-M-066

Year	Name	Type	Burden	First Name	Last Name	Length	Port State / Country	Custom In / Entered Out / Custom Out / Cleared Out / Departure	Length	Port State / Country	Custom In / Entered Out / Custom Out / Cleared Out / Departure
MSTR ID# / SHIP ID#	Registry Location										
								Source		Notes	
1721 – 1723 / M-S-063 / S-S-069	*Speedwell*	Sloop		Arnold / Arnont / Arnt	Schermerhoorn	Start	New York	[5 Jun 1721]	>	Boston	
							[New York]	[12 Jun 1721]		[Massachusetts]	
						>	New York	[24 Jul 1721]	>	Boston	[2 Sept 1721]
								[31 Jul 1721]			[2 Sept 1721]
							[New York]	[21 Aug 1721]		[Massachusetts]	
						>	New York	[25 Sept 1721]	>	Boston	
								[25 Sept 1721]			
							[New York]	[2 Oct 1721]		[Massachusetts]	
						>	New York	29 Oct 1721	>	Boston	
								[6 Nov 1721]			
							[New York]	[13 Nov 1721]		[Massachusetts]	
						>	New York	(19 Dec 1721)	>	Boston	
								(12 Feb 1722)			
							[New York]	[23 Apr 1722]		[Massachusetts]	[12 May 1722]
						>	New York	19 May 1722	>	Boston	
								[28 May 1722]			
							[New York]	[4 Jun 1722]		[Massachusetts]	[23 Jun 1722]
						>	New York	[9 Jul 1722]	>	Boston	[11 Aug 1722]
								[9 Jul 1722]			[18 Aug 1722]
							[New York]	[30 Jul 1722]		[Massachusetts]	
						>	New York	[27 Aug 1722]	>	Boston	
								[27 Aug 1722]			
							[New York]	[10 Sept 1722]		[Massachusetts]	[22 Sept 1722]
						>	New York	[8 Oct 1722]	>	Boston	
								[8 Oct 1722]			
							[New York]	[15 Oct 1722]		[Massachusetts]	
						>	New York	[10 Dec 1722]	>	Boston	[16 Feb 1723]
								(5 Feb 1723)			
							[New York]	(18 Feb 1723)		[Massachusetts]	[23 Feb 1723]
						>	New York	[11 Mar 1723]	>	Boston	[6 Apr 1723]
								[18 Mar 1723]			
							[New York]	[1 Apr 1723]		[Massachusetts]	[13 Apr 1723]
						>	New York	23 Apr 1723	>	Boston	[8 Jun 1723]
								[6 May 1723]			[8 Jun 1723]
							[New York]	[13 May 1723]		[Massachusetts]	[15 Jun 1723]
						>	New York	[1 Jul 1723]	>	Boston	[3 Aug 1723]
								[1 Jul 1723]			
							[New York]	[22 Jul 1723]		[Massachusetts]	[17 Aug 1723]
						>	New York	23 Aug 1723	>	Boston	[14 Sept 1723]
								[2 Sept 1723]			
							[New York]	[9 Sept 1723]		[Massachusetts]	[21 Sept 1723]
						>	New York	[30 Sept 1723]	>	Boston	[19 Oct 1723]
								[30 Sept 1723]			[26 Oct 1723]
							[New York]	[14 Oct 1723]		[Massachusetts]	
						>	New York	6 Nov 1723			
							[New York]				

6:58,60,84,87,94,108,111,125,130,132,148 / 7:20,45,48,60,63,67,82,92,102,108,118,122,144 /
8:16,21,26,28,34,45,50,54,70,73,81,94,96,98,106,112,126 /
20:4,41,47,54,55,60,81,82,88,89,97,98,105,107,111,112,116,117

M-B-074 / S-S-069 / Page # 97

Interact	Ship				Captain / Master		Passage	Arrival / Departure 1		Passage	Arrival / Departure 2		Page
	Year	Name	Type	Burden	First Name	Last Name	Length	Port	Arrival / Entered Inwards	Length	Port	Arrival / Entered Inwards	
									Custom In / Entered Out			Custom In / Entered Out	
26	MSTR ID#	Registry Location						State / Country	Custom Out / Cleared Out		State / Country	Custom Out / Cleared Out	97
	SHIP ID#								Departure			Departure	
	Source							Notes					

	1720 – 1721	Speedwell	Sloop		John	Beekman	Start	New York	[28 Mar 1720]	>	Boston		
	M-B-074								[11 Apr 1720]				
	S-S-069							[New York]			[Massachusetts]		
							[>]	New York		>	Boston		
									[27 Jun 1720]				
								[New York]			[Massachusetts]		
							[>]	New York	[8 Aug 1720]	>	Boston	[10 Sept 1720]	
									[29 Aug 1720]				
								[New York]			[Massachusetts]		
							>	New York	11 Oct 1720	>	Boston		
									(13 Feb 1721)				
								[New York]	(27 Feb 1721)		[Massachusetts]		
							[>]	New York	[10 Apr 1721]	>	Boston		
									[24 Apr 1721]				
								[New York]			[Massachusetts]		
	5:32,36,70,88,94,106,115 / 6:20,23,38,42												

> | M-S-063 |
> | S-S-069 |
> | Page # 96 |

MSTR ID# / SHIP ID#	Registry Location			First Name	Last Name	Length	State / Country	Custom In / Entered Out	Length	State / Country	Custom Out / Cleared Out
	Source							Custom Out / Cleared Out Departure			Departure
								Notes			
1720 / M-T-034 / S-H-001	Hempsteed / Hamstead	Sloop		John	Tickel / Tickell / Tickle	Start	New York / [New York]	[9 Dec 1719] / (22 Dec 1719)	>	Curacao / [Leeward Antilles]	
						[>]	Jamaica / [Greater Antilles]		>	New York / [New York]	5 May 1720 / [23 May 1720] / [6 Jun 1720] → M-R-004 / S-H-001 / Page # 99
						>	Jamaica / [Greater Antilles]		>	New York / [New York]	22 Nov 1720 / XX (13 Feb 1721) XX / XXXXXXXXXXXXX / XXXXXXXXXXXXX
XXXXXXXXXX XXXXXXXXXX Captain / Master Changed Ships XXXXXXXXXX XXXXXXXXXX											
1721 – 1723 / S-J-032	Jolly	Sloop				Start	New York / [New York]	XXXXXXXXXXXXX / [1 May 1721] / [15 May 1721]	>	South Carolina	
						>	New York / [New York]	13 Jul 1721 / [24 Jul 1721] / [31 Jul 1721]	>	South Carolina	
						[>]	New Providence / [Bahamas]		>	New York / [New York]	7 Nov 1721 / [28 Nov 1721]
						>	Jamaica / [Greater Antilles]		>	New York / [New York]	29 Jun 1722 / [3 Sept 1722] → M-R-027 / S-J-032 / Page # 98
						>	Jamaica / [Greater Antilles]		>	New York / [New York]	9 Dec 1722 / (18 Feb 1723)
						>	Jamaica / [Greater Antilles]		>	New York / [New York]	4 May 1723 / [27 May 1723] / [27 May 1723]
						>	Jamaica / [Greater Antilles]		15 Days	New York / [New York]	11 Aug 1723 / XX [26 Aug 1723] XX / XXXXXXXXXXXXX / XXXXXXXXXXXXX
XXXXXXXXXX XXXXXXXXXX Captain / Master Changed Ships XXXXXXXXXX XXXXXXXXXX											
1723 / S-W-023	William & Thomas	Sloop				Start	New York / [New York]	[4 Nov 1723] / [3 Dec 1723]	>	Jamaica / [Greater Antilles]	
5:2,4,50,56,60,136 / 6:44,49,79,84,87,132,138 / 7:79,105,144 / 8:21,50,60,88,122,134						(Known Passengers / Passengers) New York / Inward – 9 Dec 1722 – Count 3+ - Captain Henry Combs Crew (M-C-010) / Charles – Sloop (S-C-012) - Check Source 7:144 – Page 40 / Philadelphia Book						
1722 / M-R-027 / S-A-027 ← M-F-015 / S-A-027 / Page # 99	Anne & Catherine	Sloop		Phillip / Phil / Philip	Ryley	Start	New York / [New York]	XXXXXXXXXXXXX / XX [6 Aug 1722] XX / [3 Sept 1722]	>	Curacao / [Leeward Antilles]	→ M-F-015 / S-A-027 / Page # 99
						>	New York / [New York]	30 Oct 1722 / XX [12 Nov 1722] XX / XXXXXXXXXXXXX / XXXXXXXXXXXXX			
XXXXXXXXXX XXXXXXXXXX Captain / Master Changed Ships XXXXXXXXXX XXXXXXXXXX											
1723 / S-J-032 ← M-T-034 / S-J-032 / Page # 98	Jolly	Sloop				Start	New York / [New York]	XX 11 Aug 1723 XX / [26 Aug 1723] / [2 Sept 1723]	>	Jamaica / [Greater Antilles]	
7:105,130 / 8:94,96											

Interact	Ship				Captain / Master		Passage	Arrival / Departure 1		Passage	Arrival / Departure 2		Page
	Year	Name	Type	Burden	First Name	Last Name	Length	Port / Arrival / Entered Inwards / Custom In / Entered Out		Length	Port / Custom In / Entered Out		
27	MSTR ID#	Registry Location						Custom Out / Cleared Out			Custom Out / Cleared Out		**99**
	SHIP ID#							State / Country / Departure			State / Country / Departure		
	Source							Notes					

M-T-034 / S-H-001 / Page # 98 <

Year	Name	Type	Burden	First Name	Last Name	Length	Port	Dates	Length	Port	Dates
1721 – 1722	*Hamstead / Hemstead*	Sloop		Thomas	Randal / Randall	Start	New York	XX 22 Nov 1720 XX / (13 Feb 1721) / (27 Feb 1721)	>	Jamaica	
M-R-004							[New York]			[Greater Antilles]	
S-H-001											
						>	New York	19 Jul 1721 / [7 Aug 1721] / [28 Aug 1721]	>	Jamaica	
							[New York]			[Greater Antilles]	
						35 Days	New York	17 Nov 1721 / (29 Jan 1722) / (29 Jan 1722)	>	Jamaica	
							[New York]			[Greater Antilles]	
						>	Philadelphia	[24 May 1722] / [7 Jun 1722]	>	New York	[18 Jun 1722] / [16 Jul 1722] / [30 Jul 1722]
							[Pennsylvania]			[New York]	
						>	Jamaica				
							[Greater Antilles]				

XXXXXXXXX XXXXXXXXX Captain / Master Changed Ships XXXXXXXXX XXXXXXXXX

Year	Name	Type	Burden	First Name	Last Name	Length	Port	Dates	Length	Port	Dates
1723	*Anne & Elizabeth*	Sloop				Start	New York	[3 Jun 1723] / [10 Jun 1723]	>	Curacao	
S-A-028							[New York]			[Leeward Antilles]	

Source: 6:20,23,84,90,96,137 / 7:13,60,68,74,85,92 / 8:62,65

M-R-027 / S-A-027 / Page # 98 <

Year	Name	Type	Burden	First Name	Last Name	Length	Port	Dates	Length	Port	Notes
1722	*Anne & Catherine*	Sloop		John	Fred	Start	New York	[6 Aug 1722] / XX [3 Sept 1722] XX / XXXXXXXXXXXXXX	>	Curacao	Never Left For Port
M-F-015							[New York]			[Leeward Antilles]	See Next Ship Or Captain
S-A-027											

> M-R-027 / S-A-027 / Page # 98

XXXXXXXXX XXXXXXXXX Captain / Master Relieved And Then Retook Command XXXXXXXXX XXXXXXXXX

Year	Name	Type	Burden	First Name	Last Name	Length	Port	Dates	Length	Port	Notes
1722 – 1723						Start	New York	XX 30 Oct 1722 XX / [12 Nov 1722] / [3 Dec 1722]	>	St Thomas	
S-A-027							[New York]			[Virgin Islands]	
						>	New York	18 May 1723 / [27 May 1723] / [3 Jun 1723]	>	Curacao	
							[New York]			[Leeward Antilles]	
						>	New York	5 Aug 1723 / [26 Aug 1723] / [2 Sept 1723]	>	Curacao	
							[New York]			[Leeward Antilles]	
						>	New York	8 Nov 1723 / [25 Nov 1723] / XXXXXXXXXXXXXX / XXXXXXXXXXXXXX	>	Curacao	Never Left For Port
							[New York]			[Leeward Antilles]	See Next Ship Or Captain

XXXXXXXXX Changed Departure Location XXXXXXXXX

Year	Name	Type	Burden	First Name	Last Name	Length	Port	Dates	Length	Port	Notes
						>	New York	XXXXXXXXXXXXXX / XXXXXXXXXXXXXX / (17 Dec 1723)	>	Barbados	
							[New York]			[Lesser Antilles]	

Source: 7:94,132,144 / 8:58,60,62,86,94,96,126,130,138

	Year	Name	Type	Burden	First Name	Last Name	Length	Port	Custom In / Entered Out	Length	Port	Custom In / Entered Out	
28	MSTR ID#							State / Country	Custom Out / Cleared Out		State / Country	Custom Out / Cleared Out	100
	SHIP ID#	Registry Location							Departure			Departure	
		Source							Notes				

	1720	John & Elizabeth	Sloop		Matthew	Furbar / Furber / Turbar	Start	South Carolina		9 Days	New York	22 May 1720	
	M-F-016										[New York]	[6 Jun 1720]	
	S-J-033											[13 Jun 1720]	> M-R-028 / S-J-033 / Page # 102
							[>]	South Carolina		>	New York	12 Aug 1720	
											[New York]	XXXXXXXXXXXXXX	
												XX [29 Aug 1720] XX	
												XXXXXXXXXXXXXX	
		XXXXXXXXX XXXXXXXXX Captain / Master Changed Ships XXXXXXXXX XXXXXXXXX												
M-M-042 / S-L-017 / Page # 100 <	1720	Lucretia / Lacretia / Lucveria	Sloop				Start	New York	XXXXXXXXXXXXXX XX [29 Aug 1720] XX	>	Maryland	XXXXXXXXXXXXXX	
	S-L-017							[New York]	[12 Sept 1720]			XXXXXXXXXXXXXX	
												XXXXXXXXXXXXXX	
		XXXXXXXXX XXXXXXXXX Captain / Master Changed Ships XXXXXXXXX XXXXXXXXX												
	1720 – 1721	South River	Sloop				Start	[South River]	XXXXXXXXXXXXXX	[>]	Virginia		
	S-S-070							[Maryland]					
							13 Days	New York	30 Oct 1720	>	Maryland		> M-M-043 / S-S-070 / Page # 101
								[New York]	[14 Nov 1720]				
									[5 Dec 1720]				
							>	New York	27 May 1721				
								[New York]	XX [10 Jul 1721] XX				
									XXXXXXXXXXXXXX				
									XXXXXXXXXXXXXX				
		XXXXXXXXX XXXXXXXXX Captain / Master Changed Ships XXXXXXXXX XXXXXXXXX												
	1721 – 1722	Catherine	Sloop				Start	New York	XXXXXXXXXXXXXX [23 Oct 1721]	>	South Carolina		
	S-C-031							[New York]	[20 Nov 1721]				> M-B-075 / S-C-031 / Page # 101
							[>]	St Thomas		>	New York	12 Apr 1722	
								[Virgin Islands]			[New York]	XX [23 Apr 1722] XX	
												XXXXXXXXXXXXXX	
												XXXXXXXXXXXXXX	
		XXXXXXXXX XXXXXXXXX Captain / Master Relieved And Then Retook Command XXXXXXXXX XXXXXXXXX												
	1722 – 1723						>	New York	XX 17 Aug 1722 XX [27 Aug 1722]	>	South Carolina		
M-B-075 / S-C-031 / Page # 101 <	S-C-031							[New York]	[8 Oct 1722]				
							>	New York	10 May 1723	>	South Carolina		
								[New York]	[20 May 1723]				
									[3 Jun 1723]				
		5:56,60,63,90,99,123,129,141 / 6:56,122,137 / 7:45,102,118 / 8:54,58,62												

	1719 – 1720	Lucretia / Lacretia / Lucveria	Sloop		John	Moore / Moor / Moare / More	Start	New York	[9 Dec 1719]	>	St Christopher		
	M-M-042							[New York]	(22 Dec 1719)		[Leeward Islands]		
	S-L-017												
							[>]	Antigua		>	New York	2 May 1720	
								[Leeward Islands]			[New York]	[16 May 1720]	
												[6 Jun 1720]	> M-F-016 / S-L-017 / Page # 100
							>	Curacao	16 Aug 1720	>	New York		
								[Leeward Antilles]	[29 Aug 1720]		[New York]	XX [12 Sept 1720] XX	
												XXXXXXXXXXXXXX	
							>		Never Left For Port				
								Maryland	See Next Ship Or Captain				
		5:2,4,50,53,60,92,94												

Interact					Captain / Master		Passage	Arrival / Departure 1		Passage	Arrival / Departure 2		Page
	Year	Name	Type	Burden	First Name	Last Name	Length	Port	Arrival / Entered Inwards / Custom In / Entered Out	Length	Port	Arrival / Entered Inwards / Custom In / Entered Out	
28	MSTR ID#								Custom Out / Cleared Out			Custom Out / Cleared Out	101
	SHIP ID#	Registry Location						State / Country	Departure		State / Country	Departure	
		Source								Notes			

	Year / MSTR ID# / SHIP ID#	Name	Type	Burden	First Name	Last Name	Length	Port / State / Country	Arr/Dep 1	Length	Port / State / Country	Arr/Dep 2
	1720 – 1721 / M-B-075 / S-E-039	Expedition	Sloop		Peter	Bedlow	Start	St Thomas [Virgin Islands]		26 Days	New York [New York]	9 Mar 1720 [28 Mar 1720] [11 Apr 1720]
							>	St Thomas [Virgin Islands]		17 Days	New York [New York]	26 Jun 1720 [11 Jul 1720]
							>	St Thomas [Virgin Islands]		>	New York [New York]	[21 Nov 1720] (19 Dec 1720)
							>	St Thomas [Virgin Islands]		6 Weeks	New York [New York]	16 Mar 1721 [3 Apr 1721] [24 Apr 1721]
							>	St Thomas [Virgin Islands]		>	New York [New York]	20 Jul 1721 [31 Jul 1721] XXXXXXXXXXXXXX XXXXXXXXXXXXXX
							>	St Thomas [Virgin Islands]	Never Left For Port See Next Ship Or Captain			
							XXXXXXXXXX Changed Departure Location XXXXXXXXXX					
							Start	New York [New York]	XXXXXXXXXXXXXX XXXXXXXXXXXXXX [14 Aug 1721]	>	Jamaica [Greater Antilles]	
							[>]	Hispaniola [Greater Antilles]		>	New York [New York]	10 Nov 1721
							XXXXXXXXXX XXXXXXXXXX Captain / Master Changed Ships XXXXXXXXXX XXXXXXXXXX					
M-F-016 < / S-C-031 / Page # 100	1722 / S-C-031	Catherine	Sloop				Start	New York [New York]	XX 12 Apr 1722 XX [23 Apr 1722]	>	Jamaica [Greater Antilles]	
							>	New York [New York]	17 Aug 1722 XX [27 Aug 1722] XX XXXXXXXXXXXXXX XXXXXXXXXXXXXX			
							XXXXXXXXXX XXXXXXXXXX Captain / Master Changed Ships XXXXXXXXXX XXXXXXXXXX					
	1722 / S-S-071	Success	Sloop				Start	New York [New York]	XXXXXXXXXXXXXX [29 Oct 1722] [26 Nov 1722]	>	Jamaica [Greater Antilles]	
	5:26,32,36,70,72,75,133 / 6:4,32,36,42,84,87,92,132 / 7:48,98,126,138											

M-F-016 > / S-C-031 / Page # 100

	Year / MSTR ID# / SHIP ID#	Name	Type	Burden	First Name	Last Name	Length	Port / State / Country	Arr/Dep 1	Length	Port / State / Country	Arr/Dep 2
M-F-016 < / S-S-070 / Page # 100	1721 / M-M-043 / S-S-070	South River	Sloop		Peter	Morgat	Start	New York [New York]	XX 27 May 1721 XX [10 Jul 1721] [31 Jul 1721]	>	Barbados [Lesser Antilles]	
	6:76,87											

	MSTR ID#	Registry Location		First Name	Last Name	Length	State / Country	Custom In / Entered Out	Length	State / Country	Custom In / Entered Out
28	SHIP ID#							Custom Out / Cleared Out Departure			Custom Out / Cleared Out Departure
		Source						Notes			

	1720 – 1723	John & Elizabeth	Sloop		John	Raal / Rail / Rall / Real / Roall	Start	New York	XX 12 Aug 1720 XX	>		
	M-R-028							[New York]	[29 Aug 1720]		South Carolina	
	S-J-033						8 Days	New York	14 May 1721	>		
									[12 Jun 1721]			
								[New York]	[26 Jun 1721]		South Carolina	
							>	New York	4 Aug 1721	[>]	Boston	
								[New York]			[Massachusetts]	[2 Sept 1721]
							>	New York	[18 Sept 1721]	>		
									[25 Sept 1721]			
								[New York]	[9 Oct 1721]		South Carolina	
							>	New York	22 Nov 1721	>	Barbados	
M-F-016									[5 Dec 1721]			
S-J-033 <								[New York]	(19 Dec 1721)		[Lesser Antilles]	
Page # 100							[>]	Tortuga		>	New York	[16 Apr 1722]
												[23 Apr 1722]
								[Haiti]			[New York]	[7 May 1722]
							>	St Thomas		>	New York	[13 Aug 1722]
												[12 Nov 1722]
								[Virgin Islands]			[New York]	[3 Dec 1722]
							>			>	Boston	[8 Jun 1723]
								South Carolina			[Massachusetts]	
							>	New York	[1 Jul 1723]	>	Curacao	
									[8 Jul 1723]			
								[New York]	[22 Jul 1723]		[Leeward Antilles]	
							>	New York	15 Nov 1723	>		
									(17 Dec 1723)			
								[New York]	(31 Dec 1723)		South Carolina	
	5:94 / 6:48,60,67,90,106,108,114,138,144,148 / 7:45,48,54,96,132,144 / 8:73,76,81,128,138,142 / 20:4,97											

Interact												Page
29	**Year**	**Name**	**Type**	**Burden**	**Captain / Master** First Name	Last Name	**Passage** Length	**Arrival / Departure 1** Port / State-Country	Arrival / Entered Inwards · Custom In / Entered Out · Custom Out / Cleared Out · Departure	**Passage** Length	**Arrival / Departure 2** Port / State-Country	Arrival / Entered Inwards · Custom In / Entered Out · Custom Out / Cleared Out · Departure	**103**
	MSTR ID# / SHIP ID# / Registry Location												
	Source							Notes					

Interact	Year	Name	Type	MSTR/SHIP ID	First Name	Last Name	Passage	Port 1	State/Country 1	Dates 1	Passage	Port 2	State/Country 2	Dates 2	Notes	Page/Interact
	1719 – 1720	*Expedition*	Brigantine	M-L-035 / S-E-040	Samuel	Lawrance / Larrance / Laurance / Larrence / Lawrence	Start	New York	[New York]	(22 Dec 1719)	>	Barbados	[Lesser Antilles]			> M-L-036 / S-E-040 / Page #104
							24 Days	New York	[New York]	3 Apr 1720 / [2 May 1720] / XX [16 May 1720] XX / XXXXXXXXXXXX	>	Barbados	[Lesser Antilles]		Never Left For Port / See Next Ship Or Captain	
XXXXXXXXXX XXXXXXXXXX Captain / Master Relieved And Then Retook Command XXXXXXXXXX XXXXXXXXXX																
M-L-036 / S-E-040 / Page # 104 <	1720 – 1721			S-E-040			Start	New York	[New York]	XX 7 Aug 1720 XX / [15 Aug 1720] / [29 Aug 1720]	>	Barbados	[Lesser Antilles]			> M-W-043 / S-E-040 / Page #105
							>	New York	[New York]	24 Nov 1720 / (19 Dec 1720) / (2 Jan 1721)	>	Barbados	[Lesser Antilles]			
							>	New York	[New York]	18 Apr 1721 / [1 May 1721] / [15 May 1721]	>	Barbados	[Lesser Antilles]			
							>	New York	[New York]	30 Jul 1721 / [7 Aug 1721] / [14 Aug 1721]	>	Barbados	[Lesser Antilles]			
							>	New York	[New York]	20 Oct 1721 / XX [5 Dec 1721] XX / XXXXXXXXXXXX / XXXXXXXXXXXX						
XXXXXXXXXX XXXXXXXXXX Captain / Master Changed Ships XXXXXXXXXX XXXXXXXXXX																
M-P-034 / S-H-039 / Page #105 <	1721	*Hope*	Brigantine	S-H-039			Start	New York	[New York]	XXXXXXXXXXXX / XX [30 Oct 1721] XX / [20 Nov 1721]	>	Barbados	[Lesser Antilles]			
XXXXXXXXXX XXXXXXXXXX Captain / Master Changed Ships XXXXXXXXXX XXXXXXXXXX																
M-W-043 / S-E-040 / Page #105 <	1722 – 1723	*Expedition*	Brigantine	S-E-040			Start	Barbados	[Lesser Antilles]		>	New York	[New York]	4 Apr 1722 / [23 Apr 1722] / [14 May 1722]		
							>	Barbados	[Lesser Antilles]		>	New York	[New York]	17 Jul 1722 / [30 Jul 1722] / [20 Aug 1722]		
							>	Barbados	[Lesser Antilles]		>	New York	[New York]	[12 Nov 1722] / (18 Feb 1723) / [11 Mar 1723]		
							>	Suriname	[South America]		[>]	Barbados	[Lesser Antilles]			
							>	New York	[New York]	21 Jun 1723						

5:4,34,45,90,136 / 6:4,8,42,44,49,87,90,92,122,137 / 7:42,48,57,89,92,98,132 / 8:21,26,70

	Year	Name	Type	Burden	First Name	Last Name	Length	Port	Custom In / Entered Out	Length	Port	Custom In / Entered Out	
29	MSTR ID#							State / Country	Custom Out / Cleared Out		State / Country	Custom Out / Cleared Out	104
	SHIP ID#	Registry Location							Departure			Departure	
	Source							Notes					

	1720	*Expedition*	Brigantine		Thomas	Lawrance / Larrance	Start	New York	XXXXXXXXXXXXXX		Barbados		
M-L-035	M-L-036								XX [2 May 1720] XX	>			M-L-035
S-E-040 <	S-E-040							[New York]	[16 May 1720]		[Lesser Antilles]		S-E-040 >
Page #103							>	New York	7 Aug 1720				Page # 103
									XX [15 Aug 1720] XX				
								[New York]	XXXXXXXXXXXXXX				
									XXXXXXXXXXXXXX				
	5:53,88												

	1720	*Hope*	Sloop		Jacob	Sarly	Start	New York	(14 Mar 1720)		Barbados		
	M-S-064								[28 Mar 1720]	>			
	S-H-040							[New York]			[Lesser Antilles]		M-H-047 >
							>				New York	6 Jul 1720	S-H-040
										>		XXXXXXXXXXXXXX	Page # 104
								Virginia			[New York]	XX [15 Aug 1720] XX	
												XXXXXXXXXXXXXX	
	XXXXXXXXXX XXXXXXXXXX Captain / Master Relieved And Then Retook Command XXXXXXXXXX XXXXXXXXXX												
M-H-047 <	1720						Start	New York	XX 8 Nov 1720 XX		Barbados		M-W-043 >
S-H-040									[21 Nov 1720]	>			S-H-040
Page #104	S-H-040							[New York]	[28 Nov 1720]		[Lesser Antilles]		Page # 105
	5:27,32,75,133,136												

	1720	*Hope*	Sloop		Robert	Hood / Hoodin	Start	New York	XX 6 Jul 1720 XX		Madeira Island		
	M-H-047								XXXXXXXXXXXXXX	>			M-S-064 >
M-S-064 <	S-H-040							[New York]	[15 Aug 1720]		[Portugal]		S-H-040
S-H-040							5 Weeks	New York	8 Nov 1720				Page # 104
Page #104									XX [21 Nov 1720] XX				
								[New York]	XXXXXXXXXXXXXX				
									XXXXXXXXXXXXXX				
	5:90,129												

	1722	*Free Gift*	Sloop		William	Dobbs	Start	New York	[11 Jun 1722]		Philadelphia	[28 Jun 1722]	
	M-D-001								[11 Jun 1722]	>		[5 Jul 1722]	
	S-F-009							[New York]			[Pennsylvania]		
							>	Boston	[21 Jul 1722]		New York	[13 Aug 1722]	M-W-043 >
									[21 Jul 1722]	>		[15 Oct 1722]	S-F-009
								[Massachusetts]			[New York]	XX [21 Oct 1722] XX	Page # 105
												XXXXXXXXXXXXXX	
							>		Never Left For Port				
								Virginia	See Next Ship Or Captain				
	XXXXXXXXXX XXXXXXXXXX Captain / Master Relieved And Then Retook Command XXXXXXXXXX XXXXXXXXXX												
M-W-043 <	1723						Start	New York	XX (24 Dec 1722) XX		Boston		
S-F-009									(4 Mar 1723)	>			
Page #105	S-F-009							[New York]			[Massachusetts]		
	7:70,76,79,96 / 8:24 / 20:51												

Interact	Page
29	105

Ship					Captain / Master		Passage	Arrival / Departure 1				Passage	Arrival / Departure 2				Page
Year	Name	Type	Burden	Registry Location	First Name	Last Name	Length	Port	Arrival / Entered Inwards / Custom In / Entered Out	State / Country		Length	Port	Arrival / Entered Inwards / Custom In / Entered Out	State / Country	Notes	
				SHIP ID#					Custom Out / Cleared Out					Departure Custom Out / Cleared Out			
				MSTR ID#					Departure								
				Source													

| 1721 | Hope | Sloop | | S-H-040 M-W-043 M-S-064 | John Nathaniel | Whitfield | Start | Maryland | | | < | | New York | [7 May 1721] [5 Jun 1721] XX [19 Jun 1721] XX XXXXXXXXXXXXXXX | New York [ ] | | Page # 104 > M-P-034 S-H-040 Page # 105 |
| | | | | | | | < | Barbados [Lesser Antilles] | Never Left For Port See Next Ship Or Captain | | | | | | | | |

XXXXXXXXXX XXXXXXXXXX Captain / Master Changed Ships XXXXXXXXXX XXXXXXXXXX

| 1722 | Freegift | Sloop | | S-F-009 M-D-001 | | | Start | New York | XXXXXXXXXXXXXX XX [15 Oct 1722] XX [21 Oct 1722] | New York [ ] | > | | Virginia | | | | Page # 104 > M-D-001 S-F-009 Page # 104 |
| | | | | | | | < | New York | (24 Dec 1722) XX (4 Mar 1723) XX XXXXXXXXXXXXXX XXXXXXXXXXXXXX | New York [ ] | | | | | | | |

6:46,58 / 7:122,151

| 1721 | Hope | Sloop | | M-P-034 S-H-040 | Alexander | Phenix | Start | New York | XXXXXXXXXXXXXX XX [5 Jun 1721] XX [19 Jun 1721] | New York [ ] | < | | Barbados [Lesser Antilles] | | | | Page # 105 < M-W-043 S-H-040 |
| | | | | | | | 21 Days | New York | 27 Aug 1721 | New York [ ] | | | | | | | |

XXXXXXXXXX XXXXXXXXXX Captain / Master Changed Ships XXXXXXXXXX XXXXXXXXXX

| 1721 | Hope | Brigantine | | S-H-039 | | | Start | New York | XXXXXXXXXXXXXX [30 Oct 1721] XX [20 Nov 1721] XX XXXXXXXXXXXXXX | New York [ ] | < | | Barbados [Lesser Antilles] | Never Left For Port See Next Ship Or Captain | | | Page # 103 > M-L-035 S-H-039 Page # 103 |

XXXXXXXXXX XXXXXXXXXX Captain / Master Changed Ships XXXXXXXXXX XXXXXXXXXX

| 1721 | Expedition | Brigantine | | S-E-040 | | | Start | New York | XX 20 Oct 1721 XX [5 Dec 1721] (19 Dec 1721) | New York [ ] | < | | Barbados [Lesser Antilles] | | | | Page # 103 > M-L-035 S-E-040 Page # 103 |

6:63,96,125,144,148

	MSTR ID# / SHIP ID#	Registry Location		First Name	Last Name	Length	State / Country	Custom In / Entered Out Custom Out / Cleared Out Departure	Length	State / Country	Custom In / Entered Out Custom Out / Cleared Out Departure	
		Source						Notes				
	1720	*Sea Nymph*	Snow	Walter	Kippen / Kipin / Kippin	Start	Barbados	XXXXXXXXXXXXXX XXXXXXXXXXXXXX XXXXXXXXXXXXXX	>	Antigua	[? Apr 1720]	
	M-L-007 S-S-072	New York, New York					[Lesser Antilles]	11 Apr 1720		[Leeward Islands]	Taken / Pirates	
M-B-076 S-S-072 Page #107						>	Antigua	[? Apr 1720]	>	New York	23 May 1720 [6 Jun 1720] [4 Jul 1720]	M-B-076 S-S-072 Page # 107
							[Leeward Islands]	Released / Pirates		[New York]		
						>	Madeira Island					
							[Portugal]					
	XXXXXXXXX XXXXXXXXXX Captain / Master Changed Ships XXXXXXXXX XXXXXXXXXX											
	1720 – 1722	*Hopewell*	Brigantine			Start	New York	[7 Nov 1720] [5 Dec 1720]	>	Suriname		
	S-H-041						[New York]			[South America]		
						25 Days	New York	30 Apr 1721 [22 May 1721] [26 Jun 1721]	>	Suriname		M-W-044 S-H-041 Page # 106
							[New York]			[South America]		
						>	New York	10 Nov 1721 [19 Mar 1722] [2 Apr 1722]	>	Madeira Island		
							[New York]			[Portugal]		
						>	New York	13 Jul 1722 XX [5 Nov 1722] XX XXXXXXXXXXXXXX XXXXXXXXXXXXXX				
							[New York]					
	XXXXXXXXX XXXXXXXXXX Captain / Master Changed Ships XXXXXXXXX XXXXXXXXXX											
	1723	*Albons*	Ship			Start	New York	[11 Mar 1723] [15 Apr 1723]	>	Barbados		
	S-A-029						[New York]			[Lesser Antilles]		
	5:45,53,56,60,72,126,141 / 6:44,52,63,67,132 / 7:34,40,85 / 8:26,39						13 Jul 1722 – Passenger Captain David Linsey – Philadelphia Custom House - Master ID: M-L-005 / Ship ID: S-M-021 - Ship Lost: Hamburgh to Philadelphia on island of St Michael, Leeward Islands					
	1722 – 1723	*Hopewell*	Brigantine	John	Woodside	Start	New York	XX 13 Jul 1722 XX [5 Nov 1722] [10 Dec 1722]	>	Madeira Island		
	M-W-044 S-H-041						[New York]			[Portugal]		
M-L-007 S-H-041 Page #106						6 Weeks	New York	12 Mar 1723 [1 Apr 1723] [8 Apr 1723]	>	Curacao		
							[New York]			[Leeward Antilles]		
						[>]	Barbados		22 Days	New York	19 Jul 1723 [29 Jul 1723] [12 Aug 1723]	
							[Lesser Antilles]			[New York]		
						>	Madeira Island		>	New York	24 Nov 1723	
							[Portugal]			[New York]		
	7:130,144 / 8:28,34,81,84,88,130 / 26:177,193											

Interact	Ship				Captain / Master		Passage	Arrival / Departure 1		Passage	Arrival / Departure 2		Page
	Year	Name	Type	Burden	First Name	Last Name	Length	Port	Arrival / Entered Inwards	Length	Port	Arrival / Entered Inwards	
									Custom In / Entered Out			Custom In / Entered Out	
30	MSTR ID#							State / Country	Custom Out / Cleared Out		State / Country	Custom Out / Cleared Out	107
	SHIP ID#	Registry Location							Departure			Departure	
		Source								Notes			

	1720	Sea Nymph	Snow		Joseph	Bloodworth	Start	New York		>	Barbados	XXXXXXXXXXXXXX	> M-L-007
	M-B-076	New York, New York						[New York]			[Lesser Antilles]		S-S-072
	S-S-072												Page # 106

XXXXXXXXXX XXXXXXXXXX Captain / Master Relieved And Then Retook Command XXXXXXXXXX XXXXXXXXXX

	1720 – 1723						Start	New York	[12 Sept 1720]	>	Antigua		
									[12 Sept 1720]				
	S-S-072							[New York]			[Leeward Islands]		

| | | | | | | | [>] | Anguilla | | > | New York | 8 Dec 1720 | |
| | | | | | | | | [Leeward Islands] | | | [New York] | (2 Jan 1721) | |

							>	Curacao		>	New York	31 Mar 1721	
												[10 Apr 1721]	
								[Leeward Antilles]			[New York]	[17 Apr 1721]	
												19 Apr 1721	

| | | | | | | | > | Bristol | | > | | | |
| | | | | | | | | [England] | | | Holland | | |

							[>]	Bristol		>	New York	4 Oct 1721	
												[16 Oct 1721]	
								[England]			[New York]	[6 Nov 1721]	
									6 Aug 1721			6 Nov 1721	

M-L-007 <
S-S-072
Page #106

							>	Bristol		>	New York	20 Apr 1722	
												[7 May 1722]	
								[England]			[New York]	[14 May 1722]	
									21 Feb 1722				

| | | | | | | | > | Madeira Island | | [>] | Canary Islands | | |
| | | | | | | | | [Portugal] | | | | | |

							>	New York	[3 Sept 1722]	>	Bristol		
									[29 Oct 1722]				
								[New York]	[12 Nov 1722]		[England]		
												17 Mar 1723	

							>	New York	16 May 1723	>	Jamaica		
									[3 Jun 1723]				
								[New York]	[17 Jun 1723]		[Greater Antilles]		

| | | | | | | | [>] | Havanna | | > | New York | 6 Nov 1723 | |
| | | | | | | | | [Cuba] | | | [New York] | | |

5:26,99 / 6:4,8,36,38,40,42,114,119,122,125,130 / 7:47,54,57,105,126,132 / 8:58,62,68,126

Year / MSTR ID# / SHIP ID#	Name / Registry Location	Type	Burden	First Name	Last Name	Length	Port / State-Country	Custom In/Out / Departure	Length	Port / State-Country	Custom In/Out / Departure	Notes
1720 / M-R-029 / S-T-020	Three Brothers	Sloop		Henry	Rowe / Row	Start	Madeira Island [Portugal]		5 Weeks	New York [New York]	16 Jul 1720 [15 Aug 1720]	> M-B-077 / S-T-020 / Page # 109
						>	Jamaica [Greater Antilles]					
	XXXXXXXXXX XXXXXXXXXX Captain / Master Changed Ships XXXXXXXXXX XXXXXXXXXX											
1722 / / S-K-006	King George	Ship				Start	Holland		>	Cowes [England]	20 Feb 1722	
						>	New York [New York]	13 Apr 1722 [23 Apr 1722] [7 May 1722]	>	South Carolina		> M-L-037 / S-K-006 / Page # 111
						[>]	Bristol [England]	6 Oct 1722	>	New York [New York]	18 Nov 1722 XX [10 Dec 1722] XX	
	XXXXXXXXXX XXXXXXXXXX Captain / Master Changed Ships XXXXXXXXXX XXXXXXXXXX											
1722 – 1723 / / S-C-032	Catherine & Mary	Sloop				Start	New York [New York]	XX 7 Sept 1722 XX [10 Dec 1722] (24 Dec 1722)	>	Maryland		M-L-037 / S-C-032 / Page #111 <
						>	New York [New York]	19 Jun 1723 [8 Jul 1723] [22 Jul 1723]	>	Jamaica [Greater Antilles]		
						>	New York [New York]	24 Oct 1723 [18 Nov 1723] (17 Dec 1723)	>	Suriname [South America]		
	Source: 5:78,90 / 7:42,48,54,136,144,152 / 8:70,76,81,118,128,138											
1720 / M-W-044 / S-C-032	Catherine & Mary	Sloop		William	White	Start	Suriname [South America]		>	New York [New York]	2 Jan 1720 [16 Feb 1720] [1 Mar 1720]	
						>	Barbados [Lesser Antilles]		22 Days	New York [New York]	1 May 1720 [30 May 1720] [13 Jun 1720]	> M-L-037 / S-C-032 / Page # 111
						>	Madeira Island [Portugal]		5 Weeks	New York [New York]	12 Sept 1720 XX [24 Oct 1720] XX	
	XXXXXXXXXX XXXXXXXXXX Captain / Master Changed Ships XXXXXXXXXX XXXXXXXXXX											
1720 – 1721 / / S-S-073	Sea Flower	Sloop				Start	New York [New York]	[26 Sept 1720] [10 Oct 1720]	>	Antigua [Leeward Islands]		> M-C-046 / S-S-073 / Page # 112
						>	New York [New York]	22 May 1721 XXXXXXXXXXXXXX XX [24 Jul 1721] XX				
	XXXXXXXXXX XXXXXXXXXX Captain / Master Changed Ships XXXXXXXXXX XXXXXXXXXX											
1722 / / S-T-021	Thomas	Schooner				Start	New York [New York]	XX [5 Dec 1721] XX [29 Jan 1722] [29 Jan 1722]	>	Jamaica [Greater Antilles]		M-E-016 / S-T-021 / Page #110 < > M-R-030 / S-T-021 / Page # 109
						>	New York [New York]	20 Apr 1722 XX (8 Jan 1723) XX				
	Source: 5:8,20,24,45,58,63,102,107,112 / 6:52 / 7:13,47											

Interact	Ship				Captain / Master		Passage	Arrival / Departure 1		Passage	Arrival / Departure 2		Page
31	Year	Name	Type	Burden	First Name	Last Name	Length	Port	Arrival / Entered Inwards / Custom In / Entered Out	Length	Port	Arrival / Entered Inwards / Custom In / Entered Out	**109**
	MSTR ID# / SHIP ID#	Registry Location						State / Country	Custom Out / Cleared Out / Departure		State / Country	Custom Out / Cleared Out / Departure	
	Source								Notes				

Three Brothers — Interact: M-R-029 < / S-T-020 / Page #108

Year	Name	Type	Burden	First Name	Last Name	Passage	Port	Dates	Passage	Port	Dates
1720 – 1721	Three Brothers	Sloop		Ezekiel	Bonyott	Start			>	New York / [New York]	(19 Dec 1720) / (31 Jan 1721) / (13 Feb 1721)
M-B-077 / S-T-020							Maryland				
						>	Barbados / [Lesser Antilles]		21 Days	New York / [New York]	7 May 1721 / [10 Jul 1721]
						>	Jamaica / [Greater Antilles]		[>]	Curacao / [Leeward Antilles]	
						23 Days	New York / [New York]	17 Sept 1721 / [25 Sept 1721] / [2 Oct 1721]	>	Jamaica / [Greater Antilles]	

XXXXXXXXXX XXXXXXXXXX Captain / Master Changed Ships XXXXXXXXXX XXXXXXXXXX

Mary Anne

Year	Name	Type	Passage	Port	Dates	Passage	Port	Dates
1722 – 1723	Mary Anne	Sloop	Start	New York / [New York]	[14 May 1722] / [14 May 1722]	>	North Carolina	
S-M-067			>	New York / [New York]	8 Jul 1722 / [16 Jul 1722] / [16 Jul 1722]	>	Boston / [Massachusetts]	[21 Jul 1722]
			>	North Carolina		>	New York / [New York]	[11 Mar 1723] / [25 Mar 1723] / [1 Apr 1723]
			>	North Carolina		>	New York / [New York]	5 Jun 1723 / [24 Jun 1723] / [1 Jul 1723]
			>	Jamaica / [Greater Antilles]				

Source: 6:4,16,20,46,76,106,108,111 / 7:57,82,85 / 8:26,32,34,65,70,73 / 20:51

Thomas — Interact: M-W-044 < / S-T-021 / Page #108

Year	Name	Type	First Name	Last Name	Passage	Port	Dates	Passage	Port
1723	Thomas	Schooner	William	Richardson	Start	New York / [New York]	XX 20 Apr 1722 XX / (8 Jan 1723) / (22 Jan 1723)	>	Suriname / [South America]
M-R-030 / S-T-021					>	New York / [New York]	28 May 1723 / [10 Jun 1723] / [1 Jul 1723]	>	Suriname / [South America]
					>	New York / [New York]	6 Nov 1723 / (31 Dec 1723)	>	Suriname / [South America]

Source: 8:5,10,62,65,73,126,142

MSTR ID# / SHIP ID#		First Name	Last Name	Length	State / Country	Custom In / Entered Out Custom Out / Cleared Out Departure	Length	State / Country	Custom In / Entered Out Custom Out / Cleared Out Departure	
	Registry Location									
	Source					Notes				
1720 – 1721 M-E-014 S-J-033	*Joseph* / Sloop	William	Ellison	Start	North Carolina		>	Sandy Hook [New Jersey]	18 May 1720	
				>	Barbados [Lesser Antilles]		>	Antigua [Leeward Islands]		
				>	Perth Amboy [New Jersey]		>	New York [New York]	[10 Oct 1720] [28 Nov 1720] [5 Dec 1720]	
				>	North Carolina					
				NO SUPPORTING DATA TO LINK TIMELINE						
				Start	New York [New York]	[17 Jul 1721]	>	Boston [Massachusetts]	XXXXXXXXXXXXXX XXXXXXXXXXXXXX XXXXXXXXXXXXXX	> M-E-015 S-J-033 Page # 110
	5:56,112,136,141 / 6:79 / 23:54									
1720 – 1721 M-E-015 S-T-021	*Thomas* / Schooner	Thomas	Ellison	Start	New York [New York]	[29 Aug 1720] [29 Aug 1720]	>	North Carolina		> M-V-017 S-T-021 Page # 110
				>	New York [New York]	30 Nov 1720 XX (2 Jan 1721) XX XXXXXXXXXXXXXX XXXXXXXXXXXXXX				
XXXXXXXXXX XXXXXXXXXX Captain / Master Changed Ships XXXXXXXXXX XXXXXXXXXX										
M-E-014 S-J-033 Page #110 <	1721 S-J-033 *Joseph* / Sloop			Start	Boston [Massachusetts]	XXXXXXXXXXXXXX [5 Aug 1721] [12 Aug 1721]	>	New York [New York]	17 Aug 1721 [11 Sept 1721]	
				>	Boston [Massachusetts]					
	5:94,141 / 6:94,103 / 20:1,2									
M-E-015 S-T-021 Page #110 <	1721 M-V-017 S-T-021 *Thomas* / Schooner	Richard	Van Dam	Start	New York [New York]	XX 30 Nov 1720 XX (2 Jan 1721) (16 Jan 1721)	>	South Carolina		> M-E-016 S-T-021 Page # 110
				>	Bermuda					
	6:8,12									
M-V-017 S-T-021 Page #110 <	1721 M-E-016 S-T-021 *Thomas* / Schooner	John	Ellison Jr	>	New York [New York]	[29 May 1721] [3 Jul 1721]	>	Suriname [South America]		> M-W-044 S-T-021 Page # 108
				>	New York [New York]	[5 Dec 1721] XX [29 Jan 1722] XX XXXXXXXXXXXXXX XXXXXXXXXXXXXX				
	6:52,56,71,144									

Interact	Year / MSTR ID# / SHIP ID#	Name	Type	Burden	First Name	Last Name	Passage Length	Port / State / Country (1)	Arrival / Custom / Departure (1)	Passage Length	Port / State / Country (2)	Arrival / Custom / Departure (2)	Page
31													111

Block 1 — Catherine & Mary

- Interact (left): M-W-044 / S-C-032 / Page #108 — Interact (right): M-R-029 / S-C-032 / Page #108

Year / MSTR / SHIP	Name	Type	First Name	Last Name
1720 – 1721 / M-L-037 / S-C-032	Catherine & Mary	Sloop	John	Lawrance / Larrance

Passage Length	Port (1)	State/Country (1)	Arr/Cust/Dep (1)	Passage Length	Port (2)	State/Country (2)	Arr/Cust/Dep (2)
Start	New York	[New York]	XX 12 Sept 1720 XX / [24 Oct 1720] / [7 Nov 1720]	>	Madeira Island	[Portugal]	
[>]	Saltertuda	[Location Unkn]		28 Days	New York	[New York]	21 Apr 1721 / [15 May 1721] / [29 May 1721]
>	Suriname	[South America]		>	New York	[New York]	22 Oct 1721 / [2 Apr 1722] / [23 Apr 1722]
>	Suriname	[South America]		>	New York	[New York]	7 Sept 1722 / XX [10 Dec 1722] XX / XXXXXXXXXXXXXX XXXXXXXXXXXXXX

XXXXXXXXXX XXXXXXXXXX Captain / Master Changed Ships XXXXXXXXXX XXXXXXXXXX

King George — Interact (left): M-R-029 / S-K-006 / Page #108

Year / SHIP	Name	Type	Passage Length	Port (1)	State/Country (1)	Arr/Cust/Dep (1)	Passage Length	Port (2)	State/Country (2)
1722 – 1723 / S-K-006	King George	Ship	Start	New York	[New York]	XX 18 Nov 1722 XX / [10 Dec 1722] / (8 Jan 1723)	>	Jamaica	[Greater Antilles]

XXXXXXXXXX XXXXXXXXXX Captain / Master Changed Ships XXXXXXXXXX XXXXXXXXXX

Royal Prince — Interact (left): M-P-035 / S-R-019 / Page #111

Year / SHIP	Name	Type	Passage Length	Port (1)	State/Country (1)	Arr/Cust/Dep (1)	Passage Length	Port (2)	State/Country (2)
1723 / S-R-019	Royal Prince	Snow	Start	New York	[New York]	XX 28 Aug 1723 XX / [18 Nov 1723] / (17 Dec 1723)	>	Barbados	[Lesser Antilles]

Source: 5:120,126 / 6:42,48,56,122 / 7:40,48,108,144 / 8:5,128,138

Block 2 — Royal Prince

Year / MSTR / SHIP	Name	Type	First Name	Last Name
1720 – 1722 / M-P-035 / S-R-019	Royal Prince	Snow	Samuel	Payton / Peyton

Passage Length	Port (1)	State/Country (1)	Arr/Cust/Dep (1)	Passage Length	Port (2)	State/Country (2)	Arr/Cust/Dep (2)
Start	Cowes	[England]	5 Nov 1720 (Departure)	>	New York	[New York]	12 Jan 1721 / (27 Feb 1721) / [13 Mar 1721]
>	Madeira Island	[Portugal]		5 Weeks	New York	[New York]	2 Jun 1721 / [12 Jun 1721] / [3 Jul 1721]
>	Madeira Island	[Portugal]		7 Weeks	New York	[New York]	17 Oct 1721 / [28 May 1722] / [11 Jun 1722]
>	Madeira Island	[Portugal]		7 Weeks	New York	[New York]	14 Sept 1722 / [10 Dec 1722] / (24 Dec 1722)
>	Madeira Island	[Portugal]		29 Days	New York	[New York]	24 Mar 1723 / [8 Apr 1723] / [28 Apr 1723]
>	Madeira Island	[Portugal]		[>]	Lisbon	[Portugal]	
>	New York	[New York]	28 Aug 1723 / XX [18 Nov 1723] XX / XXXXXXXXXXXXXX XXXXXXXXXXXXXX				

Interact (right, at 4th voyage): M-L-037 / S-R-019 / Page #111

Source: 6:12,23,28,58,60,71,122 / 7:63,70,110,144,152 / 8:32,45,96 / 26:177

Year	Name	Type	Burden	First Name	Last Name	Length	Port	Custom In / Entered Out	Length	Port	Custom In / Entered Out
MSTR ID#	Registry Location						State / Country	Custom Out / Cleared Out		State / Country	Custom Out / Cleared Out
SHIP ID#								Departure			Departure
Source							Notes				
1721 – 1723	Sea Flower	Sloop		James	Craig	Start	New York	XX 22 May 1721 XX XXXXXXXXXXXXXX	>	Antigua	
M-C-046							[New York]	[24 Jul 1721]		[Leeward Islands]	
S-S-073											
						>	New York	24 Oct 1721 [30 Apr 1722]	>	Antigua	
							[New York]	[21 May 1722]		[Leeward Islands]	
						>	New York	[8 Oct 1722] [12 Nov 1722]	>	Barbados	
							[New York]	[3 Dec 1722]		[Lesser Antilles]	
M-W-044						>	Bay of Honduras		>	New York	27 Apr 1723 [27 May 1723]
S-S-073										[New York]	[17 Jun 1723]
Page #108						>	Jamaica		[>]		
							[Greater Antilles]			Maryland	
						>	New York	1 Aug 1723			
							[New York]				
	6:84,125 / 7:52,60,118,132,144 / 8:45,60,68,88										

SHARED – CAPTAIN / MASTER & SHIP INDEX --- YEARS COVERED / 9 Dec 1719 – 31 Dec 1723

The Captains & Ships in this index are the ones that are shared between Philadelphia & New York Custom House. Also they have been updated with additional information since they were published in the Philadelphia Custom House Book. The Captain & Ship ID's match in both books, so you know they are the same Captain or Ship.

Last Name	First Name	MSTR ID#	Page #	19	20	21	22	23	Date Range
B									
Barber	John	M-B-026	52			X			30 Mar 1721 – 20 Apr 1721
"	"	"	"			X			2 Oct 1721 – 16 Oct 1721
Bennett	Elisha	M-B-006	65			X			5 Jun 1721 – 19 Dec 1721
"	"	"	"					X	5 Feb 1723
"	"	"	"					X	5 Jun 1723
Bourdet	Samuel	M-B-034	11				X	X	13 Sept 1722 – 26 Aug 1723
Burch	John	M-B-028	25				X		12 Apr 1722 – 20 Aug 1722
C									
Cassly / Casely	John	M-C-011	67		X				6 Oct 1720 – 28 Nov 1720
"	"	"	"					X	26 Sept 1723 – 21 Oct 1723
Cathoone	James	M-C-006	52			X	X		5 Aug 1721 – Jun 1722
Clarke	John	M-C-003	31		X	X	X	X	27 Jun 1720 - 18 Nov 1723
Cooper	Samuel	M-C-008	57		X	X	X		23 Oct 1720 – 3 Dec 1722
D									
Dickinson	John	M-D-005	67		X				9 Jan 1720
"	"	"	"		X	X			7 Apr 1720 – 28 Sept 1721
"	"	"	"					X	15 Sept 1723 – 14 Oct 1723
Dobbs	William	M-D-001	104				X	X	11 Jun 1722 – 4 Mar 1723
G									
Gibbs	John	M-G-005	21			X			7 Aug 1721 – 7 Sept 1721
"	"	"	"				X		3 Sept 1722 – 10 Sept 1722
Gilbert	Ephraim	M-G-002	13	X	X	X			18 Nov 1719 – 11 May 1721
Gordon	James	M-G-010	66		X				18 Jun 1720 – 14 Jul 1720
"	"	"	"			X	X		3 Apr 1721 – 28 Aug 1722
"	"	"	"					X	10 Jun 1723 – 1 Jul 1723
H & P & R									
Holmes	Robert	M-H-002	10					X	25 Mar 1723 – 13 Jul 1723
Price	John	M-P-002	16				X		26 Apr 1722 – 10 Sept 1722
Randal	Thomas	M-R-004	99			X	X		13 Feb 1721 – 30 Jul 1722
"	"	"	"					X	3 Jun 1723 – 10 Jun 1723
Royal	Joseph	M-R-013	13		X				6 Jun 1720
S									
Stout	John	M-S-012	68			X			25 May 1721
"	"	"	"			X			16 Oct 1721 – 13 Nov 1721
"	"	"	"				X		26 Apr 1722 – 16 Oct 1722
"	"	"	"					X	7 Jun 1723 – 19 Aug 1723
Styles	John	M-S-025	54		X				5 May 1720 – 24 Oct 1720
V									
Vesey	John	M-V-004	87		X				12 Jun 1720 – 4 Jul 1720
"	"	"	"			X	X		7 Sept 1721 – 30 Jul 1722
"	"	"	"				X		3 Dec 1722 – 24 Dec 1722
W									
Webb	Nicholas	M-W-017	54	X	X				9 Dec 1719 – 1 Dec 1720

Ship Names	Type	Ship ID#	Page #	19	20	21	22	23	Date Range
A									
Anne	Sloop	S-A-007	10					X	25 Mar 1723 – 13 Jul 1723
Antelope	Sloop	S-A-010	11				X	X	13 Sept 1722 – 26 Aug 1723
B									
Bedminster	Ship	S-B-013	66		X				18 Jun 1720 – 14 Jul 1720
Beginning	Sloop	S-B-016	13		X				6 Jun 1720
Benjamin	Sloop	S-B-002	13	X	X	X			18 Nov 1719 – 11 May 1721
C									
Clarendon Packet	Sloop	S-C-006	65			X			5 Jun 1721 – 19 Dec 1721
Concord	Sloop	S-C-013	67		X				9 Jan 1720
Cutwater	Sloop	S-C-010	16				X		26 Apr 1722 – 10 Sept 1722
D									
Deborah	Sloop	S-D-009	67		X	X			7 Apr 1720 – 28 Sept 1721
"	"	"	67					X	15 Sept 1723 – 14 Oct 1723
E									
Elizabeth	Sloop	S-E-008	66					X	10 Jun 1723 – 1 Jul 1723
Elizabeth & Martha	Sloop	S-E-004	21			X			7 Aug 1721 – 7 Sept 1721
"	"	"	"				X		3 Sept 1722 – 10 Sept 1722
F & G & H									
Free Gift	Sloop	S-F-009	104,105				X	X	11 Jun 1722 – 4 Mar 1723
George	Sloop	S-G-007	25				X		12 Apr 1722 – 20 Aug 1722
Hamstead	Sloop	S-H-001	98,99	X	X	X	X		9 Dec 1719 – 30 Jul 1722
J									
John & Mary	Sloop	S-J-007	31		X	X	X	X	27 Jun 1720 - 18 Nov 1723
M									
Mary	Sloop	S-M-005	68				X		26 Apr 1722 – 16 Oct 1722
"	"	"	"					X	7 Jun 1723 – 19 Aug 1723
Mary Hope	Sloop	S-M-022	67		X				6 Oct 1720 – 28 Nov 1720
Mary Hope	Scallop	S-M-023	67					X	26 Sept 1723 – 21 Oct 1723
P									
Pennsylvania Merchant	Ship	S-P-014	66			X	X		3 Apr 1721 – 28 Aug 1722
S & T & W									
Speedwell	Sloop	S-S-008	52			X			30 Mar 1721 – 20 Apr 1721
"	"	"	"			X			2 Oct 1721 – 16 Oct 1721
Speedwell	Sloop	S-S-009	87,88		X	X	X	X	22 Aug 1720 – 3 Dec 1723
Speedwell	Sloop	S-S-010	52			X	X		5 Aug 1721 – Jun 1722
Three Brothers	Sloop	S-T-008	54		X				5 May 1720 – 24 Oct 1720
Three Sisters	Sloop	S-T-009	54	X	X				9 Dec 1719 – 1 Dec 1720
William	Sloop	S-W-001	57		X	X	X		23 Oct 1720 – 3 Dec 1722

The Captain & Ship ID's in both the Philadelphia & New York Custom House books are unique and do not repeat unless they are the same Captain or Ship, a shared index has been given.

Last Name	First Name	MSTR ID#	Page #	19	20	21	22	23	Date Range
?									
?	?	M-?-004	3			X			6 May 1721
?	?	M-?-005	4				X		8 Oct 1722
?	?	M-?-006	4				X		11 Nov 1722
?	?	M-?-007	6					X	Jul 1723
?	?	M-?-008	6					X	28 Jul 1723 – 19 Aug 1723
?	?	M-?-009	19		X				1720
?	?	M-?-010	41		X				1720
A									
Albin	?	M-A-014	5					X	23 Mar 1723
Albin	John	M-A-016	25		X				5 Jan 1720
Ablin	John	M-A-018	65		X	X	X		11 Jul 1720 – 29 Oct 1722
Agnew	David	M-A-019	79					X	22 Jul 1723 – 26 Aug 1723
Albony	Peter	M-A-017	48		X				14 Mar 1720 – 21 Mar 1720
Applebe	Benjamin	M-A-015	15			X	X		20 Nov 1721 – 14 May 1722
B									
Banbury	James	M-B-046	14		X				17 Aug 1720 – 12 Sept 1720
Barber	John	M-B-026	52			X			30 Mar 1721 – 20 Apr 1721
"	"	"	"			X			2 Oct 1721 – 16 Oct 1721
Barrington	Richard	M-B-067	51	X	X				22 Dec 1719 – 12 Mar 1720
Bayles	James	M-B-063	49					X	18 Mar 1723 – 1 Apr 1723
Beaudine	Vincent	M-B-058	37		X				4 Apr 1720
Beckman	William	M-B-056	36		X	X	X	X	14 Mar 1720 – 18 Nov 1723
Beekman	John	M-B-074	97		X	X			28 Mar 1720 – 24 Apr 1721
Bedlow	Isaac	M-B-045	10		X				12 Sept 1720 – 19 Sept 1720
Bedlow	Peter	M-B-075	101		X	X	X		9 Mar 1720 – 26 Nov 1722
Bennet	Christopher	M-B-052	25					X	18 Feb 1723
Bennett	Elisha	M-B-047	17		X				21 Mar 1720
Bennett	Elisha	M-B-006	65			X			5 Jun 1721 – 19 Dec 1721
"	"	"	"					X	5 Feb 1723
"	"	"	"					X	5 Jun 1723
Bret	John	M-B-057	37					X	1 Jul 1723 – 20 Sept 1723
Billop	Middleton	M-B-060	42		X	X	X	X	17 Apr 1720 – 17 Dec 1723
Birch	John	M-B-048	17			X			22 May 1721 – 29 May 1721
Birch	Thomas	M-B-050	20		X	X			4 Nov 1720 – 16 Apr 1722
Bisset	Andrew	M-B-053	27	X	X	X	X	X	22 Dec 1719 – 17 Dec 1723
Bloodworth	Joseph	M-B-076	107		X	X	X	X	12 Sept 1720 – 6 Nov 1723
Bloom	Daniel	M-B-068	69					X	1 Apr 1723 – 17 Dec 1723
Bodin	Vincent	M-B-059	37		X				25 Jul 1720 – 19 Dec 1720
Bodin	Vincent	M-B-073	92			X	X		7 May 1721 – 17 Dec 1723
Boiles	Phillip	M-B-071	77			X	X		20 Nov 1721 – 3 Apr 1722
Bonyott	Ezekiel	M-B-077	109		X	X			19 Dec 1720 – 2 Oct 1721
"	"	"	"				X	X	14 May 1722 – 1 Jul 1723
Bourdet	Samuel	M-B-034	11				X	X	13 Sept 1722 – 26 Aug 1723
Bourder Jr	Samuel	M-B-061	43	X	X				9 Dec 1719 – 18 Jun 1720
Bradick	John	M-B-062	47			X			10 Jul 1721 – 26 Aug 1721
Brasse	Richard	M-B-051	21	X	X				22 Dec 1719 – 5 Jan 1720
Broadhurst	Samuel	M-B-072	83				X		12 May 1722 – 1 Oct 1722
"	"	"	"					X	8 Jul 1723 – 6 Aug 1723
Brown	?	M-B-038	1	X					22 Dec 1719
Brown	?	M-B-066	50		X				9 Oct 1720 – 4 Dec 1720
Brown	James	M-B-049	17					X	1 Aug 1723 – 16 Aug 1723
Brown	John	M-B-069	73			X	X	X	7 May 1721 – 25 Nov 1723
Burch	?	M-B-041	4				X		4 Apr 1722
Burch	Justus	M-B-044	10		X				31 Jul 1720 – 19 Sept 1720
"	"	"	"			X			15 May 1721
Burch	John	M-B-028	25				X		12 Apr 1722 – 20 Aug 1722
Burchen	?	M-B-042	4				X		16 Apr 1722

Last Name	First Name	MSTR ID#	Page #	19	20	21	22	23	Date Range
B									
Burgis	John	M-B-055	35					X	14 Sept 1723 – 7 Oct 1723
Burras	John	M-B-054	35				X		14 May 1722
Burrough	?	M-B-039	1		X				16 Jan 1720
Burrows	Christopher	M-B-064	49					X	21 Apr 1723 – 3 Jun 1723
Burrows	William	M-B-070	76				X		14 May 1722 – 12 Nov 1722
Burt	Jos.	M-B-065	50				X		14 May 1722
Bush	?	M-B-043	5					X	24 May 1723
Buston	?	M-B-040	2		X				19 Aug 1720
Butler	Isaac	M-B-071	81		X				21 Jan 1720 – 29 Jul 1720
"	"	"	"			X			12 Jun 1721
C									
Callender	Phillip	M-C-026	29		X				8 Apr 1720 – 2 May 1720
Camerford	James	M-C-036	48		X				17 Oct 1720 – 28 Nov 1720
Campbell	Dugald	M-C-031	39					X	10 Jun 1723 – 17 Dec 1723
Carlisle	William	M-C-023	19		X				18 Jul 1720 – 28 Nov 1720
Carmer	David	M-C-043	83			X	X		19 Dec 1721 – 30 Apr 1722
"	"	"	"				X	X	4 Nov 1722 – 4 Mar 1723
"	"	"	"					X	3 Dec 1723
Carthy	Owen	M-C-041	59				X	X	3 Sept 1722 – 5 Aug 1723
Carty	Owen	M-C-022	16		X				3 Oct 1720
Cassly / Casely	John	M-C-011	67		X				6 Oct 1720 – 28 Nov 1720
"	"	"	"					X	26 Sept 1723 – 21 Oct 1723
Cathoone	James	M-C-006	52			X	X		5 Aug 1721 – Jun 1722
Chamberlain	John	M-C-039	50				X		14 May 1722 – 28 May 1722
Chamberlain	William	M-C-032	40				X		8 Oct 1722 – 29 Oct 1722
Churchill	Abel	M-C-029	38		X				5 Sept 1720 – 11 Oct 1720
Clarke	John	M-C-003	31		X	X	X	X	27 Jun 1720 – 18 Nov 1723
Clarke	Jonathan	M-C-024	21		X				23 May 1720 – 6 Jun 1720
Clarke	Joseph	M-C-020	11				X		30 Apr 1722 – 24 Dec 1722
Clarke	William	M-C-034	41		X				4 May 1720 – 21 Nov 1720
Clock	John	M-C-019	7					X	27 Apr 1723 – 3 Dec 1723
Coarten	?	M-C-028	29		X				17 Apr 1720
Coddington	Edward	M-C-033	40					X	Aug 1723 – 14 Oct 1723
Coden	James	M-C-045	93,94,95	X	X	X	X	X	13 Dec 1719 – 17 Dec 1723
Coffin	Ebenezer	M-C-037	49			X			20 Aug 1721 – 6 Oct 1721
Cogeshal	Daniel	M-C-038	50			X			17 Jul 1721
Conyars	Benjamin	M-C-044	89			X	X	X	11 Nov 1721 – 1 Apr 1723
Conyars	John	M-C-035	45			X			6 Nov 1721 – 28 Nov 1721
Cook	Ebenezer	M-C-027	29				X		19 Mar 1722
Cook	William	M-C-021	16			X			20 Sept 1721 – 20 Nov 1721
Cooper	Samuel	M-C-008	57			X	X	X	23 Oct 1721 – 3 Dec 1722
Cooper	William	M-C-040	58				X		7 May 1722
Cox	Florentius	M-C-030	38			X			26 Jun 1721 – 17 Jul 1721
Cozens	?	M-C-018	5					X	14 May 1723
Craig	James	M-C-046	112			X	X	X	24 Jul 1721 – 1 Aug 1723
Crony	Samuel	M-C-042	82					X	11 Mar 1723 – 2 Sept 1723
Cupitt / Cupittina	Richard	M-C-025	26				X	X	24 Dec 1722 – 5 Feb 1723
D									
Darkins	John	M-D-016	9				X		14 May 1722 – 22 Jul 1722
Davis	Isa.	M-D-029	76		X				26 Sept 1720
Davis	James	M-D-028	76		X				27 Aug 1720 – 19 Sept 1720
Davis	John	M-D-026	51					X	4 Nov 1723 – 3 Dec 1723
Delap	John	M-D-027	53					X	11 Mar 1723 – 4 Nov 1723
Dewilde	Henry	M-D-019	13				X		7 May 1722 – 14 May 1722
Dill	Benjamin	M-D-021	17		X				5 Sept 1720 – 19 Sept 1720

CAPTAIN / MASTER INDEX --- YEARS COVERED / 9 Dec 1719 – 31 Dec 1723

The Captain & Ship ID's in both the Philadelphia & New York Custom House books are unique and do not repeat unless they are the same Captain or Ship, a shared index has been given.

D

Last Name	First Name	MSTR ID#	Page #	19	20	21	22	23	Date Range
Dickinson	John	M-D-005	67		X				9 Jan 1720
"	"	"	"		X	X			7 Apr 1720 – 28 Sept 1721
"	"	"	"					X	15 Sept 1723 – 14 Oct 1723
Dobbs	William	M-D-001	104				X	X	11 Jun 1722 – 4 Mar 1723
Dodge	?	M-D-014	5					X	4 May 1723
Doick	Stephen	M-D-022	38		X				26 Sept 1720 – 31 Oct 1720
Downing	?	M-D-020	16			X			3 Jun 1721
Downing	Dennis	M-D-023	43			X			19 Jun 1721 – 3 Aug 1721
Drummay	John	M-D-015	7			X			19 Oct 1721
"	"	"	"				X		29 Oct 1722
"	"	"	"					X	18 Mar 1723
Dunham	Samuel	M-D-025	50			X			29 Mar 1721 – 13 Jun 1721
Dunscomb	Jonathan	M-D-018	10					X	28 Aug 1723 – 9 Sept 1723
Dunscomb	Samuel	M-D-017	10			X			23 Mar 1721
Dupler	Christopher	M-D-024	48		X				5 Jan 1720

E

Last Name	First Name	MSTR ID#	Page #	19	20	21	22	23	Date Range
Ellison Jr	John	M-E-016	110			X			29 May 1721 – 5 Dec 1721
Ellison	Thomas	M-E-015	110		X				29 Aug 1720 – 30 Nov 1720
"	"	"	"			X			5 Aug 1721 – 11 Sept 1721
Ellison	William	M-E-014	110		X				18 May 1720 – 5 Dec 1720
"	"	"	"			X			17 Jul 1721
Ellison	William	M-E-008	57			X	X	X	2 Jun 1721 – 17 Dec 1723
Ellwood	John	M-E-006	29			X			10 Jul 1721 – 4 Sept 1721
English	John	M-E-013	84					X	16 Sept 1721 – 19 Oct 1723
Erasmus	Adrian	M-E-007	50		X				22 Aug 1720
Erwing	John	M-E-005	28		X				6 Jun 1720
Eustace	?	M-E-004	1		X				8 Apr 1720
Eustace	James	M-E-010	69		X	X	X	X	14 Mar 1720 – 21 Mar 1723
Evans	David	M-E-012	77			X			2 Oct 1721 – 28 Nov 1721
Evans	Edward	M-E-011	77		X				24 Jul 1720 – 22 Aug 1720
"	"	"	"			X			25 Sept 1721
Evans	Joseph	M-E-009	58					X	26 Oct 1723 – 11 Nov 1723

F

Last Name	First Name	MSTR ID#	Page #	19	20	21	22	23	Date Range
Feaver	Henry	M-F-013	54		X				16 Feb 1720 – 1 Mar 1720
Fell	Christopher	M-F-012	50				X	X	10 Dec 1722 – 1 Jul 1723
Fitch	Thomas	M-F-011	48				X	X	9 Apr 1722 – 17 Dec 1723
Fox	Samuel	M-F-009	13			X			13 Nov 1721 – 5 Dec 1721
Fred	John	M-F-014	70	X	X	X	X		9 Dec 1719 – 8 Sept 1722
Fred	John	M-F-015	99				X	X	6 Aug 1722 – 17 Dec 1723
Furbar	Matthew	M-F-016	100		X	X	X	X	22 May 1720 – 3 Jun 1723
Furse	Silvanus	M-F-010	14				X	X	16 May 1722 – 8 Jan 1723

G

Last Name	First Name	MSTR ID#	Page #	19	20	21	22	23	Date Range
Gailaspy	Thomas	M-G-028	46			X			22 May 1721 – 31 Jul 1721
Gardner	Ebenezer	M-G-025	34				X		8 Jul 1722 – 8 Oct 1722
Gardiner	Joseph	M-G-024	28	X					3 Oct 1719
"	"	"	"		X				15 Apr 1720
"	"	"	"			X			25 Apr 1721
"	"	"	"			X	X		25 Nov 1721 – 17 Dec 1722
Garland	William	M-G-023	24					X	18 Jul 1723 – 9 Sept 1723
Geering	?	M-G-018	3			X			7 Nov 1721
Gibs	John	M-G-022	19		X				27 Jun 1720 – 4 Jul 1720
Giles	John	M-G-027	37				X		24 Sept 1722

G

Last Name	First Name	MSTR ID#	Page #	19	20	21	22	23	Date Range
Gibbs	John	M-G-005	21			X			7 Aug 1721 – 7 Sept 1721
"	"	"	"				X		3 Sept 1722 – 10 Sept 1722
Gilbert	Ephraim	M-G-002	13	X	X	X			18 Nov 1719 – 11 May 1721
Gilbert	?	M-G-019	4				X		14 Aug 1722
Gilbert	Richard	M-G-021	17			X			19 Jun 1721 – 26 Jun 1721
Gleaves	Matthew	M-G-031	72				X		26 Nov 1722 – 10 Dec 1722
Goelet	Jacob	M-G-026	34		X				2 Jan 1720
Gordon	James	M-G-010	66		X				18 Jun 1720 – 14 Jul 1720
"	"	"	"			X	X		3 Apr 1721 – 28 Aug 1722
"	"	"	"					X	10 Jun 1723 – 1 Jul 1723
"	"	"	"					X	17 Aug 1723
Gother	?	M-G-020	6				X		15 Jan 1722 – 29 Jan 1722
Gottier	Francis	M-G-032	88				X	X	13 Aug 1722 – 3 Dec 1723
Gray	Joseph	M-G-033	95					X	24 Jun 1723
Greenock	John	M-G-030	68				X		16 Jul 1722 – 30 Jul 1722
"	"	"	"				X		27 Sept 1722
Grimston	Richard	M-G-029	58		X				12 Sept 1720

H

Last Name	First Name	MSTR ID#	Page #	19	20	21	22	23	Date Range
Hall	Alexander	M-H-043	58				X		29 Oct 1722 – 5 Nov 1722
Hall	John	M-H-032	19		X				8 Aug 1720 – 15 Aug 1720
"	"	"	"			X			8 Oct 1721 – 19 Dec 1721
Hall	Nathaniel	M-H-033	21			X			16 Oct 1721 – 23 Oct 1721
Harriot	John	M-H-039	48				X		12 Mar 1722 – 27 Mar 1722
Hatch	Maletier	M-H-040	52				X		12 Nov 1722 – 3 Dec 1722
Hays	Robert	M-H-031	13	X	X				13 Dec 1719 – Feb 1720
Hester	James	M-H-046	80		X				17 Jul 1720 – 8 Aug 1720
Hickford	?	M-H-037	29		X				19 Jan 1720 – 7 May 1720
Highinton	?	M-H-028	4				X		19 Jul 1722
Hill	Benjamin	M-H-041	58		X				20 Apr 172 – 2 May 1720
Hinson	Benjamin	M-H-030	12					X	23 Aug 1723 – 30 Sept 1723
Hinson	Nicholas	M-H-042	58				X		20 Jun 1722 – 16 Jul 1722
Hodsol	James	M-H-034	21				X	X	24 Dec 1722 – 8 Jan 1723
Holmes	?	M-H-029	5				X		Dec 1722
Holmes	Robert	M-H-002	10					X	25 Mar 1723 – 13 Jul 1723
Hood	Robert	M-H-047	104		X				15 Aug 1720 – 8 Nov 1720
Hook	Thomas	M-H-045	77	X	X	X			22 Dec 1719 – 23 Oct 1721
"	"	"	"				X		28 May 1722 – 18 Jun 1722
Hopkins	Thomas	M-H-044	74			X	X		13 Feb 1721 – 20 Apr 1722
Hopper	Thomas	M-H-036	24		X	X			21 Nov 1720 – 31 Jul 1721
Hull	Tiddman	M-H-035	22					X	3 Jun 1723
Hunt	John	M-H-038	40			X			1 May 1721 – 29 May 1721

J

Last Name	First Name	MSTR ID#	Page #	19	20	21	22	23	Date Range
Jackson	John	M-J-014	24	X	X				Dec 1719 – 10 Sept 1720
Jacobs Jr	Thomas	M-J-018	71		X				23 May 1720 – 4 Nov 1720
Jandine	?	M-J-013	16		X				29 Aug 1720
Jarrat	Allan	M-J-012	6				X		26 Nov 1722 – 24 Dec 1722
Jarrett	William	M-J-010	8	X	X	X	X	X	22 Dec 1719 – 25 Nov 1723
Jefferys	Caleb	M-J-016	29					X	15 Jul 1723 – 12 Aug 1723
Jennings	?	M-J-009	1			X			17 Oct 1721
Jones	John	M-J-017	51		X				26 Feb 1720 – 6 Jun 1720
"	"	"	"			X			3 Apr 1721 – 12 Jul 1721
"	"	"	"					X	2 Apr 1723
Johnson	Isaac	M-J-011	9		X	X	X	X	31 Mar 1720 – 11 Dec 1723
Johnson	Joseph	M-J-015	26	X	X				Dec 1719 – 17 Dec 1720
Joseph	Jacobs	M-J-008	1		X				18 Mar 1720 – 1 Apr 1720

The Captain & Ship ID's in both the Philadelphia & New York Custom House books are unique and do not repeat unless they are the same Captain or Ship, a shared index has been given.

Last Name	First Name	MSTR ID#	Page #	19	20	21	22	23	Date Range
K									
Kierstead	Jacob	M-K-005	91		X				15 Aug 1720 – 24 Nov 1720
"	"	"	"			X			24 Jul 1721 – 16 Oct 1721
"	"	"	"				X		28 Apr 1722 – 4 Jun 1722
"	"	"	"					X	22 May 1723 – 3 Dec 1723
Kiersteade	Jesse	M-K-006	91					X	17 Dec 1723
Kiersted	John	M-K-004	38			X			13 Feb 1721 – 7 May 1721
Kippen	Walter	M-L-007	106		X				11 Apr 1720 – 4 Jul 1720
"	"	"	"		X	X	X	X	7 Nov 1720 – 15 Apr 1723
L									
Lancolet	?	M-L-015	5					X	4 Mar 1723
Lancolet	Samuel	M-L-033	81		X	X			29 Aug 1720 – 28 Aug 1721
Landy	?	M-L-014	3			X			1 Jun 1721
Lashbrook	Thomas	M-L-022	35		X				3 Mar 1720 – 20 Jun 1720
Lasher	Daniel	M-L-018	19			X			8 Oct 1721 – 23 Oct 1721
Laurance	Dennis	M-L-023	38				X		18 Jun 1722 – 12 Nov 1722
Law	Andrew	M-L-034	85		X				14 Mar 1720 – 28 Nov 1720
Law	Robert	M-L-032	79					X	8 Jul 1723 – 17 Dec 1723
Lawrence	Henry	M-L-031	73					X	4 Mar 1723 – 31 Dec 1723
Lawrance	John	M-L-037	111					X	24 Oct 1720 – 8 Jan 1723
"	"	"	"					X	18 Nov 1723 – 17 Dec 1723
Lawrance	Lawrance	M-L-021	34		X				14 Mar 1720
"	"	"	"			X			22 May 1721 – 29 May 1721
Lawrance	Samuel	M-L-035	103	X	X	X	X	X	22 Dec 1719 – 21 Jun 1723
Lawrance	Thomas	M-L-036	104		X				16 May 1720 – 7 Aug 1720
Lea	Thomas	M-L-017	18					X	15 Apr 1723 – 22 Apr 1723
Leacraft	Richard	M-L-026	47		X	X			6 Jul 1720 – 26 Jun 1721
Leacraft	Richard	M-L-019	20					X	1 Jul 1723 – 30 Jul 1723
Leicester	?	M-L-013	3		X				22 Nov 1720
Leonard	Robert	M-L-028	56		X	X	X	X	18 Jul 1720 – 25 Jan 1723
Lester	Terret	M-L-029	64		X				22 Aug 1720
"	"	"	"			X	X		20 Mar 1721 – 8 Oct 1722
"	"	"	"					X	28 Oct 1723 – 18 Nov 1723
Lobdell	Samuel	M-L-027	55					X	23 Apr 1723 – 27 May 1723
Long	Robert	M-L-020	23		X				19 Feb 1720 – 6 Jun 1720
Lontit	Ichabad	M-L-030	70				X		17 Sept 1722 – 24 Sept 1722
Low	Peter	M-L-025	46	X	X	X	X	X	22 Dec 1719 – 21 Oct 1723
Lusher	Benjamin	M-L-024	39		X				9 May 1720 – 16 May 1720
Lyford	William	M-L-016	15		X	X			14 Nov 1720 – 22 Nov 1721
M									
Mackintosh	?	M-M-016	1	X					22 Dec 1719
Manning	William	M-M-024	13		X				10 Oct 1720 – 31 Oct 1720
Mansfield	?	M-M-023	6					X	23 Oct 1723
Mansfield	Andrew	M-M-039	79			X	X		29 May 1721 – 2 Jul 1722
Margatt	Peter	M-M-047	47		X				2 Feb 1720 – 27 Jun 1720
Margeson	John	M-M-026	16			X	X		28 May 1721 – 20 Nov 1721
Marshall	?	M-M-021	3			X			14 Aug 1721
Marston	?	M-M-020	3			X			3 Jun 1721
Marston	John	M-M-033	44					X	11 Aug 1723 – 17 Dec 1723
Martin	John	M-M-035	47		X	X			21 Mar 1720 – 6 Mar 1721
Martindale	William	M-M-027	17					X	5 Jun 1723 – 1 Jul 1723

Last Name	First Name	MSTR ID#	Page #	19	20	21	22	23	Date Range
M									
Massey	Daniel	M-M-037	63		X				1 Apr 1720 – 2 May 1720
"	"	"	"		X	X			5 Dec 1720 – 5 Dec 1721
"	"	"	"				X		29 Oct 1722
"	"	"	"					X	10 Jun 1723 – 28 Oct 1723
Mathelin	Richard	M-M-028	20			X			19 Jun 1721 – 26 Jun 1721
Mayne	Alexander	M-M-032	38			X			12 Feb 1721 – 20 Mar 1721
Meredith	John	M-M-029	20		X				9 Jun 1720 – 12 Sept 1720
Miller	?	M-M-017	1		X				14 May 1720
Minviele	David	M-M-019	2		X				11 Oct 1720
Misereau	Joseph	M-M-031	25				X		29 Jan 1722
Moore	John	M-M-042	100	X	X				9 Dec 1719 – 29 Aug 1720
Moorsom	John	M-M-025	14				X	X	29 Oct 1722 – 8 May 1723
Morgan	Henry	M-M-030	20			X			22 May 1721 – 19 Jun 1721
Morgat	Peter	M-M-043	101			X			10 Jul 1721 – 31 Jul 1721
Morine	James	M-M-034	45					X	17 Jun 1723 – 8 Jul 1723
Moses	?	M-M-022	4				X		22 Jun 1722
Mosse	?	M-M-018	2			X			Jun 1720 – 19 Jul 1720
Moulton	John	M-M-040	80	X	X				23 Dec 1719 – 28 Aug 1720
Moyon	Benjamin	M-M-038	68				X		26 Nov 1722
"	"	"	"					X	1 Jul 1723
Mutlow	John	M-M-041	86		X				11 Jul 1720 – 26 Sept 1720
"	"	"	"				X	X	20 Aug 1722 – 11 Mar 1723
"	"	"	"					X	18 Nov 1723 – 25 Nov 1723
N									
Nicholls	Mayes	M-N-007	18					X	18 Feb 1723
Norwood	Richard	M-N-009	45				X		15 Oct 1722 – 26 Nov 1722
Noxon Jr	Thomas	M-N-008	39				X		19 Mar 1722
O									
Oivian	Richard	M-O-008	85			X	X	X	16 May 1720 – 16 Jun 1722
Outerbridge	John	M-O-005	14					X	29 Jul 1723 – 19 Aug 1723
Overy	Isaiah	M-O-007	66		X	X			23 Jun 1720 – Jan 1721
"	"	"	"			X			26 May 1721 – Oct 1721
"	"	"	"				X		15 Aug 1722 – 10 Sept 1722
Owen	?	M-O-004	4			X			10 Nov 1721
Owen	Jeremiah	M-O-006	32				X		26 Feb 1722 – 31 Mar 1722
P									
Painter	John	M-P-026	17				X		3 Dec 1722
Paymer	?	M-P-024	5				X		12 Nov 1722
Paynter	Thomas	M-P-031	78				X		15 May 1723 – 28 Oct 1723
Payton	?	M-P-022	1	X					22 Dec 1719
Payton	Samuel	M-P-035	111		X	X	X	X	5 Nov 1720 – 28 Aug 1723
Phelpes	Charles	M-P-027	32		X				26 Sept 1720 – 3 Oct 1720
Phenix	Alexander	M-P-033	87		X	X			22 Aug 1720 – 16 Jan 1721
Phenix	Alexander	M-P-032	78					X	5 Feb 1723 – 8 Apr 1723
Phenix	Alexander	M-P-034	105			X			19 Jun 1721 – 19 Dec 1721
Phenix	Jacob	M-P-030	61	X	X	X	X	X	22 Dec 1719 – 31 Dec 1723
Phillips	?	M-P-025	5					X	4 May 1723 – 22 Jul 1723
Pinfold	William	M-P-028	39					X	5 Feb 1723
Pitmore	?	M-P-023	3			X			2 Feb 1721
Pound	Samuel	M-P-029	52					X	4 Jun 1723 – 10 Jun 1723
Price	John	M-P-002	16				X		26 Apr 1722 – 10 Sept 1722

CAPTAIN / MASTER INDEX --- YEARS COVERED / 9 Dec 1719 – 31 Dec 1723

The Captain & Ship ID's in both the Philadelphia & New York Custom House books are unique and do not repeat unless they are the same Captain or Ship, a shared index has been given.

Last Name	First Name	MSTR ID#	Page #	19	20	21	22	23	Date Range
R									
Raal	John	M-R-028	102		X	X	X	X	29 Aug 1720 – 31 Dec 1723
Randal	Thomas	M-R-004	99			X	X		13 Feb 1721 – 30 Jul 1722
"	"	"	"					X	3 Jun 1723 – 10 Jun 1723
Rawlings	Phillip	M-R-019	19		X				30 Jun 1720 – 25 Jul 1720
Rhode	Joseph	M-R-025	55		X				21 Nov 1720
Richards	John	M-R-023	41		X				9 May 1720 – 13 Jun 1720
Richardson	William	M-R-030	109					X	8 Jan 1723 – 31 Dec 1723
Risden	Elisha	M-R-026	82				X		15 Jan 1722 -15 Oct 1722
Rivers	Robert	M-R-024	43		X	X			5 Dec 1720 – 15 May 1721
Roach	?	M-R-018	2		X				13 Jun 1720
Robinson	Richard	M-R-020	22			X			19 Jun 1721 – 15 Aug 1721
"	"	"	"				X	X	24 Dec 1722 – 17 Dec 1723
Robinson	Valentine	M-R-021	27			X	X		5 Dec 1721 – 15 Jan 1722
Rose	Tomut	M-R-022	32			X			2 Oct 1721
Rowe	Henry	M-R-029	108		X				16 Jul 1720 – 15 Aug 1720
"	"	"	"				X	X	20 Feb 1722 – 17 Dec 1723
Royal	Joseph	M-R-013	13		X				6 Jun 1720
Ryley	Phillip	M-R-027	98				X		3 Sept 1722 – 30 Oct 1722
"	"	"	"					X	26 Aug 1723 – 2 Sept 1723
S									
Saltus	Samuel	M-S-054	56			X	X		26 Nov 1721 – 1 Jan 1722
Sanders	?	M-S-038	1					X	23 Oct 1723
Santford	Abraham	M-S-058	71		X				5 Apr 1720
"	"	"	"			X	X	X	13 Feb 1721 – 27 May 1723
Sarly	Jacob	M-S-064	104		X				14 Mar 1720 – 28 Nov 1720
Sarly	Jacob	M-S-042	28				X	X	24 Nov 1722 – 25 Nov 1723
Satant	John	M-S-045	39					X	5 Aug 1723
Savage	?	M-S-033	1		X				5 Apr 1720
Schermerhoom	Arnold	M-S-063	96			X	X	X	5 Jun 1721 – 6 Nov 1723
Scuse	?	M-S-034	2		X				2 Aug 1720
Sergent	Peter	M-S-057	68				X		6 Oct 1722 – 21 Oct 1722
Seymour	James	M-S-050	45					X	19 Jun 1723 – 28 Oct 1723
Seymour	John	M-S-055	58		X				12 Sept 1720 – 19 Sept 1720
Shadden	?	M-S-036	3		X				11 Nov 1720
Sharp	George	M-S-061	80			X	X	X	19 Jun 1721 – 30 Jul 1723
Simmons	Ebenezer	M-S-047	40					X	17 May 1723 – 3 Jun 1723
Simmons	Peter	M-S-056	62		X	X	X		23 May 1720 – 3 Dec 1722
Singer	Isaac	M-S-049	45					X	19 Apr 1723 – 27 May 1723
Sipkins	Burger	M-S-060	75		X	X			16 Apr 1720 – 7 May 1721
"	"	"	"				X		25 Jun 1722 – Feb 1723
Skaats	Bartholemew	M-S-062	84			X		X	11 Mar 1723 – 1 Jul 1723
Smith	?	M-S-035	2		X				21 Aug 1720
Smith	John	M-S-048	40			X			22 May 1721 – 29 May 1721
Smith	Josiah	M-S-051	49		X				15 Apr 1720 – 6 Jun 1720
Smith	Thomas	M-S-040	12		X	X	X	X	26 Feb 1720 – 25 Nov 1723
Smith	William	M-S-039	10		X				13 Jun 1720 – 20 Jun 1720
Smith	William	M-S-046	39					X	3 Jun 1723 – 17 Dec 1723
Smith	William	M-S-059	75				X		10 Feb 1722 – 16 Jun 1722
Soley	John	M-S-043	35				X		22 Apr 1722 – 18 Aug 1722
Soliel	Jacob	M-S-037	3			X			2 Feb 1721
Spofforth	Percinet	M-S-052	53		X	X			7 Jul 1720 – 29 May 1721
"	"	"	"				X		26 Nov 1722 – 10 Dec 1722
Steed	John	M-S-053	54					X	21 Apr 1723 – 6 May 1723
Strahan	Charles	M-S-044	37		X				28 Aug 1720 – 19 Sept 1720
Studley	James	M-S-041	21		X	X			24 Jul 1720 – 27 Feb 1721
S									
Stout	John	M-S-012	68			X			25 May 1721
"	"	"	"			X			16 Oct 1721 – 13 Nov 1721
"	"	"	"				X		26 Apr 1722 – 16 Oct 1722
"	"	"	"					X	7 Jun 1723 – 19 Aug 1723
Styles	John	M-S-025	54		X				5 May 1720 – 24 Oct 1720
T									
Tannatt	Thomas	M-T-018	17		X				9 May 1720 – 17 Jul 1720
Tatem	John	M-T-023	37		X				3 Oct 1720 – 10 Oct 1720
"	"	"	"				X		14 May 1722 – 28 May 1722
Tempest	John	M-T-022	35					X	9 Sept 1723 – 11 Nov 1723
Tempest	William	M-T-029	54		X				14 Nov 1720
Ten Eyck	John	M-T-031	78			X			3 Apr 1721
"	"	"	"			X	X	X	28 Nov 1721 – 30 Jul 1723
Tibbe	John	M-T-013	1		X				2 May 1720
Tilion	Vincent	M-T-020	25			X			2 Oct 1721 – 28 Nov 1721
Thatcher	?	M-T-014	1		X				5 May 1720
Theobald	John	M-T-032	82				X		31 Mar 1722 – 23 Jul 1722
"	"	"	"					X	4 May 1723 – 6 Aug 1723
Thody	Michael	M-T-026	44		X	X			21 Jan 1720 – 19 Dec 1721
"	"	"	"					X	21 Apr 1723 – 18 Nov 1723
Thorpe	Richard	M-T-027	48					X	17 Jun 1723 – 19 Aug 1723
Thurman	John	M-T-025	43				X	X	29 Jan 1722 – 6 Aug 1723
Tickel	John	M-T-034	98	X	X	X	X	X	9 Dec 1719 – 3 Dec 1723
Todd	Edward	M-T-019	21				X		22 Jun 1722 – 16 Jul 1722
Tomlin	George	M-T-017	9		X				18 Jul 1720 – 25 Jul 1720
Torsh	William	M-T-028	51					X	7 Oct 1723 – 14 Oct 1723
Tregoe	?	M-T-015	4				X		15 Oct 1722
Tret	?	M-T-016	4				X		12 Nov 1722
Trot	Nicholas	M-T-024	39					X	24 May 1723 – 1 Jul 1723
Tucker	Mansfield	M-T-033	90			X			21 Apr 1721
"	"	"	"			X	X		17 Sept 1721 – 11 Jun 1722
"	"	"	"					X	21 May 1723 – 16 Sept 1723
Tuder	John	M-T-021	32				X		24 May 1722 – 1 Oct 1722
Turhill	Barnabas	M-T-030	76				X	X	24 Dec 1722 – 8 Jan 1723
U									
Unran	?	M-U-001	2		X				4 Nov 1720
V									
Van Dam	Richard	M-V-017	110			X			2 Jan 1721 – 16 Jan 1721
Van Heese	?	M-V-006	2		X				27 Jun 1720
Vanbrugh	John	M-V-015	72		X	X	X	X	20 Apr 1720 – 12 Aug 1723
Vandick	Francis	M-V-013	55			X			17 Jul 1721 – 20 Nov 1721
"	"	"	"				X		30 Jul 1722
Vangeider	Tunis	M-V-016	82					X	5 Feb 1723 – 6 Aug 1723
"	"	"	"					X	8 Jul 1723 – 15 Jul 1723
"	"	"	"					X	31 Dec 1723
Vanpelt	?	M-V-008	6					X	1 Aug 1723 – 18 Nov 1723
Vanscise	Cornelius	M-V-009	15				X	X	27 Aug 1722 – 5 Aug 1723
Vantuyl	Richard	M-V-010	17				X		4 Jun 1722 – 2 Jul 1722
Vantyle	Richard	M-V-007	3			X			21 Oct 1721- 6 Nov 1721
Vear	John	M-V-011	25			X	X		7 May 1721 – 1 Jan 1722
Veare	John	M-V-014	58					X	20 May 1723
Vesey	Joseph	M-V-012	48		X				22 Aug 1720 – 5 Sept 1720

The Captain & Ship ID's in both the Philadelphia & New York Custom House books are unique and do not repeat unless they are the same Captain or Ship, a shared index has been given.

Last Name	First Name	MSTR ID#	Page #	19	20	21	22	23	Date Range
V									
Vesey	John	M-V-004	87		X				12 Jun 1720 – 4 Jul 1720
"	"	"	"			X	X		7 Sept 1721 – 30 Jul 1722
"	"	"	"				X		3 Dec 1722 – 24 Dec 1722
W									
Waldron	?	M-W-032	34			X			6 Feb 1721 – 29 Apr 1721
Walker Jr	Thomas	M-W-029	30		X				9 Jun 1720 – 4 Jul 1720
Wallis	Benjamin	M-W-041	78				X		22 May 1722 – 25 Jun 1722
Ware	Thomas	M-W-038	54		X				4 Jul 1720 – 11 Jul 1720
Waring	Rupert	M-W-034	48					X	8 Aug 1723 – 18 Nov 1723
Watson	Abraham	M-W-028	28					X	5 Aug 1723
Webb	George	M-W-031	33		X				16 Feb 1720 – 5 Sept 1720
Webb	Nicholas	M-W-017	54	X	X				9 Dec 1719 – 1 Dec 1720
Wells	?	M-W-026	2		X				13 Jun 1720
Wells	William	M-W-035	49				X		4 Jun 1722 – 25 Jun 1722
"	"	"	"					X	1 Apr 1723 – 19 Aug 1723
Welman	Jehoshaphat	M-W-037	53		X				21 Nov 1720 – 19 Dec 1720
Whippo	James	M-W-036	53		X				22 Apr 1720 – 19 Dec 1720
White	William	M-W-044	108		X	X	X		2 Jan 1720 – 20 Apr 1722
Whitfield	John	M-W-043	105			X			7 May 1721 – 5 Jun 1721
"	"	"	"				X		21 Oct 1722 – 24 Dec 1722
Willary	Robert	M-W-030	33					X	15 Nov 1723
Williams	William	M-W-033	35				X		8 Apr 1722 – 24 Dec 1722
Wilson	Joseph	M-W-042	79		X	X			2 Feb 1720 – 27 Apr 1721
Wilson	Joseph	M-W-040	74				X	X	7 May 1722 – 11 Nov 1723
Wolf	Matthew	M-W-039	60		X				16 May 1720
"	"	"	"			X	X	X	24 Apr 1721 – 14 Oct 1723
Woodberry	Jonathan	M-W-027	15				X		5 Nov 1722 – 26 Nov 1722
Woodside	John	M-W-044	106				X	X	5 Nov 1722 – 24 Nov 1723

Last Name	First Name	MSTR ID#	Page #	19	20	21	22	23	Date Range
Y									
Yeaman	David	M-Y-002	32			X			5 Dec 1721 – 19 Dec 1721
"	"	"	"				X		7 Jul 1722 – 30 Jul 1722
Yeats	John	M-Y-003	47		X				7 Nov 1720 – 14 Nov 1720
Young	Joseph	M-Y-001	19				X		20 Aug 1722 – 3 Sept 1722

SHIP INDEX --- YEARS COVERED / 9 Dec 1719 – 31 Dec 1723

The Captain & Ship ID's in both the Philadelphia & New York Custom House books are unique and do not repeat unless they are the same Captain or Ship, a shared index has been given.

?

Ship Names	Type	Ship ID#	Page #	19	20	21	22	23	Date Range
?	?	S-?-019	1	X					22 Dec 1719
?	?	S-?-020	1	X					22 Dec 1719
?	?	S-?-021	1	X					22 Dec 1719
?	Sloop	S-?-022	1		X				16 Jan 1720
?	Sloop	S-?-023	1		X				18 Mar 1720 – 1 Apr 1720
?	Sloop	S-?-024	1		X				5 Apr 1720
?	Sloop	S-?-025	1		X				8 Apr 1720
?	Sloop	S-?-026	1		X				2 May 1720
?	Brigantine	S-?-027	1		X				5 May 1720
?	Sloop	S-?-028	1		X				14 May 1720
?	Sloop	S-?-029	2		X				13 Jun 1720
?	Sloop	S-?-030	2		X				13 Jun 1720
?	Sloop	S-?-031	2		X				27 Jun 1720
?	Sloop	S-?-032	2		X				Jun 1720 – 19 Jul 1720
?	Sloop	S-?-033	2		X				2 Aug 1720
?	Sloop	S-?-034	2		X				19 Aug 1720
?	Sloop	S-?-035	2		X				21 Aug 1720
?	Brigantine	S-?-036	2		X				11 Oct 1720
?	Sloop	S-?-037	2		X				4 Nov 1720
?	Scallop	S-?-038	3		X				11 Nov 1720
?	Sloop	S-?-039	3		X				22 Nov 1720
?	?	S-?-040	3			X			2 Feb 1721
?	?	S-?-041	3			X			2 Feb 1721
?	Brigantine	S-?-042	3			X			6 May 1721
?	?	S-?-043	3			X			1 Jun 1721
?	?	S-?-044	3			X			3 Jul 1721
?	Sloop	S-?-045	3			X			14 Aug 1721
?	Sloop	S-?-046	3			X			17 Oct 1721
?	Sloop	S-?-047	3			X			6 Nov 1721
?	Sloop	S-?-048	3			X			7 Nov 1721
?	Sloop	S-?-049	4			X			10 Nov 1721
?	Sloop	S-?-050	4				X		4 Apr 1722
?	Schooner	S-?-051	4				X		16 Apr 1722
?	Brigantine	S-?-052	4				X		22 Jun 1722
?	?	S-?-053	4				X		19 Jul 1722
?	Sloop	S-?-054	4				X		14 Aug 1722
?	Sloop	S-?-055	4				X		8 Oct 1722
?	Sloop	S-?-056	4				X		15 Oct 1722
?	Sloop	S-?-057	4				X		11 Nov 1722
?	Sloop	S-?-058	4				X		12 Nov 1722
?	Sloop	S-?-059	5				X		12 Nov 1722
?	Brigantine	S-?-060	5				X		Dec 1722
?	Sloop	S-?-061	5					X	4 Mar 1723
?	?	S-?-062	5					X	23 Mar 1723
?	Sloop	S-?-063	5					X	4 May 1723
?	Sloop	S-?-064	5					X	14 May 1723
?	Sloop	S-?-065	5					X	24 May 1723
?	Sloop	S-?-066	5					X	4 May 1723 – 22 Jul 1723
?	Sloop	S-?-067	6					X	Jul 1723
?	Sloop	S-?-068	6					X	1 Aug 1723 – 18 Nov 1723
?	Sloop	S-?-069	6					X	17 Aug 1723
?	Schooner	S-?-070	6					X	28 Jul 1723 – 19 Aug 1723
?	Sloop	S-?-071	6					X	23 Oct 1723
?	Sloop	S-?-072	6					X	23 Oct 1723
?	?	S-?-073	7			X	X	X	19 Oct 1721 – 18 Mar 1723
?	Sloop	S-?-074	7					X	27 Apr 1723 – 3 Dec 1723

?

Ship Names	Type	Ship ID#	Page #	19	20	21	22	23	Date Range
?	?	S-?-075	24		X				10 Sept 1720
?	Sloop	S-?-076	32				X		7 Jul 1722 – 30 Jul 1722
?	Sloop	S-?-077	65					X	5 Jun 1723
?	Sloop	S-?-078	68			X			25 May 1721
?	Schooner	S-?-079	68				X		27 Sept 1722
?	Sloop	S-?-080	68				X		6 Oct 1722 – 15 Oct 1722
?	Sloop	S-?-081	68				X		26 Nov 1722
?	Sloop	S-?-082	90			X			21 Apr 1721

A

Ship Names	Type	Ship ID#	Page #	19	20	21	22	23	Date Range
Abigail	Sloop	S-A-020	8	X	X	X	X	X	22 Dec 1719 – 25 Nov 1723
Abigail	Sloop	S-A-021	9				X		14 May 1722 – 22 Jul 1722
Adventure	Sloop	S-A-022	9		X				18 Jul 1720 – 25 Jul 1720
Adventure	Sloop	S-A-027	82					X	31 Dec 1723
Albany	Brigantine	S-A-023	9		X	X	X	X	31 Mar 1720 – 11 Dec 1723
Albons	Ship	S-A-029	106					X	11 Mar 1723 – 15 Apr 1723
Anne	Sloop	S-A-015	10		X				13 Jun 1720 – 20 Jun 1720
Anne	Sloop	S-A-016	10		X				31 Jul 1720 – 19 Sept 1720
"	"	"	"			X			15 May 1721
Anne	Sloop	S-A-017	10		X				12 Sept 1720 – 19 Sept 1720
Anne	Sloop	S-A-018	10			X			23 Mar 1721
Anne	Sloop	S-A-019	10					X	28 Aug 1723 – 9 Sept 1723
Anne	Sloop	S-A-025	63		X				1 Apr 1720 – 2 May 1720
"	"	"	"		X	X			5 Dec 1720 – 5 Dec 1721
"	"	"	"				X		29 Oct 1722
Anne	Sloop	S-A-026	64		X				22 Aug 1720
Anne	Sloop	S-A-007	10					X	25 Mar 1723 – 13 Jul 1723
Anne & Catherine	Sloop	S-A-027	98,99				X	X	6 Aug 1722 – 17 Dec 1723
Anne & Elizabeth	Sloop	S-A-028	99					X	3 Jun 1723 – 10 Jun 1723
Antelope	Sloop	S-A-024	11				X		30 Apr 1722 – 24 Dec 1722
Antelope	Sloop	S-A-010	11				X	X	13 Sept 1722 – 26 Aug 1723

B

Ship Names	Type	Ship ID#	Page #	19	20	21	22	23	Date Range
Barbados Packet	Sloop	S-B-034	72				X	X	10 Dec 1722 – 12 Aug 1723
Beaver	Ship	S-B-022	12		X	X	X	X	26 Feb 1720 – 25 Nov 1723
Bedminster	Ship	S-B-013	66		X				18 Jun 1720 – 14 Jul 1720
Beginning	Sloop	S-B-016	13		X				6 Jun 1720
Benjamin	Sloop	S-B-002	13	X	X	X			18 Nov 1719 – 11 May 1721
Benjamin	Sloop	S-B-023	12					X	23 Aug 1723 – 30 Sept 1723
Benjamin	Ship	S-B-024	13	X	X				13 Dec 1719 – Feb 1720
Benjamin	Sloop	S-B-037	89			X	X	X	6 Nov 1721 – 1 Apr 1723
Bermuda	Sloop	S-B-035	76				X	X	14 May 1722 – 8 Jan 1723
Bersheba	Sloop	S-B-025	13		X				10 Oct 1720 – 31 Oct 1720
Bersheba	Sloop	S-B-026	13			X			13 Nov 1721 – 5 Dec 1721
Bersheba & Mary	Sloop	S-B-027	13				X		7 May 1722 – 14 May 1722
Blessing	Pink	S-B-028	14				X	X	29 Oct 1722 – 8 May 1723
Blessing	Sloop	S-B-029	14					X	5 Aug 1723 – 19 Aug 1723
Boneta	Sloop	S-B-030	14		X				17 Aug 1720 – 12 Sept 1720
Brown Betty	Brigantine	S-B-033	64					X	28 Oct 1723 – 18 Nov 1723
Burnet	Sloop	S-B-031	6				X		26 Nov 1722 – 24 Dec 1722
Burnet	Sloop	S-B-036	86					X	18 Nov 1723 – 25 Nov 1723
Burnet	Pink	S-B-032	14				X	X	16 May 1722 – 8 Jan 1723

The Captain & Ship ID's in both the Philadelphia & New York Custom House books are unique and do not repeat unless they are the same Captain or Ship, a shared index has been given.

C

Ship Names	Type	Ship ID#	Page #	19	20	21	22	23	Date Range
Catherine	Sloop	S-C-018	15				X		5 Nov 1722 – 26 Nov 1722
Catherine	Sloop	S-C-028	62		X				9 May 1720
Catherine	Sloop	S-C-031	100,101			X	X	X	23 Oct 1721 – 3 Jun 1723
Catherine & Mary	Sloop	S-C-019	15			X	X		20 Nov 1721 – 14 May 1722
Catherine & Mary	Sloop	S-C-020	15				X	X	27 Aug 1722 – 5 Aug 1723
Catherine & Mary	Sloop	S-C-032	108,111	X	X	X	X	X	2 Jan 1720 – 17 Dec 1723
Charlotte	Pink	S-C-030	85,86		X				14 Mar 1720 – 26 Sept 1720
Clarendon Packet	Sloop	S-C-006	65			X			5 Jun 1721 – 19 Dec 1721
Concord	Sloop	S-C-013	67	X					9 Jan 1720
Content	Sloop	S-C-021	15		X	X			14 Nov 1720 – 22 Nov 1721
Content	Sloop	S-C-022	16			X			20 Sept 1721 – 20 Nov 1721
Content	Brigantine	S-C-027	60				X	X	10 Dec 1722 – 14 Oct 1723
Cornelia	Sloop	S-C-029	77	X	X	X	X		22 Dec 1719 – 3 Apr 1722
Crane / Crean	Snow	S-C-023	16		X				29 Aug 1720
Crane / Crean	Snow	S-C-024	16		X				3 Oct 1720
Crane / Crean	Snow	S-C-025	16			X			28 May 1721 – 20 Nov 1721
Crown Galley	Ship	S-C-026	16			X			3 Jun 1721
Cutwater	Sloop	S-C-010	16				X		26 Apr 1722 – 10 Sept 1722

D

Ship Names	Type	Ship ID#	Page #	19	20	21	22	23	Date Range
Deborah	Sloop	S-D-009	67		X	X			7 Apr 1720 – 28 Sept 1721
"	"	"	67					X	15 Sept 1723 – 14 Oct 1723
Devonshire	Sloop	S-D-013	17					X	5 Jun 1723 – 1 Jul 1723
Devonshire	Ship	S-D-014	17		X				21 Mar 1720
Devonshire	Sloop	S-D-015	17			X			19 Jun 1721 – 26 Jun 1721
Diamond	Sloop	S-D-016	17		X				5 Sept 1720 – 19 Sept 1720
Diamond	Sloop	S-D-017	17			X			22 May 1721 – 29 May 1721
Dolphin	Schooner	S-D-018	17					X	1 Aug 1723 – 16 Aug 1723
Dolphin	Snow	S-D-019	17		X				9 May 1720 – 17 Jul 1720
Dolphin	Sloop	S-D-020	17				X		4 Jun 1722 – 2 Jul 1722
Dolphin	Sloop	S-D-021	17				X		3 Dec 1722
Dolphin	Schooner	S-D-022	18					X	18 Feb 1723
Dreadnought	Sloop	S-D-023	18					X	15 Apr 1723 – 22 Apr 1723

E

Ship Names	Type	Ship ID#	Page #	19	20	21	22	23	Date Range
Eagle	Snow	S-E-014	19		X				1720
Eagle	Brigantine	S-E-036	69		X	X	X	X	14 Mar 1720 – 17 Dec 1723
Easter	Sloop	S-E-015	19		X				8 Aug 1720 – 15 Aug 1720
"	"	"	"			X			8 Oct 1721 – 19 Dec 1721
Elizabeth	Sloop	S-E-016	19				X		20 Aug 1722 – 3 Sept 1722
Elizabeth	Sloop	S-E-017	19		X				27 Jun 1720 – 4 Jul 1720
Elizabeth	Sloop	S-E-018	19		X				18 Jul 1720- 28 Nov 1720
Elizabeth	Sloop	S-E-019	19			X			8 Oct 1721 – 23 Oct 1721
Elizabeth	Brigantine	S-E-020	19		X				30 Jun 1720 – 25 Jul 1720
Elizabeth	Sloop	S-E-021	20		X	X	X		4 Nov 1720 – 16 Apr 1722
Elizabeth	Sloop	S-E-022	20			X			19 Jun 1721 – 26 Jun 1721
Elizabeth	Sloop	S-E-037	77		X	X	X		24 Jul 1720 – 22 Aug 1722
"	"	"	"			X			25 Sept 1721 – 2 Oct 1721
Elizabeth	Sloop	S-E-039	93	X					13 Dec 1719 – 25 Dec 1719
Elizabeth	Sloop	S-E-008	66					X	10 Jun 1723 – 1 Jul 1723
Elizabeth & Martha	Sloop	S-E-004	21			X			7 Aug 1721 – 7 Sept 1721
"	"	"	"				X		3 Sept 1722 – 10 Sept 1722
Elizabeth & Anne	Ship	S-E-023	20		X				9 Jun 1720 – 12 Sept 1720
Elizabeth & Anne	Sloop	S-E-024	20			X			22 May 1721 – 19 Jun 1721
Elizabeth & Anne	Sloop	S-E-025	20					X	1 Jul 1723 – 30 Jul 1723
Elizabeth & Catherine	Brigantine	S-E-035	66		X	X			23 Jun 1720 – Jan 1721
Endeavor	Sloop	S-E-026	21			X			16 Oct 1721 – 23 Oct 1721

E

Ship Names	Type	Ship ID#	Page #	19	20	21	22	23	Date Range
Endeavor	Sloop	S-E-027	21		X				23 May 1720 – 6 Jun 1720
Endeavor	Sloop	S-E-028	21	X	X				22 Dec 1719 – 5 Jan 1720
Endeavor	Sloop	S-E-029	21		X	X			24 Jul 1720 – 27 Feb 1721
Endeavor	Sloop	S-E-030	21				X		22 Jun 1722 – 16 Jul 1722
Endeavor	Sloop	S-E-031	21				X	X	24 Dec 1722 – 8 Jan 1723
Endeavor	Sloop	S-E-032	22					X	3 Jun 1723
Endeavor	Sloop	S-E-033	22			X			19 Jun 1721 – 15 Aug 1721
"	"	"	"				X	X	24 Dec 1722 – 17 Dec 1723
Endeavor	Sloop	S-E-038	88				X		15 Jan 1722 – 29 Jan 1722
Evelyn	Ship	S-E-034	23		X				19 Feb 1720 – 6 Jun 1720
Expedition	Sloop	S-E-039	101		X	X			9 Mar 1720 – 10 Nov 1721
Expedition	Brigantine	S-E-040	103-105	X	X	X	X	X	22 Dec 1719 – 21 Jun 1723

F

Ship Names	Type	Ship ID#	Page #	19	20	21	22	23	Date Range
Fame	Sloop	S-F-012	24					X	18 Jul 1723 – 9 Sept 1723
Free Gift	Sloop	S-F-009	104,105				X	X	11 Jun 1722 – 4 Mar 1723
French Merchant	Brigantine	S-F-013	24		X	X			21 Nov 1720 – 31 Jul 1721
Friends Adventure	Sloop	S-F-014	24	X	X				Dec 1719 – 14 Mar 1720
Friendship	Sloop	S-F-015	85,86		X	X	X		16 May 1720 – 11 Mar 1723

G

Ship Names	Type	Ship ID#	Page #	19	20	21	22	23	Date Range
George	Sloop	S-G-007	25				X		12 Apr 1722 – 20 Aug 1722
George	Sloop	S-G-009	25		X				5 Jan 1720
George	Sloop	S-G-010	25			X	X		7 May 1721 – 1 Jan 1722
George	Sloop	S-G-011	25					X	18 Feb 1723
George	Sloop	S-G-016	60		X				16 May 1720
"	"	"	"			X	X		24 Apr 1721 – 23 Jul 1722
Good Intent	Boat	S-G-012	25			X			2 Oct 1721 – 28 Nov 1721
Good Intent	Sloop	S-G-013	25				X		29 Jan 1722
Good Intent	Sloop	S-G-017	63					X	10 Jun 1723 – 28 Oct 1723
Goodwill	Sloop	S-G-014	26	X	X				Dec 1719 – 17 Dec 1720
Greyhound	Snow	S-G-015	26				X	X	24 Dec 1722 – 5 Feb 1723

H

Ship Names	Type	Ship ID#	Page #	19	20	21	22	23	Date Range
Hamilton	Sloop	S-H-036	80		X	X	X	X	17 Jul 1720 – 30 Jul 1723
Hamilton Galley	Snow	S-H-018	27	X	X	X	X	X	22 Dec 1719 – 17 Dec 1723
Hamstead	Sloop	S-H-001	98,99	X	X	X	X		9 Dec 1719 – 30 Jul 1722
Hannah	Sloop	S-H-035	75				X	X	10 Feb 1722 – Feb 1723
Happy Margaret	Sloop	S-H-021	28					X	5 Aug 1723
Happy Return	Brigantine	S-H-022	28	X					3 Oct 1719
"	"	"	"		X				15 Apr 1720
"	"	"	"			X			25 Apr 1721
"	"	"	"			X	X		25 Nov 1721 – 17 Dec 1722
Haywood Galley	Ship	S-H-037	81			X			11 Aug 1721 – 28 Aug 1721
Hester	Sloop	S-H-038	95					X	17 Jun 1723 – 17 Dec 1723
Hester & Sarah	Sloop	S-H-019	27			X	X		5 Dec 1721 – 15 Jan 1722
Hope	Brigantine	S-H-020	28				X	X	24 Nov 1722 – 25 Nov 1723
Hope	Brigantine	S-H-032	66			X			26 May 1721 – 21 Oct 1721
Hope	Brigantine	S-H-039	103,105			X			30 Oct 1721 – 20 Nov 1721
Hope	Sloop	S-H-033	71		X	X	X		5 Apr 1720 – 27 May 1723
Hope	Sloop	S-H-040	104,105		X	X			14 Mar 1720 – 27 Aug 1721
Hopewell	Brigantine	S-H-023	28		X				6 Jun 1720
Hopewell	Brigantine	S-H-041	106		X	X	X	X	7 Nov 1720 – 24 Nov 1723
Hopewell	Sloop	S-H-025	29			X			10 Jul 1721 – 4 Sept 1721
Hopewell	Sloop	S-H-031	65				X		28 May 1722 – 29 Oct 1722
Hopewell	Sloop	S-H-024	29					X	15 Jul 1723 – 12 Aug 1723

SHIP INDEX --- YEARS COVERED / 9 Dec 1719 – 31 Dec 1723

The Captain & Ship ID's in both the Philadelphia & New York Custom House books are unique and do not repeat unless they are the same Captain or Ship, a shared index has been given.

H

Ship Names	Type	Ship ID#	Page #	19	20	21	22	23	Date Range
Humbird	Sloop	S-H-026	29		X				8 Apr 1720 – 2 May 1720
Humbird	Sloop	S-H-027	29				X		19 Mar 1722
Hunter	Sloop	S-H-028	29		X				19 Jan 1720 – 7 May 1720
Hunter	Sloop	S-H-030	65		X	X	X		11 Jul 1720 – 2 Apr 1722
Huntington	Sloop	S-H-034	72		X	X	X	X	20 Apr 1720 – 23 Mar 1723
Hunter Galley	?	S-H-029	29		X				17 Apr 1720

I & J

Ship Names	Type	Ship ID#	Page #	19	20	21	22	23	Date Range
Industry	Sloop	S-I-004	30		X				9 Jun 1720 – 4 Jul 1720
Jacob	Sloop	S-J-022	61				X	X	7 May 1722 – 31 Dec 1723
James & Joseph	Snow	S-J-027	79					X	17 Dec 1723
James & Mary	Ship	S-J-028	79					X	8 Jul 1723 – 26 Aug 1723
Jenny	Sloop	S-J-015	32			X			5 Dec 1721 – 19 Dec 1721
Joanna	Ship	S-J-025	78				X	X	22 May 1722 – 28 Oct 1723
Joanna & Judith	Sloop	S-J-023	68					X	1 Jul 1723
John Galley	Ship	S-J-029	81		X	X			21 Jan 1720 – 3 Apr 1721
John & Catherine	Sloop	S-J-016	32				X		24 May 1722 – 1 Oct 1722
John & Elizabeth	Sloop	S-J-017	32		X				26 Sept 1720 – 3 Oct 1720
John & Elizabeth	Sloop	S-J-018	32			X			2 Oct 1721
John & Elizabeth	Sloop	S-J-033	100,102		X	X	X	X	22 May 1720 – 31 Dec 1723
John & Henry	Sloop	S-J-026	78			X			3 Apr 1721
"	"	"	"			X	X	X	28 Nov 1721 – 30 Jul 1723
John & Mary	Sloop	S-J-007	31		X	X	X		27 Jun 1720 – 18 Nov 1723
John & Rebekah	Ship	S-J-019	32				X		26 Feb 1722 – 14 Apr 1722
Jolly	Sloop	S-J-021	33		X				16 Feb 1720 – 5 Sept 1720
Jolly	Sloop	S-J-030	82				X		31 Mar 1722 – 23 Jul 1722
"	"	"	"					X	4 May 1723 – 2 Sept 1723
Jolly	Sloop	S-J-032	98			X	X	X	1 May 1721 – 2 Sept 1723
Joseph	Sloop	S-J-031	82				X	X	15 Jan 1722 – 15 Jul 1723
Joseph	Sloop	S-J-033	110		X				18 May 1720 – 5 Dec 1720
"	"	"	"			X			17 Jul 1721 – 11 Sept 1721
Joseph & Betty	Ship	S-J-020	33					X	15 Nov 1723
Judith	Sloop	S-J-024	73					X	25 Nov 1723 – 31 Dec 1723

K

Ship Names	Type	Ship ID#	Page #	19	20	21	22	23	Date Range
King Fisher	Sloop	S-K-002	34				X		8 Jul 1722 – 8 Oct 1722
King George	Snow	S-K-003	34		X				2 Jan 1720
King George	Ship	S-K-004	34		X				14 Mar 1720
"	"	"	"			X			22 May 1721 – 29 May 1721
King George	Snow	S-K-005	34		X				6 Feb 1721 – 29 Apr 1721
King George	Ship	S-K-006	108,111				X	X	20 Feb 1722 – 8 Jan 1723

L

Ship Names	Type	Ship ID#	Page #	19	20	21	22	23	Date Range
Lark	Sloop	S-L-011	35				X		14 May 1722
Lark	Pink	S-L-012	35				X		22 Apr 1722 – 18 Aug 1722
Levett	Ship	S-L-013	35		X				3 Mar 1720 – 20 Jun 1720
Leve	Sloop	S-L-014	35					X	14 Sept 1723 – 7 Oct 1723
Lucretia	Sloop	S-L-017	100	X	X				9 Dec 1719 – 12 Sept 1720
Lydia	Brigantine	S-L-015	35				X		8 Apr 1722 – 24 Dec 1722
Lyon	Ship	S-L-016	35					X	9 Sept 1723 – 11 Nov 1723

M

Ship Names	Type	Ship ID#	Page #	19	20	21	22	23	Date Range
Mackworth	Brigantine	S-M-059	66				X		15 Aug 1722 – 10 Sept 1722
Margaret	Sloop	S-M-058	62		X	X	X		23 May 1720 – 3 Dec 1722
Marianne	Sloop	S-M-056	40			X			22 May 1721 – 29 May 1721
Martha & Jane	Sloop	S-M-034	37		X				28 Aug 1720 – 19 Sept 1720
Mary	Sloop	S-M-032	36		X	X	X	X	14 Mar 1720 – 18 Nov 1723
Mary	Sloop	S-M-037	37		X				4 Apr 1720
Mary	Sloop	S-M-038	37		X				25 Jul 1720 – 19 Dec 1720
Mary	Sloop	S-M-039	38		X				5 Sept 1720 – 11 Oct 1720
Mary	Sloop	S-M-040	38			X			13 Feb 1721 – 7 May 1721
Mary	Sloop	S-M-041	38		X				26 Sept 1720 – 31 Oct 1720
Mary	Sloop	S-M-042	38				X		18 Jun 1722 – 12 Nov 1722
Mary	Ship	S-M-043	38			X			12 Feb 1721 – 20 Mar 1721
Mary	Sloop	S-M-044	38			X			26 Jun 1721 – 17 Jul 1721
Mary	Sloop	S-M-045	39					X	5 Feb 1723
Mary	Sloop	S-M-046	39					X	24 May 1723 – 1 Jul 1723
Mary	Sloop	S-M-047	39					X	5 Aug 1723
Mary	Sloop	S-M-061	75			X			7 May 1721
Mary	Sloop	S-M-063	77				X		28 May 1722 – 18 Jun 1722
Mary	Sloop	S-M-064	79		X	X	X		2 Feb 1720 – 2 Jul 1722
Mary	Sloop	S-M-066	93,94,95		X	X	X	X	3 Mar 1720 – 24 Jun 1723
Mary	Ship	S-M-065	80	X	X				23 Dec 1719 – 28 Aug 1720
Mary	Schooner	S-M-060	68				X		21 Oct 1722
Mary	Schooner	S-M-048	39					X	10 Jun 1723 – 17 Dec 1723
Mary	Sloop	S-M-005	68				X		26 Apr 1722 – 16 Oct 1722
"	"	"	"					X	7 Jun 1723 – 19 Aug 1723
Mary Hope	Sloop	S-M-022	67		X				6 Oct 1720 – 28 Nov 1720
Mary Hope	Scallop	S-M-023	67					X	26 Sept 1723 – 21 Oct 1723
Mary & Anne	Sloop	S-M-049	39				X		19 Mar 1722
Mary & Anne	Schooner	S-M-050	39					X	3 Jun 1723 – 17 Dec 1723
Mary Anne	Schooner	S-M-033	37					X	1 Jul 1723 – 20 Sept 1723
Mary Anne	Sloop	S-M-067	109				X	X	14 May 1722 – 1 Jul 1723
Mary & Hannah	Sloop	S-M-057	61	X	X	X			22 Dec 1719 – 31 Jul 1721
Mary & Martha	Sloop	S-M-035	37		X				3 Oct 1720 – 10 Oct 1720
"	"	"	"				X		14 May 1722 – 28 May 1722
Mary & Martha	Sloop	S-M-036	37				X		24 Sept 1722
Mayflower	Sloop	S-M-051	39		X				9 May 1720 – 16 May 1720
Mayflower	Sloop	S-M-052	40				X		8 Oct 1722 – 29 Oct 1722
Mayflower	Brigantine	S-M-053	40					X	Aug 1723 – 14 Oct 1723
Medara	Sloop	S-M-054	40					X	17 May 1723 – 3 Jun 1723
Mermaid	Sloop	S-M-062	75		X	X			16 Apr 1720 – 24 Apr 1721
Miriam	Sloop	S-M-055	40			X			1 May 1721 – 29 May 1721

N & O

Ship Names	Type	Ship ID#	Page #	19	20	21	22	23	Date Range
Nassau	Brigantine	S-N-013	64			X	X		20 Mar 1721 – 8 Oct 1722
Neut	Ship	S-N-012	41		X				9 May 1720 – 13 Jun 1720
New York	Sloop	S-N-010	41		X				1720
New York	Pink	S-N-011	41		X				4 May 1720 – 21 Nov 1720
Overplus	Sloop	S-O-001	89,90		X	X	X		11 Nov 1720 – 11 Jun 1722
"	"	"	90					X	21 May 1723 – 16 Sept 1723

P

Ship Names	Type	Ship ID#	Page #	19	20	21	22	23	Date Range
Paddock	Sloop	S-P-019	43				X	X	29 Jan 1722 – 6 Aug 1723
Pennsylvania Merchant	Ship	S-P-014	66			X	X		3 Apr 1721 – 28 Aug 1722
Peter	Sloop	S-P-018	42		X	X	X	X	17 Apr 1720 – 17 Dec 1723
Peter	Sloop	S-P-024	44					X	11 Aug 1723 – 17 Dec 1723
Phenix	Sloop	S-P-020	43		X	X			5 Dec 1720 – 15 May 1721
Postilion	Ship	S-P-021	43			X			19 Jun 1721 – 3 Aug 1721
Pearl	Sloop	S-P-022	43	X	X				9 Dec 1719 – 18 Jun 1720
Phenix Galley	Ship	S-P-025	45					X	17 Jun 1723 – 8 Jul 1723

The Captain & Ship ID's in both the Philadelphia & New York Custom House books are unique and do not repeat unless they are the same Captain or Ship, a shared index has been given.

P

Ship Names	Type	Ship ID#	Page #	19	20	21	22	23	Date Range
Phillipsburgh	Ship	S-P-023	44		X	X			21 Jan 1720 – 19 Dec 1721
"	"	"	"					X	21 Apr 1723 – 18 Nov 1723
Phoebe & Mary	Sloop	S-P-026	45				X		15 Oct 1722 – 26 Nov 1722
Port Royal	Sloop	S-P-030	70	X	X	X	X		9 Dec 1719 – 24 Sept 1722
Prophet Elias	Ship	S-P-031	81			X			12 Jun 1721
Providence	Sloop	S-P-027	45					X	19 Apr 1723 – 27 May 1723
Prudence	Sloop	S-P-028	45			X			6 Nov 1721 – 28 Nov 1721
Prudence	Sloop	S-P-029	45					X	19 Jun 1723 – 28 Oct 1723

R

Ship Names	Type	Ship ID#	Page #	19	20	21	22	23	Date Range
Rachael	Brigantine	S-R-018	85		X				17 Oct 1720 – 28 Nov 1720
Revenge	Sloop	S-R-013	47		X				2 Feb 1720 – 27 Jun 1720
Revenge	Sloop	S-R-014	47		X				7 Nov 1720 – 14 Nov 1720
Revenge	Sloop	S-R-015	47			X			10 Jul 1721 – 26 Aug 1721
Rubie	Sloop	S-R-016	47		X	X			6 Jul 1720 – 26 Jun 1721
Rubie	Sloop	S-R-011	46	X	X	X	X	X	22 Dec 1719 – 21 Oct 1723
Rubie	Sloop	S-R-012	46			X			22 May 1721 – 31 Jul 1721
Rose	Sloop	S-R-017	47		X	X			21 Mar 1720 – 6 Mar 1721
Royal Prince	Snow	S-R-019	111		X	X	X	X	5 Nov 1720 – 17 Dec 1723

S

Ship Names	Type	Ship ID#	Page #	19	20	21	22	23	Date Range
St Christophers	Snow	S-S-037	48					X	17 Jun 1723 – 19 Aug 1723
St George	Sloop	S-S-038	48					X	8 Aug 1723 – 18 Nov 1723
Saint Michael	Sloop	S-S-039	48		X				5 Jan 1720
Samuel	Sloop	S-S-040	48		X				22 Aug 1720 – 5 Sept 1720
Samuel	Ship	S-S-041	48				X	X	9 Apr 1722 – 17 Dec 1723
Samuel & Elizabeth	Sloop	S-S-042	48		X				17 Oct 1720 – 28 Nov 1720
Sarah	Sloop	S-S-043	48		X				14 Mar 1720 – 21 Mar 1720
Sarah	Sloop	S-S-044	48				X		12 Mar 1722 – 27 Mar 1722
Sarah	Scallop	S-S-045	49					X	18 Mar 1723 – 1 Apr 1723
Sarah	Sloop	S-S-046	49			X			20 Aug 1721 – 6 Oct 1721
Sarah	Sloop	S-S-047	49					X	21 Apr 1723 – 3 Jun 1723
Sarah	Sloop	S-S-048	49		X				15 Apr 1720 – 6 Jun 1720
Sarah & Elizabeth	Sloop	S-S-049	49				X		4 Jun 1722 – 25 Jun 1722
"	"	"	"					X	1 Apr 1723 – 19 Aug 1723
Sarah & Mary	Sloop	S-S-050	50				X		14 May 1722
Sarah & Rebekah	Sloop	S-S-051	50			X			17 Jul 1721
Seabrook	Sloop	S-S-052	50				X		14 May 1722 – 28 May 1722
Sea Flower	Sloop	S-S-053	50		X				22 Aug 1720 – 5 Sept 1720
Sea Flower	Sloop	S-S-054	50			X			29 Mar 1721 – 13 Jun 1721
Sea Flower	Sloop	S-S-073	108,112		X	X	X	X	26 Sept 1720 – 1 Aug 1723
Sea Flower	Schooner	S-S-055	50				X		10 Dec 1722 – 24 Dec 1722
"	"	"	"					X	1 Jul 1723 – 20 Sept 1723
Sea Nymph	Snow	S-S-072	106,107		X	X	X	X	11 Apr 1720 – 6 Nov 1723
Seneca	Snow	S-S-057	51		X				26 Feb 1720 – 6 Jun 1720
"	"	"	'			X			3 Apr 1721 – 12 Jul 1721
"	"	"	"					X	2 Apr 1723
Shareham	Sloop	S-S-058	51					X	7 Oct 1723 – 14 Oct 1723
Shepherd	Pink	S-S-059	51	X	X				22 Dec 1719 – 12 Mar 1720
Sparrow	Sloop	S-S-060	51					X	4 Nov 1723 – 3 Dec 1723
South River	Sloop	S-S-070	100,101		X	X			30 Oct 1720 – 31 Jul 1721
Speedwell	Scallop	S-S-061	52					X	4 Jun 1723 – 10 Jun 1723
Speedwell	Sloop	S-S-062	52				X		12 Nov 1722 – 3 Dec 1722
Speedwell	Sloop	S-S-069	97		X	X			28 Mar 1720 – 24 Apr 1721
"	"	"	96			X	X	X	5 Jun 1721 – 6 Nov 1723

S (continued)

Ship Names	Type	Ship ID#	Page #	19	20	21	22	23	Date Range
Speedwell	Sloop	S-S-008	52			X			30 Mar 1721 – 20 Apr 1721
"	"	"	"			X			2 Oct 1721 – 16 Oct 1721
Speedwell	Sloop	S-S-009	87,88		X	X	X	X	22 Aug 1720 – 3 Dec 1723
Speedwell	Sloop	S-S-010	52			X	X		5 Aug 1721 – Jun 1722
Stanhope	Snow	S-S-063	53					X	11 Mar 1723 – 4 Nov 1723
Success	Sloop	S-S-064	53		X				22 Apr 1720 – 19 Dec 1720
Success	Sloop	S-S-065	53		X	X			7 Jul 1720 – 29 May 1721
"	"	"	"				X		26 Nov 1722 – 10 Dec 1722
Success	Sloop	S-S-071	101				X		29 Oct 1722 – 26 Nov 1722
Sunderland	Ship	S-S-068	74			X	X	X	13 Feb 1721 – 11 Nov 1723
Susanna	Sloop	S-S-066	53		X				21 Nov 1721 – 19 Dec 1720
Susanna & Judith	Sloop	S-S-067	65					X	5 Feb 1723
Swanswick	Ship	S-S-056	50		X				9 Oct 1720 – 4 Dec 1720
Sweet Fancy	Sloop	S-S-069	76		X				27 Aug 1720 – 26 Sept 1720

T

Ship Names	Type	Ship ID#	Page #	19	20	21	22	23	Date Range
Tempest	Brigantine	S-T-010	54		X				14 Nov 1720
Three Brothers	Sloop	S-T-018	91,92		X	X		X	15 Aug 1720 – 17 Dec 1723
Three Brothers	Sloop	S-T-020	108,109		X	X			16 Jul 1720 – 2 Oct 1721
Three Brothers	Sloop	S-T-008	54		X				5 May 1720 – 24 Oct 1720
Three Sisters	Sloop	S-T-009	54	X	X				9 Dec 1719 – 1 Dec 1720
Thomas	Schooner	S-T-021	108-110		X	X	X	X	29 Aug 1720 – 31 Dec 1723
Thomas & Mary	Schooner	S-T-017	73			X	X	X	7 May 1721 – 25 Nov 1723
Trampoose	Sloop	S-T-013	54					X	21 Apr 1723 – 6 May 1723
Trial	Sloop	S-T-014	55			X			17 Jul 1721 – 20 Nov 1721
"	"	"	"				X		30 Jul 1722
"	"	"	"					X	5 Feb1723 – 6 Aug 1723
Tryall	Sloop	S-T-015	55		X				21 Nov 1720
Two Brothers	Sloop	S-T-011	54		X				16 Feb 1720 – 1 Mar 1720
Two Brothers	Sloop	S-T-012	54		X				4 Jul 1720 – 11 Jul 1720
Two Brothers	Sloop	S-T-019	91			X			24 Jul 1721 – 16 Oct 1721
"	"	"	"				X		28 Apr 1722 – 4 Jun 1722
"	"	"	"					X	22 May 1723 – 17 Dec 1723
Two Brothers	Sloop	S-T-016	55					X	23 Apr 1723 – 27 May 1723

U, V, W & Y

Ship Names	Type	Ship ID#	Page #	19	20	21	22	23	Date Range
Unity	Snow	S-U-002	56		X	X	X	X	18 Jul 1720 – 25 Jan 1723
Unity	Sloop	S-U-003	83,84			X	X	X	19 Dec 1721 – 3 Dec 1723
Victory	Sloop	S-V-003	56			X	X		26 Nov 1721 – 1 Jan 1722
Warwick	Sloop	S-W-022	87		X				12 Jun 1720 – 4 Jul 1720
"	"	"	"				X		16 Jul 1722 – 30 Jul 1722
"	"	"	"				X		3 Dec 1722 – 24 Dec 1722
William	Sloop	S-W-001	57		X	X	X		23 Oct 1720 – 3 Dec 1722
William	Sloop	S-W-011	57			X	X	X	2 Jun 1721 – 17 Dec 1723
William	Sloop	S-W-012	58		X				20 Apr 1720 – 2 May 1720
William	Sloop	S-W-013	58		X				12 Sept 1720 – 19 Sept 1720
William	Sloop	S-W-014	58				X		7 May 1722
William	Sloop	S-W-015	58				X		20 Jun 1722 – 16 Jul 1722
William	Sloop	S-W-016	58					X	26 Oct 1723 – 11 Nov 1723
William & John	Sloop	S-W-017	58					X	20 May 1723
William & John	Sloop	S-W-021	68				X		16 Jul 1722 – 30 Jul 1722
William & Mary	Sloop	S-W-018	58		X				12 Sept 1720 – 19 Sept 1720
William & Sarah	Schooner	S-W-019	58				X		29 Oct 1722 – 5 Nov 1722
William & Sarah	Sloop	S-W-020	68			X			16 Oct 1721 – 13 Nov 1721
William & Thomas	Sloop	S-W-023	98					X	4 Nov 1723 – 3 Dec 1723
Young Benjamin	Sloop	S-Y-001	59				X	X	3 Sept 1722 – 5 Aug 1723

Sources Index

Source #	Title	Publisher	Year	Vol
3	Minutes of the Provincial Council of Pennsylvania	Jo. Severns & Co	1852	III
5	The American Weekly Mercury / 1719 – 1720	The Colonial Society of Pennsylvania	1898	I
6	The American Weekly Mercury / 1720 – 1721	The Colonial Society of Pennsylvania	1898	II
7	The American Weekly Mercury / 1721 – 1722	The Colonial Society of Pennsylvania	1905	III
8	The American Weekly Mercury / 1722 – 1723	The Colonial Society of Pennsylvania	1907	IV
14	Public Records of the Colony of Connecticut / May 1717 To Oct 1725	Hartford	1872	VI
20	The New England Courant / 7 Aug 1721 – 4 Jun 1726	James & Benjamin Franklin	1721+	ISSUES
21	The Boston News Letter / 1704 +→		1704+	ISSUES
22	The American Weekly Mercury / 1724 +→	Andrew Bradford	1724+	ISSUES
23	New Jersey Colonial Records / 1704 – 1739	The Press Printing and Publishing Co.	1894	XI
25	History of New London Connecticut	H. D. Utley	1895	
26	The Boston Gazette / 1719 +→		1719+	ISSUES
45	Diary of Joshua Hempstead / 1711 – 1758	New London County Historical Society	1901	I